HEWITT—DONLON CATALOG OF UNITED STATES SMALL SIZE PAPER MONEY

EDITOR
MARC HUDGEONS

SPECIAL BOARD OF CONTRIBUTORS

MR. NATHAN GOLDSTEIN II
MR. CHUCK O'DONNELL
MR. HARRY J. FORMAN

MR. AUBREY E. BEBEE
MR. HARRY JONES
MR. STEVE MICHAELS

LAWS REGULATING ILLUSTRATIONS OF U.S. PAPER MONEY

Section 504 of title 18, United States Code permit illustrations of paper money, provided the illustrations are in black and white; are of a size less than three-fourths or more than one and one-half times the size of the genuine obligations; and appear in articles, books, journals, newspapers, or albums for historical, educational, numismatic, or newsworthy purposes.

The Treasury Department has taken the position that in order for an illustration of currency to come within the permissible uses outlined above, the illustration must be accompanied by information about the particular items that is reproduced. In other words, an illustration of currency cannot be used merely for decorative or eye-catching purposes.

14th ANNUAL EDITION
1979

Copyright 1964, 1965, 1966, 1967, 1968, 1969, 1970, 1971, 1972, 1973, 1974, 1975, 1976, 1977
Copyright 1979© House of Collectibles
ISBN: 0-87637-112-8

Published by
HOUSE OF COLLECTIBLES
773 KIRKMAN RD.
SUITE 120
ORLANDO, FLORIDA 32811

SERIES NUMBERING SYSTEM

The series System is very simple. The first letter denotes the class. This letter is followed by denomination digit, then the series number (19 being understood). Example: S5-34A denotes Silver Certificate $5.00 series of 1934A. An asterisk after the denomination digit is used to denote a star note. Where space permits the series may be followed by two letters to indicate the Treasurer and Secretary signatures, such as JM denoting Julian and Morgenthau.

The six classes of small size notes are denoted as follows:
 U—United States Notes (Legal Tender)
 S—Silver Certificates (H is used for Hawaii overprints; A for World War II Africa Yellow Seals and E for the Experimental R and S Notes).
 N—National Bank Notes
 FB—Federal Reserve Bank Notes
 F—Federal Reserve Notes
 G—Gold Certificates

A SPECIAL NOTE

It is a genuine pleasure to be a part of the 14th Edition of the Hewitt Donlon Catalog. Having served on many of these editions, and having worked with Bill Donlon at the start, I feel in a position of complete awe at the surge of interest that has taken place in our hobby since the introduction of this Catalog some fifteen years ago.

It was the foresight of Bill Donlon, and the faith and confidence of Lee Hewitt, that started this project. This work has been brought to the present as the "father" of all small sized paper money catalogs. The offspring have been many, and they have gone into various areas of our hobby. All are welcome and even necessary for the help to collectors has been tremendous.

It is our hope that this new edition will bring to the collector a better insight into the production of our currency, as well as current values. We hear the talk about obsoleting the $1 note, and I personally feel this is a lot of hot air, for this denomination will be with us for a long time.

As the Bureau of Engraving and Printing continues its experimental work, and adds new dimensions to paper money production, we will see bigger and faster presses, larger printing plates, and even more secure intaglio printed notes. Today we have the finest product in the world, and we will have no less tomorrow. Follow your hobby, for it is a fascinating one, and will bring you much pleasure and enjoyment.

Our thanks for the great boost given to our hobby by both Donlon and Hewitt. Let's accept this catalog as our heritage, and keep it going strongly...

NATHAN GOLDSTEIN II

TABLE OF CONTENTS

General Information	3	Federal Reserve Notes	66
Official Serial Number Data	27	Gold Certificates	154
United States Notes	28	World War II Emergency Series	158
Silver Certificates	38	Special Printing	164
1929 Series National Bank Notes	50	Errors and Misprints	165

GENERAL INFORMATION

GRADING CONDITIONS

Advanced or serious collectors of current size notes usually insist upon these notes being in uncirculated or at least extra fine condition, the exception being the real scarce numbers and possibly the 1929 series of National Currency from one's own state, or bearing a family name in bank or signatures. However, the beginner, if limited in funds, should acquire the first specimen available needed for his collection and later endeavor to improve. As with coins a collection of choice currency will appreciate more in value than one of poor quality.

UNCIRCULATED OR NEW

UNCIRCULATED, or New means just that! Never in Circulation. However, new notes right out of a bank pack and which have seen no circulation will sometimes be found with light thumb soil marks by tellers, or with slightly bent corners. These minor flaws should be noted in any description of a new note.

A so-called "clean and crisp" note is not necessarily a new note, and some series of notes absolutely new, appear to lack crispness due to different grades of paper used in printing currency. This is especially true of notes printed by wet process.

EXTRA FINE

Notes to measure up to EXTRA FINE grading must at first glance appear to be uncirculated. Examination might reveal slight creases vertically, horizontally, or on one or more corners. However, these folds or creases must not have broken the paper to the extent that the engraving is impaired. There can be no cuts, smudges, stains, marks or evidences of washing, to be considered extra fine.

VERY FINE

To merit the VERY FINE grading, a note must show only slight evidence of circulation or handling. Any folds or creases must be so faint that they do not impair the general appearance. Only minor pin-holes may exist, and there should be no cuts or tears. In short the note should have an overall acceptable appearance. Non-collectors usually describe such a note as being "in nice conditions."

FINE OR LESS

A note to be grade FINE might show quite a bit of handling, but must not be worn, badly stained, or have a washed out faded appearance. Only the scarcer current size notes are usually collected in fine condition and in less than fine condition are seldom worth saving with the possible exception of low issues from some states.

IMPORTANT TO NOTE FOLLOWING INFORMATION ON OFF-COLOR BACKS AND SEALS AND ALTERED SERIAL NUMBERS

Numerous inquiries have been received relative to so-called "blue back" and "yellow back" notes, also United States Notes with "yellow seals." Without exception every off-color back or seal examined by the writer, has been chemically treated to cause the change in color. Possibly this was done accidentally by certain detergents or acids, but more likely, intentionally.

Collectors should also beware of notes with missing signatures or serial numbers, or missing portions of these details. Errors do occur in the printing, but almost all of these "errors" submitted have been found to be deliberate removal of portions of the printing by erasing.

Notes with altered serial numbers and altered series date have also been reported. Careful examination with a good glass will usually reveal this attempt to make the serial number more attractive. Notes under suspicion should be so examined.

"Errors" artificially created have no premium value.

PIN HOLES

Pin holes or needle holes frequently found in early large size notes, fortunately are not encountered to any great extent in current size currency. Packages of early issues of large size notes were frequently fastened together with needle and thread, or pierced by a pin in banding, and sometimes even punctured by a spindle on a teller's desk.

Today, pins for fastening bands have been outmoded by the use of paper bands with gummed ends. Notes are received by the member banks from the Federal Reserve Banks, nicely banded in packs of 100. Pin holes in a current size note usually indicate it has seen circulation and has perhaps been pinned to an invoice or letter, or possibly to a shirt pocket. This note is definitely not in new or uncirculated condition.

FORMING A COLLECTION

The currency collector should not be discouraged by the thought that he will be unable to acquire every issue with every combination of seals and signatures. Coin collectors are fortunate if they complete a single series.

It is doubtful that a complete collection of current size notes has ever been formed. Unfortunately, there were relatively few collectors of currency until recent years, and many of these issues have not been preserved in sufficient quantity to make a complete collection possible. The notes possibly exist but they are widely scattered. As the years go by if they are offered for sale, some fortunate persistent collector will perhaps be successful in acquiring a note of each series, signature combination and denomination.

A beautiful prize-winning collection which will afford much enjoyment in assembling and exhibiting, may be formed by collecting major designs of each issue of United States Notes, Silver Certificates, National Currency and Federal Reserve Notes, in denominations to suit one's budget. Gold Certificates may be included, as these are now legal to hold.

The collection may be extended to include a Federal Reserve Bank Note, 1929 series, brown seal, from each District, or possibly a Federal Reserve Note, green seal, from any one District in every series 1928 to date. Some collectors select one series and endeavor to obtain one note from every District in that series. Suggestions for collecting 1929 series of National Currency are given in the text preceding the valuations for this series.

One of the most popular "type" collections today is BLOCK collecting. This specialization started with the small size Silver Certificates, but really came into vogue with the appearance of the $1 Federal Reserve Notes. As different suffixes (for FR notes) and prefixes (for Silvers) appeared, one note with each change was saved. Each change in alphabetic designation is called a "BLOCK." Some of these Blocks are released in small numbers, whereas others are available in limited numbers as large amounts were not saved. To form a complete block collection is a great challenge to any collector.

HOUSING A COLLECTION

The present day currency collector need not resort to the use of old envelopes, or wallets to house his collection. Single notes may be handled and preserved if placed in acetate cellulose holders, but beware of holders made of nitrate cellulose which will cause the notes to become brittle and crack. These may usually be detected by the yellowish color of the holder. The use of polyethylene holders is also not advisable, as these tend to soften and wrinkle the notes. Flip-up type albums are available, both for large and small size currency, with capacity of 50 to 100 notes. Vinyl pages to hold 3 notes each, when placed in acetate holders, are also available. These pages will fit any 3-ring binder. Some foreign made pages have been foud to be detrimental to notes, causing brittleness. All types of vinyl binders and currency holders are available from ANCO Coin & Stamp Supplies, P.O. Box 782, Florence, Alabama 35630 See ad in the back of this book for more information.

INVENTORY

An inventory of a currency collection using serial numbers provides an immediate means of identification and is easily kept up to date as new items are added to a collection. The inventory should be kept in a separate place, not with the collection, and should show cost, date and from whom acquired.

INTERESTING SERIAL NUMBERS

A fascinating phase of currency collecting is the search for interesting serial numbers such as low numbers, numbers with all digits alike, numbers that read the same both ways called radar numbers or palindromes, block numbers such as 11114444, pairs of digits such as 14141414, poker hands and countless others. The search for these is challenging and unending.

OBVERSE AND REVERSE OR FACE AND BACK?

While the two sides of a coin have always been designated as obverse and reverse, the Bureau of Engraving and Printing designates the two sides of currency as face and back. Due to the large number of coin collectors now adding currency to their collections, and who are accustomed to the designation of obverse and reverse, it will be difficult probably to put correct designation of face and back into universal use. Whether you call it obverse and reverse, or face and back, you will surely enjoy both sides of every piece of currency you add to your collection.

STAR NUMBERED CURRENCY

Star numbered notes are used to replace plain numbered notes damaged in production, as it would be impractical to match the serial number of a defective note.

A star numbered note is now used as a substitute for the number 100,000,000 as the numbering machines print eight digits only, consecutively to 99,999,999. However several notes of earlier issues bearing number "One Hundred Million" are known to exist. Five such notes, some accompanied by the preceding number, 99,999,999, were offered in the Grinnell sales, over thirty years ago. Quite recently a series 1928 A $1.00 silver certificate with serial 100,000,000, was publicly sold, and many new collectors learned of this unusual numbering for the first time.

From information at hand, it is believed that this nine digit number was used only on Series 1928, 1928 A, 1928 B and 1934 $1.00 silver certificates. Listed in the Grinnell sale of Nov. 30, 1946, were the following:

$1.00 1928A, Woods-Mellon, C99,999,999B and C100,000,000B
$1.00 1928B, Woods-Mills, G99,999,999B and G100,000,000B
$1.00 1934, Julian-Morgenthau, A99,999,999A with A100,000,000A and the next note, B00,000,001A.
$1.00 1934, Julian-Morgenthau, B99,999,999A with B100,000,000A and C00,000,001A.
$1.00 1934, Julian-Morgenthau, F99,999,999A and F100,000,000A.

Notes so numbered and with prefix C, D or E, were not offered, but possibly exist. Series 1935 $1.00 silver certificate, serial number G99,999,999A was offered with H00,000,001A, the latter being listed as the next highest serial number.

We may assume from this pair of notes, that the system of specially numbered 100,000,000 serials, was discontinued with the 1935 series. There is no record of this unusual serial number appearing on silver certificates of higher denominations or on any other issues.

On Federal Reserve Notes, the star or asterisk, is placed after the serial number, replacing the suffix letter. On all other issues, the star precedes the serial number.

In the last brick (4000 notes) of the $1 Federal Reserve Notes for Boston (brick number 25,000) a note was printed, and released with serial number A00000000 A. This was Series 1969 A, and is the only example of this all zero note to be actually released (though in error), for this is normally replaced with a star note. This note, along with brick label, was on display at the A.N.A. Convention in Boston, 1973.

A very large quantity of star numbered notes have been printed in recent issues, and have been released in solid bank packs of one hundred consecutive numbers. This procedure apparently was not followed on earlier issues, with the result that star numbers on early issues are scarcer.

STAR SERIAL NUMBER VALUATIONS

Valuations of U. S. Legal Tender Notes, and Silver Certificates with Star serial numbers, are given on pages 25, 26, 27. Suggestions from dealers and collectors have been carefully weighed and averaged. These prices are intended as a guide for collectors buying or selling, but actual price will be a matter between buyer and seller. Comments from dealers and collectors are always appreciated, and will be considered carefully for future editions.

VALUATIONS

Valuations of the various issues have been compiled from information as to scarcity and availability, gathered from dealers and collectors and from public offering of these items, and are given as a guide as to what you might be expected to pay. these prices are not to be construed as an offer to sell on the part of the publisher or the authors.

These are not the prices a collector might hope to obtain should be dispose of this collection to a dealer. The legitimate established dealer must add cost of advertising, overhead and profit to the price he pays for an item, and therefore must discount these valuations depending upon the availability, his present supply and whether his experience tells him it is a fast or slow moving item.

Valuations given are for notes with average centering of designs. Notes with perfect centering might command a higher premium. Notes badly centered will be worth less than those with good average centering.

CLEANING PAPER MONEY

Whether paper money should be cleaned is a subject of difference of opinion. Many collectors feel very strongly that notes should not be cleaned and probably just as many take the opposite position. Washing paper money does cause some characteristic changes as to paper color, feel, etc., therefore cleaning generally does not increase value.

Those who use notes obtained from circulation as starter items or fillers generally feel that a cleaned note is personally more desirable that a dirty one, and for those who want to clean up such a note—here are a few hints.

Before attempting to clean a note which has any premium value, experiment first with a few notes from your billfold. As the bank overprint on 1929 National Currency is easily washed off, cleaning notes of that series is very risky.

Soak the note thoroughly in warm water, smooth it out on the side of the basin, then rub gently with a mild soap on both sides. Rinse with more warm water and watch the soiling flow away. Pencil marks, etc. should be removed with a soft eraser before washing.

Wrinkles and folds can be removed by placing the wet note on a piece of glass or your Formica top kitchen counter. Flatten out the note and roll the edge of your hand over the wet note, starting at the middle and work to the ends. Use paper toweling, napkin or white blotting paper to soak up as much moistoure as possible. Place the note between the pages on a heavy book and let dry. If your heavy book does not contain blank pages, use two pieces of plain paper top and bottom of the moist note.

Some collectors have developed the knack of ironing out wrinkles. This is a procedure that requires a good deal of practice to avoid curling and new wrinkling, so the natural drying in a heavy book is generally the preferred method.

"HOLD-OVER," "TURN-OVER' OR "CHANGE-OVER"?

For want of a more appropriate designation, notes with consecutive serial numbers but from two different series, have been commonly called "change-over" pairs. This is certainly a misnomer and infers that when numbering reached those particular serial numbers the printing of one series was discontinued and a new one started. This would only be possible if notes were printed from single plates. Further proof that there was no actual change-over is the fact that several of these pairs have been discovered in a single pack of 100 notes, with some pairs in reverse order the higher serial number being on the earlier series.

The term "hold-over" pair seems to be a better name for these attention-getters, as held over plates were used in conjunction with plates of later series. This interesting mix-up seems to have occurred only in the printing of our early series of small sizes notes.

In this edition we are not attempting to evaluate these difficult-to-find pairs, some of which are much scarcer than others. The consensus seems to be that the pairs should be valued at 5 to 10 times the value of the single notes comprising the pair. For the present we will accept this valuation as being approximately correct. Reader's comments will be appreciated, as will information as to series and serial numbers of existing pairs.

Illustration of above pair of $1. silver certificates is additional proof that these are not "change-over" pairs, as numbering skips from series 1928B to 1928D.

No. 140504110B series 1928B has face plate #48, back plate #2451.
No. 140504111B series 1928 has face #49, back plate #2260.

No. L50330563A series 1934B with face place #1785, plate #1650.
No. L50330562A series 1934C with face plate #1879, back plate #1650.
It will be noted that the serial number on series 1934B is higher than that on the later series 1934C.

No. B80851308B series 1934A with face plate #464, back plate #1151.
No. 80851309B series 1934B with face plate #496, back plate #1150.
A good pair in the $10 denomination of Federal Reserve Notes. These pairs

are found more frequently in denominations lower than $10.
Known existing "hold-over" pairs are:

- $ 1 Silver Certificate: Series 1928/1928A; 28A/28B; 28A/28C; 28A/28D;
- $ 2 U S N Series 1928C, 28D, 28E and 28F were being printed at the same time. "Hold over" pairs of these are suspected, some known. Can you report any?
- $ 5 F R for Series 1934, 1934A, 1934B, 1934C and 1934D were being printed at the same time.
- $ 5 S C Series 1934, 1934A, 1934B, 1934C and 1934D were also being printed at the same time.
- $ 5 U S N Series 1828D, 1928E and 1928F were also being printed at the same time.
- $10 F R Series 1934A and 1934B were printed at the same time, and "hold-over" pairs have been reported from New York and Philadelphia. It is possible that others exist, and should be reported.

Chuck O'Donnell in his Standard Handbook has done a great job in bringing to our attention many simultaneous printings, thru the study of press records of this period.

For the record, these "hold-over" pairs ar the result of the Bureau of Engraving and Printing making use of all "fit" plates until they were worn to the point of discard. As a new series cam into existence, it was necessary to make new plates, and engrave these Flat Press plates on which the series designation and signatures were also engraved (and not overprinted). Therefore, when a printing was called for, four plates (which were the plates required for the Flat Press) were taken and put on the press for duty. It might have been that three of the plates were of one Series, while the fourth plate was of another. As these plates of 12 subjects were numbered in series of 6 for each plate, the seventh note would be numbered on the next sheet (and this sheet could have been of a different series). Thus we get pairs of notes in consecutive order from two series, sometimes the later series is first, other times last in the pair. With later series, this was discontinued, as the series designation and signatures were overprinted on the note at the same time as the serial numbers.

SERIAL NUMBER PREFIX AND SUFFIX LETTERS

Collecting the various combinations of serial number prefix and suffix letters has stimulated increased interest in many series, with a gradually increasing number of collectors now striving to obtain all possible combinations.

While many combinations appeared on a full run of one hundred million notes, and are therefore usually available, some combinations of "block letters" were used only on a relatively limited quantity of starting and closing serial numbers of series.

In placing a valuation on "block letters" or any other items of collector interest, much consideration must be given to the collector-demand. As stated above the increase in the number of collectors of prefix and suffix letters, has been very gradual.

(See also section on Forming a Collection)

BLOCK LETTERS UNITED STATES NOTES, red seals
Valuations in the price section seem adequate for most combinations.

One Dollar and Two Dollars
U1-28	1928	A-A
U2-28	1928	A-A
U2-28A	1928A	A-A and B-A
U2-28B	1928B	A-A and B-A
U2-28C	1928C	B-A and C-A
U2-28D	1928D	B-A, C-A, D-A
U2-28E	1928-E	D-A
U2-28F	1928F	D-A
U2-28G	1928G	D-A and E-A
U2-53	1953	A-A
U2-53A	1953A	A-A
U2-53B	1953B	A-A
U2-53C	1953C	A-A
U2-63	1963	A-A
U2-63A	1963A	A-A

Five Dollars
U5-28	1928	A-A, B-A, C-A, and D-A
U5-28A	1928A	C-A and D-A
U5-28B	1928B	D-A and E-A
U5-28C	1928C	F-A, F-A, G-A
U5-28D	1928D	G-A
U5-28E	1928E	G-A and H-A
U5-28F	1928F	H-A and J-A
U5-53	1953	A-A and B-A
U5-53A	1953A	B-A and C-A
U5-53B	1953B	C-A
U5-53C	1953C	C-A
U5-63	1963	A-A

One Hundred Dollars
U100-66	1966	A-A
U100-66A	1966A	A-A

BLOCK LETTERS SILVER CERTIFICATES

One Dollar Silver Certificates
S1-28	1928	A-A thru L-A
S1-28A	1928A	E-A thru J-B, Experimentals: X-B, Y-B, Z-B
S1-28B	1928C	B-B thru J-B
S1-28C	1928B	V-A thru J-B
S1-28D	1928D	D-B thru J-B
S1-28E	1928E	F-B thru J-B
S1-34	1934	A-A thru G-A
S1-35	1935	A-A thru P-A
S1-35A	1935A	M-A thru D-D
S1-35C	1935C	K-D thru U-E
S1-35D	1935DW	R-E thru M-G (except G-G)
S1-35D	1935DN	U-E thru M-G (except G-G) (12-subject)
S1-35D	1935D	G-G thru N-G (18-subject)
S1-35E	1935E	N-G thru J-I
S1-57	1957	A-A thru B-B
S1-57F	1957F	P-I thru E-J
S1-57A	1957A	A-A thru Q-A
S1-35G	1935G	B-J thru D-J
S1-35G	1935G	motto D-J
S1-57B	1957B	Q-A thru Y-A
S135H	1935H	D-J and E-J
S1-35A	1935A	Hawaii Y-B, C-C, F-C, L-C, P-C, S-C
S1-35A	1935A	Africa B-C, C-C, I-C, R-C

Five Dollar Silver Certificates
S5-34	1934	A-A thru E-4
S5-34A	1934A	E-A thru L-A
S5-34B	1934B	K-A thru M-A
S5-34C	1934C	L-A thru Q-A
S5-53	1953	A-A thru D-A
S5-53A	1953A	D-A thru E-A
S5-53B	1953B	F-A
S5-34-A	1934A	Africa K-A

Ten Dollar Silver Certificates
S10-33	1933	A-A
S10-34	1934	A-A
S10-34A	1934A	A-A, B-A
S10-34B	1934B	B-A
S10-34C	1934C	B-A
S10-34D	1934D	B-A
S10-53	1953	A-A
S10-53A	1953A	A-A
S10-53B	1953B	A-A

BLOCK LISTING FOR $1 FEDERAL RESERVE NOTES

Prices shown are for specific blocks listed, and can change should large supplies become available (supplies could still be in Federal Reserve vaults, and be released some time later). These prices are averages of listed prices by dealers who offer these BLOCKS.

Series 1963
A A	...	3.50
A *	....	4.50
B A	...	3.50
B B	...	6.75
B C	...	125.00
B *	....	4.00
C A	...	4.00
C B	...	32.50
C *	...	4.00
D A	...	3.50
D B	...	100.00
D *	....	4.00
E A	....	4.00
E B	...	6.75
E *	....	4.00
F A	...	3.50
F B	....	25.00
F C	....	50.00
F *	....	4.00
G A	...	3.50
G B	...	19.50
G C	...	3.25
G *	....	4.00
H A	...	4.00
H *	....	5.00
I A	....	3.50
I *	....	4.50
J A	....	3.50
J *	....	4.50
K A	...	3.50
K *	....	4.50
L A	....	3.50
L B	....	25.00
L *	....	4.00

Series 1963 A
A A	...	3.25
A B	...	3.25
A C	...	3.25
A D	...	3.25
A *	...	3.50
B A	...	3.25
B B	...	25.00
B C	...	19.50
B D	...	4.50

Series 1963 A Continued
B E	....	22.50
B F	....	3.25
B G	...	3.25
B *	....	3.50
C A	...	3.25
C B	...	8.00
C C	...	3.25
C D	...	3.25
C *	...	3.50
D A	...	3.25
D B	...	6.75
D C	...	3.25
D D	...	3.25
D *	....	3.50
E A	....	3.25
E B	....	5.50
E C	....	5.50
E D	....	4.50
E E	....	4.50
E F	....	3.25
E *	....	3.50
F A	....	3.25
F B	....	5.50
F C	....	5.50
F D	....	5.50
F E	....	3.25
F F	....	3.75
F G	....	3.25
F *	....	3.50
G A	...	3.25
G B	...	7.75
G C	...	7.75
G D	...	3.75
G E	...	3.25
G F	...	5.50
G G	...	3.25
G H	...	3.25
G *	....	3.50
H A	...	3.25
H B	...	3.25
H C	...	4.50
H *	....	3.50
I A	....	3.25
I B	....	5.50
I *	....	3.75
J A	....	3.25
J B	....	3.25
J C	....	3.25
J *	....	3.50
K A	...	3.25
K B	...	3.25
K C	...	3.25
K *	....	3.50
L A	...	3.25
L B	....	19.50
L C	....	32.50
L D	....	13.50
L E	....	3.25
L F	....	3.25
L *	....	3.50

Series 1963 A
B G	...	3.25
B H	...	3.25
B *	....	3.75
E F	....	3.25
E G	...	3.25
E *	....	6.75
G H	...	5.50
G I	...	3.25
G *	....	3.75
J C	....	4.50
L F	....	3.25
L G	...	3.25
L *	....	3.75

Series 1969
A A	...	2.75
A *	....	3.25
B A	...	2.75
B B	...	2.75
B C	...	2.75
B *	...	3.25
C A	...	2.75
C *	...	3.25
D A	...	2.75
D B	...	3.25
D *	...	3.25
E A	...	2.75
E B	....	2.75
E C	....	2.75
E *	....	3.25
F A	....	2.75
F B	....	2.75
F *	....	3.25
G A	...	2.75
G B	...	2.75
G C	...	2.75
G D	...	2.75
G *	....	3.50
H A	...	2.75
H *	....	3.25
I A	...	2.75
I *	....	3.75
J A	...	2.75
J *	....	3.25
K A	...	2.75
K B	...	2.75
K *	...	3.25
L A	...	2.75
L B	...	2.75
L C	....	2.75
L *	....	3.50

Series 1969 A
A A	...	5.50
A B	...	2.75
A *	....	3.25
B C	...	2.75
B D	...	2.75
B *	....	3.25
C A	...	2.75
C B	...	2.50
C *	....	3.25
D B	...	2.75
D *	....	3.25
E C	....	2.75
E D	....	2.50
E *	....	2.75
F B	....	2.75
F C	....	2.75
F *	....	3.25
G D	...	2.75
G E	...	2.75
G *	....	3.25
H A	...	2.75
H B	...	3.00

BLOCK LISTING FOR $1 FEDERAL RESERVE NOTES—continued

1969—Cont.
H *	3.75
I A	2.75
I *	6.75
J A	3.25
J B	2.75
J *	3.25
K B	2.75
NO STAR	
L C	2.75
L *	3.25

B *	2.50
C A	2.25
C B	2.25
C *	3.25
D A	2.25
D *	2.50
E A	2.25
E B	2.25
E *	2.50
F A	2.25
F B	2.25
F *	2.50
G A	2.25
G B	2.25
G C	3.25
G *	2.50
H A	2.25
H *	2.50
I A	2.25

I *	2.50
J A	2.50
J *	2.50
K A	2.25
K B	2.25
K *	2.50
L A	2.25
L B	2.25
L C	2.25
L *	3.25

F B	2.25
F C	2.25
F *	2.75
G C	2.25
G D	2.25
G *	2.75
H A	2.50
H *	4.50
I A	2.50
I *	4.50
J A	2.25

Series 1969 B
A A	2.25
A *	2.50
B A	2.25
B B	2.50
B C	2.25
B D	2.25

Series 1969 C
B D	2.25
D A	2.50
D B	3.25
D *	4.50
E B	2.25
E C	2.25
E *	4.50

J B	2.75
J *	3.50
K B	2.50
K *	3.25
L C	2.25
L D	2.25
L *	4.50

Series 1969 D
A A	2.00	C *	2.50	F D	2.00	J B	2.00
A B	2.00	D A	2.00	F *	2.50	J *	2.50
A *	2.50	D B	2.00	G A	2.00	K A	2.00
B A	2.00	D *	2.50	G B	2.00	K B	2.00
B B	2.00	E A	2.00	G C	2.00	K *	2.50
B C	2.00	E B	2.00	G D	2.00	L A	2.00
B D	2.00	E C	2.00	G *	2.00	L B	2.00
B E	2.00	E D	2.00	H A	2.00	L C	2.00
B *	2.50	E *	2.50	H B	2.00	L D	2.00
C A	2.00	F A	2.00	H *	2.50	L E	4.00
C B	2.00	F B	2.00	I A	2.00	L *	2.50
C C	2.00	F C	2.00	J A	2.00		

(NOTE: COPE started with this series, and some of early COPE groups are very scarce and difficult to find. These are strictly specialist items.)

Series 1974
A A	1.75	C *	2.00	F E	1.75	J B	1.75
A B	1.75	D A	1.75	F F	1.75	J C	1.75
A C	1.75	D B	1.75	F *	2.00	J *	2.00
A *	2.00	D C	1.75	G A	1.75	K A	1.75
B A	1.75	D *	2.00	G B	1.75	K B	1.75
B B	1.75	F A	1.75	G C	1.75	K C	1.75
B C	1.75	E B	1.75	G D	1.75	K D	1.75
B D	1.75	E C	1.75	G E	1.75	K *	2.00
B E	1.75	E D	1.75	G *	2.00	L A	1.75
B F	1.75	E E	1.75	H A	1.75	L B	1.75
B G	1.75	E F	1.75	H G	1.75	L C	1.75
B H	1.75	E G	1.75	H C	1.75	L D	1.75
B *	2.00	E *	2.00	H *	2.00	L E	1.75
C A	1.75	F A	1.75	I A	1.75	L F	1.75
C B	1.75	F B	1.75	I B	1.75	L G	1.75
C C	1.75	F C	1.75	I *	2.00	L H	1.75
C D	1.75	F D	1.75	J A	1.75	L *	2.00

BLOCK LISTING FOR $1 FEDERAL RESERVE NOTES—continued
Series 1977 (Current-to date)

A A ...	1.75	D A ...	1.75	F *	2.00	J B	1.75
A B ...	1.75	D B ...	1.75	G A ...	1.75	J C	1.75
A *	2.00	D *	2.00	G B ...	1.75	J *	2.00
B A ...	1.75	E A	1.75	G C ...	1.75	K A ...	1.75
B B ...	1.75	E B	1.75	G D ...	1.75	K B ...	1.75
B C ...	1.76	E C	1.75	G E ...	1.75	K C ...	1.75
B D ...	1.75	E D	1.75	G *	2.00	K *	2.00
B E	1.75	E *	2.00	H A ...	1.75	L A	1.75
B F	1.75	F A	1.75	H B ...	1.75	L B ...	1.75
B *	2.00	F B	1.75	H *	2.00	L C ...	1.75
C A ...	1.75	F C	1.75	I A	1.75	L D ...	1.75
C B ...	1.75	F D	1.75	I *	2.00	L E	1.75
C *	2.00	F E	1.75	J A	1.75	L *	2.00

THE MINOR VARIETIES KNOWN AS "MULES"

Notes with a back plate number designed for use on an earlier or later series than that on which it is found, constitute a minor variety commonly called "mules." The difference is in the size of the check number on the back plate.

The earlier series were designed with microscopic check numbers, while later series had larger check numbers on the backplate. The difference is not readily detectable by the less ardent collector and usually requires a good magnifying glass to detect. Perhaps for this reason, the collecting of mules has not become as popular as other forms of collecting.

Trading in these minor, difficult to discover varieties, has not been sufficiently widespread to warrant placing factual valuations. Listing or offering at any price by a very limited number of dealers, does not constitute a conclusive valuation. The following tables of known back plate numbers will assist the neophyte in determining whether or not he owns a mule.

This group of notes with Julian-Morganthau face plate check numbers, and a larger size back plate check number which was designed for the next succeeding series:

U2-28C	$ 2.	1928C U. S. note. Black plate No. 289 or higher, designed for 1928D
U5-28D	5.	1928B U.S. note. Black plate No. 939 or higher, designed for 1928C
S1-35	1.	1935 Silver Certificate. Back plate No.930 or higher, designed for 1935A

"MULES"—Continued

The following 1934 series, Julian-Morgenthau notes have microscopic face plate check numbers, and a larger size back plate check number designed for series 1934A.

S5-34	$ 5.	1934	Silver Certificates	Back plate No. 939 or higher
S10-34	10.	1934	Silver Certificate	Back plate No. 585 or higher
F5-34	5.	1934	Federal Reserve	Back plate No. 939 or higher
F10-34	10.	1934	Federal Reserve	Back plate No. 585 or higher
F20-34	20.	1934	Federal Reserve	Back plate No. 318 or higher
H5-34	5.	1934	Hawaii overprint	Back plate No. 939 or higher
H20-34	20.	1934	Hawaii overprint	Back plate No. 318 or higher
A10-34	10.	1934	African invasion	Back plate No. 585 or higher

The following Julian-Morgenthau notes have a large size face plate check number and a microscopic back plate check number, designed for use on the preceding series.

U2-28D	$ 2.	1928D U.S. note. Back plate No. 288 or lower, designed for 1928C
U5-28C	5.	1928C U.S. note. Back plate No. 938 or lower, designed for 1928B
S1-35A	1.	1935A Silver certificate. Back plate No. 929 or lower, designed for 1935.

The following 1934A Julian-Morgenthau notes have a microscopic back plate check number, designed for the 1934 series:

S5-34A	$ 5.	Silver Certificate	Back plate No. 938 or lower
S10-34A	10.	Silver Certificate	Back plate Nos. 404, 553, 578
F5-34A	5.	Federal Reserve note	Back plate No. 938 or lower
F10-34A	10.	Federal Reserve note	Back plate Nos. 404, 553, 578
F20-34A	20.	Federal Reserve note	Back plate No. 317 or lower
H20-34A	20.	Hawaii overprint	Back plate No. 317 or lower

This group of Julian-Snyder and Julian-Vinson notes also have a larger size face plate check number and microscopic back plate check numbers 629 or 637 designed for a much earlier series:

U5-28D	$ 5.	United States note, Julian-Vinson, 1928D. 1928B back plate
U5-28E	5.	United States note, Julian-Snyder, 1928E. 1928B back plate
S5-34B	5.	United States note, Julian-Snyder, 1928E. 1928B back plate.
S5-34B	5.	Silver Certificate, Julian-Vinson, 1934B. 1934 back plate.
S5-34C	5.	Silver Certificate, Julian-Snyder, 1934C. 1934 plate.
F5-34B	5.	Federal Reserve, Julian-Vinson, 1934B. 1934 back plate.
F5-34C	5.	Federal Reserve, Julian-Snyder, 1934C. 1934 back plate.

TREASURERS AND SECRETARIES AND TERM OF OFFICE

Treasurer	Secretary	Began	Ended	yr.	mo.	da.
H. T. Tate	A. W. Mellon	4-30-1928	1-17-1929		8	17
Walter O. Woods	A. W. Mellon	1-18-1929	2-12-1932	3		25
Walter O. Woods	Ogden L. Mills	2-13-1932	3-3-1933	1		18
Walter O. Woods	W. H. Woodin	3-4-1933	5-31-1933		2	27
W. A. Julian	W. H. Woodin	6-1-1933	12-31-1933		7	
W. A. Julian	Henry Morgenthau, Jr.	1-1-1934	7-22-1945	11	6	22
W. A. Julian	Fred M. Vinson	7-23-1945	7-23-1946	1		
W. A. Julian	John W. Snyder	7-25-1946	5-29-1949	2	10	4
Georgia Neese Clark	John W. Snyder	6-21-1949	1-20-1953	3	7	
Ivy Baker Priest	George M. Humphrey	1-28-1953	7-28-1957	4	6	
Ivy Baker Priest	Robert B. Anderson	7-29-1957	1-20-1961	3	5	23
Elizabeth Rudel Smith	C. Douglas Dillon	1-30-1961	4-13-1962	1	3	14
Kathryn O'Hay Granahan	Douglas Dillon	1-3-1963	3-31-1965	2	2	28
Kathryn O'Hay Granahan	Henry H. Fowler	4-1-1965	10-13-1966	1	6	13
Kathryn O'Hay Granahan	Joseph W. Barr	1-1-1969	1-20-1969			20
Dorothy Andrews Elston	David M. Kennedy	5-8-1969	2-30-1971		9	22
Dorothy Andrews Kabis	John B. Connally	2-11-1971	7-3-1971		4	21
Romana Banuelos	John B. Connally	12-17-1971	5-16-1972-		4	30
Romana Banuelos	George P. Shultz	6-12-1972	5-8-1973	1	10	9
Francine Neff	William E. Simon	6-21-1974				
Francine Neff	William E. Simon		1-13-77			
			1-19-1977			
	Werner M. Blumenthal	1-23-77				
Azie Taylor Morton		9-12-77				

HOW SMALL NOTES ARE PRINTED
FLAT PRESS

Flat pressed have produced our currency for many years, and it was on these flat presses that our first small sized notes were produced. In 1928 notes were printed in sheets of 12 subjects, and the numbering was consecutive beginning with the note in the upper left corner, (except National Bank Notes which had a separate numbering system and the WW II emergency issues). Collectors were able to assemble notes that were originally printed on one sheet. Such a set is known as a "reconstructed" our "cut" sheet. Many of these early issues were also released in uncut sheet form.

In 1953 there was a change to 18-subject printing plates, and improved printing presses were brought into use. The consecutive numbering system was discontinued, and the ability to reconstruct full sheets became almost impossible (tho some of the early 18-subject issues were also released in uncut sheet form). The numbering system is illustrated below, and it will be noted that the numbers jump 8000 from one position to the next.

The small capital letter near the upper left corner of the face of the note and the same letter in lower right indicates the position of the note in the sheet. The note in upper left corner is "A" and the last note, 18th, is "R". With the number of each note advancing 8000 numbers, we would (for example) find note in position "A" as A 00000001 A, and "B" position A 0000800001 A, "C" position A 00016001 A, and on to each position through "R". The next sheet would be position "A" A 00000002 A, and so on through the printing.

NUMBERING LAYOUT OF 18-SUBJECT SHEET

A N46944040G	G N46992040G	M N47040040G
B N46952040G	H N47000040G	N N47048040G
C N46960040G	I N47008040G	O N47056040G
D N46968040G	J N47016040G	P N47064040G
E N46976040	K N47024040G	Q N47072040G
F N46984040G	L N47032040G	R N47080040G

Undoubtedly, to simplify inspection at the Bureau of Engraving and Printing at this period, the 8000 increase between each sheet position, the ending numbers on all 18 notes would be the same. On the chart we show, note that all 18 notes end in "040"-and the beginning and ending alphabet employed is identical.

United States notes (and formerly Silver Certificates) are delivered to the Treasurer of the United States, Federal Reserve Notes to the Federal Reserve

Full sheet 18-subject numbering advances 8,000 starting at upper left note

vault, under the supervision of the Comptroller of the Currency.

Flatbed presses handling 18-subject plates were continued in use until September 1968, the last notes being of Series 1950-E. The last delivery of notes from this press was made on September 16, 1968.

The special currency paper used on these flatbed presses was furnished in a mill-wet condition. When the contractor delivered the paper to the Bureau of Engraving and Printing, it was ready for printing. Printing was accomplished on four-plate intaglio power presses. The engraved plates, moving counter-clockwise around the bed of the press, were covered with a film of ink by means of an ink roller which was affixed to an ink fountain. Surplus ink on the surface of the plate was removed with the aid of an oscillating paper wiper. leaving the engraved (recessed) lines of the engraved plate filled with sufficient ink for printing. The plates then passed under a polisher which removed the thin film of ink on the face of plate left from the initial wiping.

The late flat presses were automatically fed, automatically wiped, whereas the earlier models were almost entirely hand operated, with one man feeding the sheets of paper on the press, another hand wiping the excess ink from the plate, and a third mand removing the printed sheet and stacking same on a pile with an interleaf sheet between every two printed sheets (to prevent offset of the wet ink). There was also a drying period, and there was a period of several days before the face of the plate was printed, after the reverse had been printed, and a like similar period before the overprinting was performed.

ROTARY PRESSES

During the calendar year 1957 nine high speed rotary intaglio printing presses were ordered, and the first two were installed at the Bureau of Engraving and Printing. Experimentation had been performed for several years prior to this time to find a suitable type of press for faster operation, equal printing ability, and to develop a rapid drying ink to prevent offsetting and do away with costly interleaving. These presses were of sufficient size to take a printing plate of 32-subjects. This almost doubled the plate size of the old 18-subject sheets. A dry process (rather than the wet paper of the flat press) gave much greater stability dimensionally to the printed sheet, as well as individual notes, and simplified the trimming and cutting operations to produce the individual notes. The rapidly drying inks developed enabled printing of the green reverse one day and the black faces (obverse) the following day, if desired.

The first notes printed on the Rotary press were $1 Silver Certificates, Series 1957, and were released for circulation on October 1, 1957. These notes were printed on presses ordered from the R. Hoe & Co but built by Thomas DeLaRue & Co, Ltd of London. The presses accommodate a single plate (32-subject). The inscription "In God We Trust" was added to the reverse of these notes, and was to be added to the other denominations at a later date. Robert Anderson was Secretary of the Treasury and Ivy Baker Priest Treasurer of the United States when these notes were printed, and the notes bear their signatures, which were printed on the notes at the same time the serial numbers and seals were applied.

During this period, production was being made on both the new Rotary presses, as well as the flatbed presses. The first flatbed notes to bear the inscription "In God We Trust" were released during the production of Series 1935G. This series is found both with and without the motto, and the following and final silver certificate series 1935H also had the motto. Silver Certificates continued until the release of the $1 Federal Reserve Notes in 1963 at which time all production and shipment of silver certificates, was discontinued.

The Series 1963 $1 Federal Reserve notes were printed, and shipped to

Full sheet—12 subject. Numbering is consecutive starting with upper left note.

various Federal Reserve Banks during the early part of November 1963, and general release to the public was made on Nov 26.

Early in 1965 the Bureau put into operation a modified Giori Rotary Press. This new high speed press carried a complement of four 32-subject plates. This represented a much speedier method of printing. It should be noted that notes printed on this press have a run of four different plate numbers (check numbers) within a run of notes (face and/or reverse) with the numbers alternating. The original nine rotary presses had carried single plates, the same number being found during a press run (the same applied to either reverse or face). It is quite interesting to note that during this period of change-over, it was possible to find a single number face dated used in conjunction with 4-plate reverses, and vice versa. Today, both types of equipment are used, but the vast majority of printing is on the 4-plate presses. Over a period of time, printing of the higher denominations was performed on the 4-plate presses. Some work is still performed on the single plate presses.

A new generation of Giori 4-plate presses were added to the Currency Printing Section at the Bureau. As the presses differed somewhat from the earlier models in the plate locking mechanism, it was necessary to distinguish the printing plates. Therefore, all plates for use on the new presses were given a "-1" after the master plate number (note this number is found at the top of the printing plate and is normally trimmed off when the sheet is cut into individual notes. It is NOT found on the notes themselves).

MAGNA PRESSES

A new type of Rotary press was installed at the Bureau during 1976, production therefrom was found acceptable, and four of the MAGNA 2010 presses were placed in operation. Manufactured by the American Bank Note Company, the presses have a capability of about 8,000 sheets per hour (still 32-subject) from a two-plate complement (whereas the 4-plate Giori turned out only 8,500 sheets per hour). This press uses different types of plates than master plate number (not to be found on the individual notes). These notes can be identified in two ways; first, alternating check numbers in the run, or second, the solid run of a single number, as this press can put the finished sheets in separate stacks for each plate, or alternate them as printed. There is no difference to be noted in the finished product from any of these presses. All plates are made from the same master die. As far as is known to date, only the $1 denomination has been printed on these presses.

There have been more problems encountered with the MAGNA presses, and they do not seem as completely dependable as the other presses. However, they have turned out a lot of stock and continue in operation.

PROCESSING NOTES

After the backs and faces of the 32-subject sheets are printed, they are sent to the inspection area. Here they are checked, sheet by sheet on both sides for imperfections, and the faulty sheets are put aside. The passed stock is then placed on a flat, and each 100 sheets denoted with a strip of paper (or flag as they are called). These are trimmed to a uniform size, and all of the sheet margins (which contain the master plate number, and other markings that serve as guides) are thus removed. These sheets then pass to the overprinting section, where they are run through the two-color overprinting press which applies the serial numbers, seal, series designation and signatures of the Treasurer and Secretary of Treasury (this method continued from the beginning of Rotary work until the Series 1963B and continued for the Series 1969 and all later series which had the series designation and signatures engraved on the printing plates). After the overprinting, the 32-subject sheets were cut into 16 subject (half sheets) with a single vertical cut, and these half sheets went to inspection. There defective notes were marked for removal, and insertion of star notes (replacement notes). If sufficient damage was found on a pane, it was removed and a 16-subject star sheet was substituted.

The half sheets are then sent to the guuillotine where they are separated into individual notes in large stacks of several hundred sheets at a time. The notes remain in numeral sequence within each of the stacks of 100 notes. Then the final inspection and assembly, and the marked defective notes are removed, a star note substituted and the count of 100 notes is verified on a machine, they are strapped and passed on to the assembly area where they are assembled into a run of 4,000 notes. Here they are put between two wooden blocks, banded with two steel straps, and wrapped with a large sheet of kraft paper with the brick designation pasted to one end.

In mid-1975 a sheet of plastic material was used to wrap the bricks (in place of the kraft paper). This new material is clear and moisture resistant, and could well be less expensive and will be continued until a better method is found.

The sheets of 32-subject notes, introduced in Series 1957, are printed in four quadrants of eight notes. The upper left quadrant sheet positions are A 1 to H 1; the lower left quadrant A 2 to H 2; the upper right quadrant A 3 to H 3; and the lower left quadrant A 4 to H 4. The numbering on the 32-subject sheets advances 20,000 numbers per note starting with A 1 and on thru H 4 so there is a total of 620,000 on one sheet. Unless all of the notes from one sheet were shipped to one bank and a sheet reconstructed before the notes reached circulation, the chances of a reconstructed sheet are mighty slim.

COPE OVERPRINTING

COPE (Currency Overprinting and Processing Equipment) was in experimental stages at the Bureau for a long period of time. From 1971 to 1976 a single COPE machine was in operation and having passed experimental stage, six new COPE machines were ordered, and installed at the Bureau. COPE is the combination of a German Koenug & Bauer two-color letter press and a Biel cutting line, this equipment allows the automation of overprinting, trimming, and packaging operations.

One cylinder of the press carries 32 numbering machines, and 32 seals with lower cylinders carrying equal number of black forms to overprint the second required color; the second set of cylinders is identical and on the opposited side of the equipment, and each will overprint a 16-subject sheet (so an entire 32-subject sheet will be processed at the same time). The press prints in groups of 100 notes, then stops, moving the completed sheets to the side of the press and to the cutting line. Automatic scanning equipment assures that the numbering devices turn properly with each sheet imprinted, and will automatically stop the press and signal the trouble spot should one of the numbering devices malfunction. As the sheets move to the cutter line, the stack of 100 sheets are cut into groups of two notes, and then into single notes. 100 notes, as a unit, are moved to a bander; and the banded pad of 100 notes moved into its proper position within a carousel. Each pocket is filled in one minute and the 32-pocket carousel accommodates 4000 notes, which go to make up the brick.

Originally only $1 denominations were COPE processed, but later the $5 and $10 were added; and then the $20, and even later the $50 and $100. It was not possible to overprint star notes on COPE as no provision for the asterik or star was made. However, new numbering wheels have been installed which now allows for star production, and which will soon lead to the obsolescence of the old overprinting machines.

The last process of a BLOCK (which consists of 100 million notes) which consisted of 160,000 notes (20,000 sheets) was a problem, for in this final process regular notes from 99840001 thru 99999999 were printed in first quadrant (A 1 to H 1), and the other three quadrants produced star notes. For some time, this quadrant was printed and processed on the older equipment; and a decision was finally made which simply ended the printing at note 99840000, and no last process wass produced. This meant that the possibility of finding a note with 99999999 was now impossible, as it just was not printed.

The numbering devices used on COPE are to BEP specifications and manufactured in Italy, wereas the ones used on conventional overprinting equipment are manufactured in the United States. There appears (to some collectors) to be a difference in the numbers of the two pieces of equipment to allow indentification of the two overprinting processes.

All denominations, including the $2, have been COPE produced.

Inspection procedure has been changed for COPE, and allows for much closer check on the product prior to overprinting. After printing, the sheets are cut in half, and inspection for COPE is strictly in units of 16-subjects. All inspected work found to have any defects is removed, whether one note or an entire 16-subjects. The rejected sheets were at first used for convention overprinting, but later were scrapped as it was found less expensive than additional inspections, etc.

Therefore, the supposition was that only perfect sheets would be sent to COPE, and there has been a very marked drop in star note usage in this process. However, as in everything that has the human element involved, there are some slips. Some less than perfect work is passed, and an inserted sheet (or more) might be placed in the stack in an inverted position (in relation to the other sheets), or in an upside down position (the face where the reverse should be). The first would result in inverted overprint, and the latter with the overprinting on the back side of the note, rather than on the face.

After the notes have been banded and ready to be made into a brick, a final spot check is made. A random sampling is made of several pads of 100 notes, and if a relatively small number of defects is found the brick is passed. If larger than norm, then 100% inspection of the entire 4000 notes is made. Here we would likely find more star notes; tho sometimes a defective printing, or a defective printing of a position in the sheet will result in an entire brick of 4000 star notes, or a large run of stars; but this is rather unusual.

The pads of 100 notes have a strap that is imprinted BEP and shows the denomination of the notes.

The following table of notes have been overprinted on COPE. Note that all numbers NOT listed, were overprinted on conventional equipment. We are listing only the early COPE printings, Series 1969B through 1969D.

Series 1969B

New York
B31 360 001B   B37 760 000B
B42 880 001B   B99 840 000B
B00 000 001C   B99 840 000C
B0 000 001D   B29 440 000D

Richmond
E57 600 001B   E77 440 00B

Chicago
G01 290 001C   G04 480 000C
                L99 840 000A

San Francisco
L92 160 001A   L08 960 000B
L00 000 001A

Series 1969C
New York
B29 440 001D   B76 160 00D
Richmond   E41 600 000C
E09 600 001C   G95 360 000C

Chicago
G04 480 001C

Series 1969D
Boston
A39 040 001A   A52 480 000A

New York
B03 840 001A   B26 240 000A
B32 640 001A   B56 320 000A
B75 520 001A   B99 840 000A
B00 000 001B   B11 520 000B
B34 560 001B   B53 120 000B
B60 800 001B   B99 840 000B
B00 000 001C   B99 200 000C
B01 920 001D   B99 840 000D
B00 000 001E   B02 560 000E
B11 520 001E   B68 480 000E

Philadelphia
C60 800 001A   C76 800 000A

Richmond
E17 280 001A   E63 360 000A
E84 480 001A   E99 840 000A
E00 000 001B   E33 280 00B
E14 720 001C   E46 720 000C
E27 520 001D   E48 640 000D
E51 840 001D   E74 240 000D

Atlanta
F45 440 001A   F64 000 000A
F00 000 001A   F46 080 000B
F79 360 001A   F99 840 000B
F00 000 001C   F31 360 000C
F71 040 001C   F90 240 000C
F67 200 001D   F77 440 000D

Chicago
G37 120 001A   G66 560 000A
G53 760 001B   G99 840 000B
G15 360 001C   G99 840 000C
G00 000 001D   G39 680 000D
G46 080 001D   G78 080 000D

St. Louis
H29 440 001A   H42 240 000A

Dallas
K29 440 001B   K42 240 000B

San Francisco
L52 480 001A   L96 000 000A
L20 480 001B   L99 840 000B
L02 560 001C   L28 800 000C
L35 200 001C   L52 480 000C
L87 680 001C   L99 840 000C
L00 000 001D   L08 960 000D

The $1 Series, 1974, was mostly overprinted on COPE, with Star note production being entirely conventional. With introduction of 6 new COPE machines the new overprint wheels included a " ★ " so that it was possible to overprint Star notes on COPE. All denominations through the $100 have been overprinted, and in future series we will have almost 100% COPE.

There is a very specialized group of collectors who watch on the various breaks in overprint in serials, but this information is for a very specialized catalog.

NEW TREASURY SEAL

The United States Treasury Department has adopted a new seal now in use on all current issues of United States paper money. The seal appeared first on series 1966 U.S. note, $100 denomination, issued in October, 1967.

Previous to these issues, the seal in use since 1862 bore the Latin inscription, "Thesaur. Amer. Serpent, Sigil." Many collectors have endeavored to translate the Latin inscription, which had several interpretations and which designated that it was the Seal of the North American Treasury.

Minor changes were made in the seal throughout the years but the Latin inscripcion remained. This now gives way to the very clear English inscription: "The Department of the Treasury 1789." The scales of justice remain, simplified and slightly enlarged, also the key. Thirteen stars complete the streamlined ornamentation.

New design

Former Design

In addition to printing our current issues of paper money, the Bureau also has the task of printing U.S. postage stamps, Treasury bonds, certificates of indebtedness, customs, revenue and savings stamps, food coupons and many engraved items for use in the various departments and independent agencies of the Federal Government, its insular possessions, and the Panama Canal Zone Government, also engraved invitations and White House stationery.

United States paper money with a face value of over $12 billion is printed annually, with an average daily production of approximately 9 million notes. Designs of our discontinued large size paper money, 1861-1923, were frequently changed. However, since the small size currency was first issued in 1929, all notes of like denomination bear the same portrait of a great American on the face of the note throughout all the series issues. The back also has undergone little change. The Treasury Department states that these designs eliminate confusion on the part of the public, and also is a protection against counterfeiting.

Face and back designs of all current issues, are as follows:

Denomination	Portrait	Back Design
$1	Washington	Obverse and reverse of Great Seal of U.S.
$5	Lincoln	Lincoln Memorial
$10	Hamilton	U.S. Treasury Building
$20	Jackson	White House
$50	Grant	U.S. Capitol
$100	Franklin	Independence Hall

Discontinued issues had these designs

$2 (United States Note)		
	Jefferson	Monticello
$2 (Federal Reserve Note)		
	Jefferson	Signing of Declaration of Independence
$500	McKinley	Ornate Five Hundred
$1000	Cleveland	Ornate One Thousand
$5000	Madison	Ornate Five Thousand
$10,000	Chase	Ornate Ten Thousand

A GUIDE TO STAR NUMBER VALUATIONS

In evaluating paper money, or coins, consideration must be given not only to estimated available supply but more especially to "collector demand." Demand for "stars" has increased considerably as many collectors formerly content with "regular numbers," turned their attention to "star numbers." This increased demand is reflected in rising values of star serial numbers.

Further information on star numbered currency will be found on page 6.

UNITED STATES NOTES, red seals, 1928-1966
with STAR prefix and suffix letter "A"

				V.F.	Unc.
U1*-28	$1.	1928	Woods-Woodin	600.00	1500.00

Records show 24,000 of above assigned. Issue unknown.

				V.F.	Unc.
U2*-28	2.	1928	Tate-Mellon	65.00	150.00
U2*-28A	2.	1928A	Woods-Mellon	150.00	350.00
U2*-28B	2.	1928B	Woods-Mills	350.00	1,500.00
U2*-28C	2.	1928C	Julian-Morgenthau	100.00	260.00
U2*-28D	2.	1928D	Julian-Morgenthau	25.00	50.00
U2*-28E	2.	1928E	Julian-Vinson	250.00	900.00
U2*-28F	2.	1928F	Julian-Snyder	20.00	40.00
U2*-28G	2.	1928G	Clark-Snyder	10.00	25.00
U2*-53	2.	1953	Priest-Humphrey	6.00	15.00
U2*-53A	2.	1953A	Priest-Anderson	—	10.00
U2*-53B	2.	1953B	Smith-Dillon	—	7.50
U2*-53C	2.	1953C	Granahan-Dillon	—	5.00
U2*-63	2.	1963	Granahan-Dillon	—	5.00
U2*-63A	2.	1963A	Granahan-Fowler	—	5.00
U5*-28	$5.	1928	Woods-Mellon	45.00	80.00
U5*-28A	5.	1928A	Woods-Mills	150.00	350.00
U5*-28B	5.	1928B	Julian-Morgenthau	35.00	80.00
U5*-28C	5.	1928C	Julian-Morgenthau	35.00	75.00
U5*-28D	5.	1928D	Julian-Vinson	200.00	500.00
U5*-28E	5.	1928E	Julian-Snyder	30.00	65.00
U5*-28F	5.	1928F	Clark-Snyder	25.00	60.00
U5*-53	5.	1953	Priest-Humphrey	30.00	75.00
U5*-53A	5.	1953A	Priest-Anderson	10.00	25.00
U5*-53B	5.	1953B	Smith-Dillon	10.00	22.50
U5*-53C	5.	1953C	Granahan-Dillon	8.50	10.00
U5*-63	5.	1963	Granahan-Dillon	8.00	10.00
U100*-66	$100.	1966	Granahan-Fowler	—	175.00

STAR NUMBER VALUATIONS
ONE DOLLAR SILVER CERTIFICATES
with STAR prefix, and suffix letter as shown.

	Series	Suffix		V.F.	Unc.
S1*-28	1928	"A"	Tate-Mellon	18.00	55.00
S1*-28A	1928A	"A"	Woods-Mellon	10.00	32.50
S1*-28B	1928B	"A"	Woods-Mills	17.50	75.00
S1*-28C	1928C	"A"	Woods-Woodin	1,000.00	2,000.00
S1*-28D	1928D	"A"	Julian-Woodin	800.00	1,750.00
S1*-28E	1928E	"A"	Julian-Morgenthau*	Rare	
S1*-34	1934	"A"	Julian-Morgenthau	40.00	120.00
S1*-35	1935	"A"	Julian-Morgenthau	30.00	100.00
S1*-35A(a)	1935A	"A"	Julian-Morgenthau	10.00	20.00
S1*-35A(b)	1935A	"B"	Julian-Morgenthau	75.00	155.00
S1*-35B	1935B	"B"	Julian-Vinson	15.00	55.00
S1*-35C	1935C	"B"	Julian-Snyder	6.00	17.50
S1*-35D(b)	1935D	"B"	Clark-Snyder (W)	4.00	10.00
S1*-35D(c)	1935D	"C"	Clark-Snyder (W)	175.00	275.00
S1*-35D(b)	1935D	"B"	Clark-Snyder (N)	4.00	10.00
S1*-35D(c)	1935D	"C"	Clark-Snyder (N)	8.00	20.00
S1*-35D(d)	1935D	"D"	Clark-Snyder (N)	20.00	55.00
S1*-35E(d-e-f)	1935E	"D-E-F"	Priest-Humphrey	—	8.50
S1*-57(a-b-c)	1957	"A-B-C"	Priest-Anderson	—	5.00
S1*-57	1957	"D"	Priest-Anderson	5.00	15.00
S1*-35F(f-g)	1935F	"F-G"	Priest-Anderson	—	8.00
S1*-57A	1957A	"A"	Smith-Dillon	—	4.50
S1*-35G(g)	1935G	"G"	Smith-Dillon	—	7.00
S1*-35G (M)	1935G	"G"	Smith-Dillon (motto)	5.00	17.50
S1*-57B(a)	1957B	"A"	Granahan-Dillon	5.00	10.00
S1*-57B(b)	1957B	"B"	Granahan-Dillon	—	4.00
S1*-35H	1935H	"G"	Granahan-Dillon	—	8.50

FIVE DOLLAR SILVER CERTIFICATES

	Series	Suffix		V.F.	Unc.
S5*-34	1934	"A"	Julian-Morgenthau	25.00	55.00
S5*-34A	1934A	"A"	Julian-Morgenthau	17.50	35.00
S5*-34B	1934B	"A"	Julian-Vinson	35.00	115.00
S5*-34C	1934C	"A"	Julian-Snyder	16.00	35.00
S5*-34D	1934D	"A"	Clark-Snyder	15.00	35.00
S5*-53	1953	"A"	Priest-Humphrey	13.00	30.00
S5*-53A	1953A	"A"	Priest-Anderson	10.00	17.50
S5*-53B	1953B	"A"	Smith-Dillon	225.00	400.00

TEN DOLLAR SILVER CERTIFICATES

	Series	Suffix		V.F.	Unc.
S10*-33	1933	"A"	Julian-Woodin	Unknown	
S10*-33A	1933A	"A"	Julian-Morgenthau	Very Rare‡	
S10*-34	1934	"A"	Julian-Morgenthau	40.00	100.00
S10*-34A	1934A	"A"	Julian-Morgenthau	45.00	100.00
S10*-34B	1934B	"A"	Julian-Vinson	750.00	2,250.00
S10*-34C	1934C	"A"	Julian-Snyder	17.50	45.00
S10*-34D	1934D	"A"	Clark-Snyder	22.50	60.00
S10*-53	1953	"A"	Priest-Humphrey	22.50	60.00
S10*-53A	1953A	"A"	Priest-Anderson	22.50	60.00

*Only 3 circulated copies known. ‡One copy reported, Standard Handbook, possibly unique.

STAR NUMBER VALUATIONS — WORLD WAR II AND EXPERIMENTAL ISSUES

WORLD WAR II HAWAII EMERGENCY ISSUES

The $1 note is a silver certificate with *-A (J-M)

The higher denominations are Federal Reserve notes of the San Francisco District with prefix letter "L." All have Julian-Morgenthau signatures.

				V.F.	Unc.
H 1*35A	$ 1.	1935A	Julian-Morgenthau	130.00	300.00
H 5*-34	$ 5.	1934	Julian-Morgenthau	125.00	400.00
H 5*-34A	$ 5.	1934A	Julian-Morgenthau	55.00	125.00
H10*-34A	$10.	1934A	Julian-Morgenthau	50.00	125.00
H20*-34	$20.	1934	Julian-Morgenthau		Rare
H20*-34A	$20.	1934A	Julian-Morgenthau	75.00	175.00

W.W. II NORTH AFRICAN INVASION ISSUES

All are silver certificates, Julian-Morgenthau signatures, suffix letter "A."

		V.F.	Unc.
A 1*-35A	1935A	125.00	275.00
A 5*-34A	1934A	60.00	125.00
A10*-34	1934		Rare
A10*-34A	1934A	50.00	100.00

RED "R" AND "S" EXPERIMENTAL ISSUE

			V.F.	Unc.
ER1*-35A	1935A	12,000 printed	950.00	1,500.00
ES1*-35A	1935A	12,000 printed	800.00	1,350.00

All are silver certificates, Julian-Morgenthau signatures with star prefix letter "A".

OFFICIAL SERIAL NUMBER DATA

We are indebted to the Bureau of Engraving and Printing for the information contained in the serial number data. Please note that for convenience in reference this information has been placed after each of the groups of notes in the pricing section of this catalog. We have also listed the uncut sheets in the same areas as the notes, so that all information will be more readily available.

The printing totals, and first and last serial numbers, are believed to be correct as to the TOTAL of notes printed through any one series date. For example, it is believed that the combined total of 430,752,800 United States Notes is correct for the eight different 1928 series: 1928 through 1928E.

Please note, however, that the breakdown for each series has been found to be incorrect. The system formerly in use of continuing the usage of old plates with engraved signatures, and to overprint serial numbers even long after the next series appeared, makes the errors in totals understandable. Many notes have been reported out of the "official" serial number range, and this appears to be the rule rather than the exception.

Starting with Series 1953 of the $2.00 U.S. Notes, and Series 1935E of the $1.00 Silver Certificates, the total given for each series is assumed to be correct. Serial numbers have not been found outside the official ending numbers.

UNITED STATES NOTES
Usually designated as LEGAL TENDER NOTES
All have red seals and serial numbers

The current size United States notes, usually designated as Legal Tender notes, have been issued in $1.00, $2.00, $5.00 and $100.00 denomination. The $1.00 note is a type note, having been issued in series 1928 only. The printing of $2.00 notes was discontinued in 1966, series 1963A being the last to be released. Final delivery of $5.00 1963 series was Nov. 27, 1967. Collector interest in both the $2.00 and $5.00 red seal notes has increased since their discontinuance.

SERIES 1928 $1.00 UNITED STATES NOTE

This series is unique as it is the only $1.00 note bearing a red seal in the current size notes. The seal is to the left of the note, with large "ONE" in grey at right of note.

The inscription at left of note reads: "This note is legal tender at its face value for all debts public and private except duties on imports and interest on the public debt."

The obligation of the United States to pay reads: "The United States of America will pay to the bearer on demand One Dollar."

Only 1,872,012 $1.00 notes were printed and most of these were released in Puerto Rico. The original issue of 5,000, numbered A00000001A to A00005000A is very scarce. The first 120 numbers were released in uncut sheets of twelve. There also exist uncut sheets with much higher numbers. This series bears the signatures of W. O. Woods, Treasurer, and W. H. Woodin, Secretary of the Treasury.

FACE AND BACK DESIGNS $2.00 UNITED STATES NOTES

The first face design, series 1928 to 1928G has the red Treasury seal to the left and large "TWO" to the right. The series date occurs once at lower left. A very minor change in face design occurs in the lower left and right corners of scroll on series 128C-D-E-F and G. This added beading does not occur on series 1953 or later.

The second face design, series 1953 to 1953C, 1963 and 1963A has the large numeral "2" in grey to the left and a smaller red Treasury seal is printed over "TWO" at right. The series date with the word "of" omitted has been moved to the lower right in place of "Washington, D.C." which is now under the red serial number at upper right.

The back design of all $2.00 notes shows the Monticello, Virginia, home of Thomas Jefferson, third president of the United States. The motto "In God we Trust" was added to the series of 1963 and 1963A.

INSCRIPTIONS AND OBLIGATIONS $2.00 UNITED STATES NOTES

On the 1928 and 1928B series, the inscription at left of note reads: "This note is legal tender at its face value for all debts public and private except duties on imports and interest on the public debt."

On series 1928C through 1928G and on series 1953 to 1953C the inscription read: "This note is legal tender at its face value for all debts public and private."

The obligation on all of the above series reads: "The United States of America will pay to the bearer on demand Two Dollars."

The 1963 series brought a change in the inscription and obligation. The inscription reading: "This note is legal tender for all debts public and private." The words "at its face value" have been eliminated. From the obligation appearing on all earlier issues, the words "will pay to the bearer on demand" have been removed. The wording in the scroll under Thomas Jefferson simply reads "The United States of America Two Dollars." Should the "bearer" infer that the United States will not meet its obligation, he may take comfort in the motto now appearing on back of note!

FACE AND BACK DESIGNS $5.00 UNITED STATES NOTES

The first face design series 1928 to 1928F has the red Treasury seal to the left and "FIVE" to right.

On the second face design, series 1953 to 1953C, series 1963 and 1963A the large numeral "5" in grey at left and a smaller red Treasury seal is struck over grey "FIVE" at right.

The back design of all $5.00 series of United States notes is the same as used on all $5.00 Silver Certificates and all types of $5.00 issues. It pictures the Lincoln Memorial at Potomac Park, Washington, D.C.

INSCRIPTIONS AND OBLIGATIONS $5.00 UNITED STATES NOTES

On series 1928 and 1928A the inscription reads: "This note is a legal tender at its face value for all debts public and private except duties on imports and interest on the public debt."

On series 1928B and 1928F and series 1953 to 1953C the words "except on duties and imports and interest on the public debt" were eliminated as these restictions were removed by the Act of May 12, 1933.

Starting with the 1963 series the inscription is further abbreviated to read "This note is legal tender for all debts public and private."

NEW $100.00 UNITED STATES NOTE, SERIES 1966

The issuance of the series 1966 $100 red seal United States note came as a surprise and delight to collectors who have eagerly awaited new designs in United States paper money.

This high denomination note has found a place in more collections than any other issue of $100 notes. Still sold at a premium over face for strictly uncirculated specimens, it is a worthwhile addition to any collection.

ONE DOLLAR UNITED STATES NOTES

Face Design $1.00, Series 1928

Back Design $1.00, Series 1928

No.	Series	Treasurer-Secretary	Printed	VF	EF	Unc.
U1-28	1928	Woods-Woodin*	1,872,012	25.00	40.00	80.00
With close margins frequently found*				20.00	35.00	65.00
Serial numbers under 5000				35.00	50.00	95.00
Star numbers 24,000 assigned. Issue unknown				600.00	800.00	1600.00

$1 UNITED STATES NOTE
12-subject Sheet

		First Serial	Last Serial	Deliveries		
Series	Sec'y. & Treas.	Number Printed	Number Printed	First Note	Last Note	Total Notes
1928	Woods-Woodin	A00 000 001A	A01 872 012A	4-26-33	5- 5-33	1,872,012

The first of the above series, numbered A00000001A to A00005000A were released in 1933. Very few of the first 5000 number were preserved by collectors and are now eagerly sought by collectors of low and special numbers.

The balance of this issue was held in Treasury vaults until 1948 when approximately one million notes were sent to Puerto Rico for release. In 1949 the balance of the stock of this issue was also sent to Puerto Rico.

*Note: Average copies are generally found and bring a much lower price than well centered notes. Note the dual pricing.

Very poor margins are frequently found on the higher serial numbers. Therefore a special evaluation is given above.

TWO DOLLAR UNITED STATES NOTES

The discontinuance of the $2 United States notes in 1966 awakened collector interest and demand for this series.

Face Design $2.00, Series 1928 to 1928G

Back Design $2.00, Series 1928 to 1953C

No.	Series	Treasurer-Secretary	Printed	VF	EF	Unc.
U2-28	1928	Tate-Mellon		16.00	27.50	60.00
U2-28A	1928A	Woods-Mellon		35.00	75.00	150.00
U2-28B	1928B	Woods-Mills		150.00	240.00	500.00
U2-28C	1928C	Julian-Morgenthau		12.00	20.00	50.00
U2-28D	1928D	Julian-Morgenthau		7.50	12.00	25.00
U2-28E	1928E	Julian-Vinson	6,480,000	12.50	25.00	50.00
U2-28F	1928F	Julian-Snyder	42-360,000	7,50	12.50	25.00
U2-28G	1928G	Clark-Snyder*	52,208,000	4.50	7.50	16.00

$2 UNITED STATES NOTE
12-subject Sheet

Series	Sec'y. & Treas.	First Serial Number Printed	Last Serial Number Printed	Deliveries First Note	Last Note	Total Notes
1928	Mellon-Tate	A00 000 001A	A18 000 000A	4-24-29	6- 5-29	18,000,000
1928A	Mellon-Woods	A18 000 001A	A73 860 000A	7- 2-29	3-17-32	55,860,000
1928B	Mills-Woods	A73 860 001A	B09 008 000A	4-20-32	4-26-34	35,148,000
1928C	Morgenthau-Julian	B09 008 001A	B09 012 000A	6-15-34	6-15-34	4,000
1928D	Morgenthau-Julian	B09-012-001A	D29 712 000A	6-15-34	1- 7-46	220,700,000
1928E	Vinson-Julian	D29 712 001A	D36 192 000A	2-25-46	8- 7-46	6,480,000
1928F	Snyder-Julian	D36 192 001A	D78 552 000A	9-25-46	12- 6-49	42,360,000
1928G	Snyder-Clark	D78 552 001A	E30 760 000A	1-16-50	5- 6-53	52,208,000

*Note: Due to a flemish at the end of Mrs. Clark's signature, the name appears to be Clarke, Clark is correct spelling.

TWO DOLLAR UNITED STATES NOTES

Face Design $2.00, Series 1953 to 1953C

No.	Series	Treasurer-Secretary	Printed	VF	EF	Unc.
U2-53	1953	Priest-Humphrey	45,360,000	3.50	5.00	12.50
U2-53A	1953A	Priest-Anderson	18,000,000	3.00	4.50	12.00
U2-53B	1953B	Smith-Dillon	10,800,000	3.00	4.00	17.00
U2-53C	1953C	Granahan-Dillon	5,760,000	3.00	4.00	9.50

Face Design $2.00, Series 1963 to 1963A

U2-63	1963	Granahan-Dillon	15,360,000	—	3.50	8.50
U2-63A	1963A	Granahan-Fowler	3,200,000	—	3.50	8.50

$2 UNITED STATES NOTES
18-subject Sheet

Series	Sec'y. & Treas.	First Serial Number Printed	Last Serial Number Printed	Deliveries First Note	Last Note	Total Notes
1953	Humphrey-Priest	A00 000 001A	A45 360 000A	5- 2-53	8-20-57	45,360,000
1953A	Anderson-Priest	A45 360 001A	A63,360,000A	2-19-58	9- 8-60	18,000,000
1953B	Dillon-Smith	A63 360 001A	A74 160 000A	9-21-61	7- 9-62	10,800,000
1953C	Dillon-Granahan	A74 160 001A	A79 920 000A	10-15-63	11- 7-63	5,760,000

32-subject Sheet

1963	Dillon-Granahan	A00 000 001A	A15 360 000A	3-11-64	6- 3-64	15,360,000
1963A	Fowler-Granahan	A15 360 001A	A18 560 000A	7-29-65	7-29-65	3,200,000

TWO DOLLAR UNITED STATES NOTES

Back Design $2.00, "In God We Trust" added above dome.

FIVE DOLLAR UNITED STATES NOTES

As with the $2 red seal United States note, the announcement of the discontinuance of the $5 denomination turned collectors to this series. The final delivery of the $5 notes was made Nov. 27, 1967.

Face Design $5.00, Series 1928 to 1928F

FIVE DOLLAR UNITED STATES NOTES

Back design $5.00 used on United States Notes, Silver Certificates and Federal Reserve Notes

No.	Series	Treasurer-Secretary	Printed	VF	EF	Unc.
U5-28	1928	Woods-Mellon		11.00	20.00	45.00
U5-28A	1928A	Woods-Mills		22.50	38.00	85.00
U5-28B	1928B	Julian-Morgenthau		15.00	25.00	35.00
U5-28C	1928C	Julian-Morgenthau		12.00	18.00	35.00
U5-28D	1928D	Julian-Vinson	11,868,000	25.00	50.00	100.00
U5-28E	1928E	Julian-Snyder	109,096,000	12.00	20.00	35.00
U5-28F	1928F	Clark-Snyder	104,194,704	12.00	20.00	32.50

$5 UNITED STATES NOTE
12-subject Sheet

Series	Sec'y. & Treas.	First Serial Number Printed	Last Serial Number Printed	Deliveries First Note	Last Note	Total Notes
1928	Mellon-Woods	A00 000 001A	B19 700 000A	5-27-29	12-19-30	119,700,000
1928A	Mills-Woods	B19 700 001A		1- 8-31		
1928B	Morgenthau-Julian		D15 228 000A		6-18-34	
1928C	Morgenthau-Julian	D15 228 001A	G50 628 000A	6-19-34	2-25-46	334,400,000
1928D	Vinson-Julian	G50 628 001A	G62 496 000A	3-11-46	9-19-46	11,868,000
1928E	Snyder-Julian	G62 496 001A	H71 592 000A	9-20-46	3-21-50	109,096,000
1928F	Snyder-Clark	H71 592 001A	I 79 468 000A	3-21-50	4-27-53	104,194,704

Face Design $5.00, Series 1953 to 1953C

FIVE DOLLAR UNITED STATES NOTES

No.	Series	Treasurer-Secretary	Printed	VF	EF	Unc.
U5-53	1953	Priest-Humphrey	120,880,000	15.00	20.00	30.00
U5-53A	1953A	Priest-Anderson	90,280,000	10.00	15.00	22.50
U5-53B	1953B	Smith-Dillon	44,640,000	10.00	15.00	20.00
U5-53C	1953C	Granahan-Dillon	8,640,000	10.00	15.00	20.00

Face Design $5.00, Series 1963

Motto added. Back Design

U5-63	1963	Granahan-Dillon	63,360,000	—	9.50	12.50

$5 UNITED STATES NOTES
18-subject Sheet

Series	Sec'y. & Treas.	First Serial Number Printed	Last Serial Number Printed	Deliveries First Note	Last Note	Total Notes
1953	Humphrey-Priest	A00 000 001A	B20 880 000A	5- 6-53	8-28-57	120,880,000
1953A	Anderson-Priest	B20 880 001A	C11 160 000A	2-10-58	1-13-61	90,280,000
1953B	Dillon-Smith	C11 160 001A	C55 800 000A	10- 5-61	2-25-63	44,640,000
1953C	Dillon-Granahan	C55 800 001A	C64 440 000A	2-26-63	11- 8-63	8,640,000

32-subject Sheet

1963	Dillon-Granahan	A00 000 001A	A63 360 000A	3- 2-64	11-27-67	63,360,000

UNITED STATES NOTE — ONE HUNDRED DOLLARS

Face Design $100, showing new seal

Back Design, $100 with motto

No.	Series	Treasurer-Secretary	Printed	Unc.
U100-66	1966	Granahan-Fowler	768,000	185.00
U100-66A	1966A	Elston-Kennedy	512,000	155.00

$100 UNITED STATES NOTES

Series	Sec'y. & Treas.	First Serial Number Printed	Last Serial Number Printed	Deliveries First Note	Last Note
1966	Granahan-Fowler	A00 000 001A	A00 768 000A	10-14-68	11- 5-68
1966A	Elston-Kennedy	A00 768 001A	A01 280 000A	1-26-71	1-26-71

Star Series — 1966

First Serial Number Printed	Last Serial Number Printed
*00 000 001A	*00 128 000A

Note: All Star Notes were not distributed.

The 1966 note marked a real "first" in the printing of small size paper money. It is the first $100 small size United States note; the first to carry the new seal with English inscription; the first in over 20 years to be printed from plates with engraved signatures and engraved dates; and the only note to bear series 1966. The red seal and serial numbers are overprinted.

The signatures are those of Kathryn O'Hay Granahan, former U.S. Treasurer, and Henry H. Fowler, former secretary of the Treasury.

By act of Congress, May 3, 1878, the amount of United States notes outstanding must be maintained at $346,681,016.00.

UNCUT SHEETS

This catalog pioneered the pricing of uncut sheets. New collector interest has been awakened and the demand exceeds the supply.

The issuance of limited numbers of uncut sheets for numismatic and educational purposes was discontinued shortly after the first printing of 18 subject sheets. The actual number existing is unknown. Uncut sheets are considered to be uncirculated if minor corner or margin flaws, as they are frequently found.

LEGAL TENDER — UNITED STATES NOTE
ONE DOLLAR, 12 Subjects

No.	Series	Treasurer-Secretary	Valuation
U1-28	1928	Walter O. Woods-W. H. Woodin (Very Rare)	9,500.00

Out of 11 issued only 8 are known to exist

TWO DOLLARS, 12 subjects

U2-28	1928	H. T. Tate-A. W. Mellon	2,750.00
U2-28A	1928A	Walter O. Woods-Odgen L. Mills	Very Rare*
U2-28B	1928B	Walter O. Woods-Ogden L. Mills	Very Rare*
U2-28C	1928C	W. A. Julian-Henry Morgenthau, Jr.	3,000.00
U2-28D	1928D	W. A. Julian-Henry Morgenthau, Jr.	Very Rare*
U2-28E	1928E	W. A. Julian-Fred W. Vinson	2,000.00
U2-28F	1928F	W. A. Julian-John W. Snyder	1,600.00
U2-28G	1928G	Georgia Neese Clark-John W. Snyder	1,500.00

TWO DOLLARS, 18 subjects

U2-53	1953	Ivy Baker Priest-George H. Humphrey	2,250.00

FIVE DOLLARS, 12 subjects

U5-28	1928	Walter O. Woods-A. W. Mellon	1,500.00
U5-28A	1928A	Walter O. Woods-Ogden L. Mills	Very Rare*
U5-28B	1928B	W. A. Julian-Henry Morgenthau, Jr.	Very Rare*
U5-28C	1928C	W. A. Julian-Henry Morgenthau, Jr.	Very Rare*
U5-28D	1928D	W. A. Julian-Fred M. Vinson	3,000.00
U5-28E	1928E	W. A. JUlian-John W. Snyder	1,750.00
U5-28F	1928F	Georgia Neese Clark-John W. Snyder	1,600.00

FIVE DOLLARS, 18 subjects

U5-53	1953	Ivy Baker Priest-George M. Humphrey	3,000.00

*No sheet verified

SILVER CERTIFICATES

All have blue seals and serial numbers

Current size Silver Certificates were issued in denominations of $1, $5 and $10. There were twenty series of the $1. denomination, exceeding by far the number of series of any other denomination.

FACE DESIGNS $1.00 SILVER CERTIFICATE

There are three designs on the face of the $1 certificates, and two major changes and one minor change on the back design.

The first face design, series 1928 to 1928E has the blue Treasury seal to the left, and "ONE" in large grey letters to the right.

The second face design, series 1934 has a large blue numeral "1" on the left and the blue Treasury seal has been moved to the right. This is the only series with this design, and it is therefore a type note in demand by collectors.

The third face design series 1935 through 1935H, also 1957 and 1957A and B has a smaller numeral "1" in grey on left side, and the blue Treasury seal on the right is also slightly smaller.

The series date appears twice on series 1928 through 1935 on upper left and lower right, on face of note. On series 1935A and subsequent series, the series date appears only on lower right. On the 1935 series the date appears under the plate letter at upper left, and over the plate letter at lower right.

BACK DESIGNS $1.00 SILVER CERTIFICATE

The first back design (same as 1928 U.S. notes) appears on all series 1928 to 1928E and also on series 1934.

The second back design appears on all issues of the 1935 series.

The addition of the motto "In God We Trust" gave us a minor change in the back design of some of the 1935G series as well as the 1935H series and the 1957, 1957A and 1957B series.

INSCRIPTIONS AND OBLIGATIONS $1.00 SILVER CERTIFICATES

On series 1928 to 1928D the inscription to left of notes reads: "This certificate is receivable for all public dues and when so received may be reissued." The obligation reads: "This certifies that there has been deposited in the Treasury of the United States of America One Silver Dollar payable to the bearer on demand."

The wording on the 1928E series is unique. The obligation is that of the 1928 to 1928D series, but the inscription is the same as 1934 and all subsequent series and reads:

"This certificate is legal tender for all debts public and private." The obligation has been changed to read: "This certifies that there is on deposit in the Treasury of the United States of America, one dollar in silver, payable to the bearer on demand."

ORDER OF RELEASE ON ALL 1957 SERIES

Some confusion has been caused among collectors by the order in which the last seven series of $1.00 Silver Certificates were released. The 1957 series was the first series to be printed in sheets of 82 notes, by the dry process, and also the first series to bear the motto "In God We Trust." Sheets of 18 1935F series continued to be printed by wet process on the older presses. This series was released after the 1957. It thus became the 15th series.

The 1957A series was printed next becoming the 16th series. This was followed by 1935G series without motto, and 1935G with motto. The 19th series to be printed was 1957B followed by the 20th and final issue of our $1.00 Silver Certificates, 1935H.

SPECIAL ISSUES OF 1935 $1.00 SILVER CERTIFICATES

In addition to the above regular issues of $1.00 Silver Certificates, the 1935A series has been used for several special issues. A total of 35,052,000 notes of this series have the Hawaii overprint on back. The face shows a brown seal and numbers, with "Hawaii" printed on left and right ends.

Another lot of 26,916,000 notes of the 1935A series were printed for the African invasion with yellow seals. The yellow seal is the only change in the notes of this issue.

An experiment to test two grades of paper was also conducted with 1935A series of $1.00 Silver Certificates. 1,184,000 notes were imprinted near the right end of the face of the note with the red letter "R," indicating regular paper. A like number were imprinted with the red letter "S" denoting a special paper or sizing. After a period of circulation almost all of these notes found their way back to the Treasury, making the supply very short for collectors.

FACE AND BACK DESIGNS $5.00 SILVER CERTIFICATES

Series 1934 marked the first issue of $5.00 Silver Certificates, small size. The first face design series 1934 to 1934D has a large numeral "5" in blue at left, and the blue Treasury seal at right of note.

The second face design, series 1953 to 1953C has a slightly smaller numeral "5" and a small Treasury seal in blue.

The back design of all series of $5.00 Silver Certificates, has a view of the Lincoln Memorial as used on all types of small size $5.00 notes.

INSCRIPTION AND OBLIGATION ON $5.00 SILVER CERTIFICATES

The inscription and obligation remained the same throughout the $5.00 Silver Certificate issues.

The inscription reads: "This certificate is legal tender for all debts public and private."

The obligation reads: "This certifies that there is on deposit in the Treasury of the United States of America, Five Dollars in silver payable to the bearer on demand."

FACE AND BACK DESIGNS $10.00 SILVER CERTIFICATES

The first face design of the $10.00 Silver Certificate was used on the first series only, 1933, making this a type note, very much in demand with a small issue of 216,000. The Treasury seal is in blue at the left, the denomination "TEN" is at the right.

The second face design, series 1934 to 1934D has the large blue numeral "10" at the left, and the blue Treasury seal at right.

The third face design 1953 to 1953B series has a smaller numeral "10" in grey at the left, and the blue Treasury seal at the right is slightly smaller.

The back design of the $10.00 Silver Certificate has a view of the United States Treasury building, the same as used on all current size notes of this denomination.

INSCRIPTION AND OBLIGATION $10.00 SILVER CERTIFICATES

As with the face design, the inscription on the 1933 series $10.00 Silver Certificate, is different than that of any other note. It reads: "This certificate issued pursuant to sections of the Act of May 12, 1933, and is legal tender at its face value for all debts public and private."

The obligation is also different and reads: "Ten Dollars in silver COIN to the bearer on demand."

All issues of the 1934 series and all issues of the 1953 series bear the same inscriptions: "This certificate is legal tender for all debts public and private." The obligation remains the same throughout these series and reads: "This certifies there is on deposit in the Treasury of the United States of America, Ten Dollars in silver, payable to the bearer on demand."

SILVER CERTIFICATES DISCONTINUED

Issuance of all denominations of Silver Certificates has been discontinued. Last delivery of these Certificates by the Bureau of Engraving and Printing to the Treasury Department was as follows:

$1.00 1957B November 6, 1963, $5.00 1953B April 25, 1962 and $10.00 1953B March 14, 1962.

THE FUTURE FOR SILVER CERTIFICATES

In the mad scramble to find silver certificates for redemption previous to June 24, 1968, hoards were discovered resulting in a temporary lessening of demand. No great quantity of the scarcer issues is known to have been discovered. This fact bore out the previous belief that some issues do not exist in sufficient quantity to supply all collectors.

Thousands of new collectors were added to the paper money field. The numismatic value of silver certificates has leveled off, and we can anticipate a gradual increase in value over the years, as these new collectors strive to obtain needed notes. Some of these items are decidedly scarce and in short supply, while others will attain a greater value as present supplies are exhausted.

ONE DOLLAR SILVER CERTIFICATES

Face Design $1.00, Series 1928 to 1928E

No.	Series	Treasurer-Secretary	Printed	VF	EF	Unc.
S1-28	1928	Tate-Mellon		6.00	9.00	20.00
S1-28A	1928A	Woods-Mellon		4.50	6.50	12.00
S1-28B	1928B	Woods-Mills		5.00	7.50	15.00
S1-28C	1928C	Woods-Mellon		165.00	250.00	400.00
S1-28D	1928D	Julian-Woodin		125.00	175.00	359.00
S1-28E	1928E	Julian-Morgenthau		375.00	575.00	975.00

$1 SILVER CERTIFICATE — 12-subject Sheet

Series	Sec'y. & Treas.	First Serial Number Printed	Last Serial Number Printed	Deliveries First Note	Last Note	Total Notes†
1928	Mellon-Tate	A00 000 001A	D15 136 000A	1-10-29	6-18-29	315,136,000
1928A	Mellon-Woods	D15 136 001A	V51 000 000A	6-18-29	4- 4-32	1,735,864,000
1928B	Mills-Woods	V51 000 001A	B29 448 000B	3-31-32	3-28-33	578,448,000
1928C	Woodin-Woods	B29 448 001B	D82 596 000B	3-28-33	9- 1-33	253,148,000
1928D	Woodin-Julian	D82 596 001B	F72 000 000B	9- 1-33	2-19-34	189,404,000
1928E	Morgenthau-Julian	F72 000 001B	J55 796 000B	5-31-35	5-31-35	383,796,000
Experimental paper Issue of 1928 A and B:						
	Morgenthau-Julian	X00 000 001B	X10 728 000B	1-30-33	2-17-33	10,728,000
	Morgenthau-Julian	Y00 000 001B	Y10 248 000B	2- 7-33	2-21-33	10,248,000
	Morgenthau-Julian	Z00 000 001B	Z10 248 000B	2-13-33	2-28-33	10.248,000

†Walter Breen's research in archives indicates following printing: 1928 638,296,908; 1928A 2,267,-809,500; 1928B 674,597,808; 1928C 5,364,348; 1928D 14,451,372; 1928E 3,519,324.

UNCUT SHEETS OF SILVER CERTIFICATES ONE DOLLAR, 12 subjects

No.	Series	Treasurer-Secretary	Valuation
S1-28	1928	H. T. Tate-A. W. Mellon	1,650.00
S1-28A	1928A	Walter O. Woods-A. W. Mellon	Very Rare*
S1-28B	1928B	Walter O. Woods-Ogden L. Mills	Very Rare*
S1-28C	1928C	Walter O. Woods-W. H. Woodin	Rare
S1-28D	1928D	W. A. Julian-W. H. Woodin	Rare
S1-28E	1928E	W. A. Julian-Henry Morgenthau, Jr.	Very Rare
S1-34	1934	W. A. Julian-Henry Morgenthau, Jr.	1,950.00
S1-35	1935	W. A. Julian-Henry Morgenthau, Jr.	1,400.00
S1-35A	1935A	W. A. Julian-Henry Morgenthau, Jr.	1,400.00
S1-35B	1935B	W. A. Julian-Fred M. Vinson	1,500.00
S1-35C	1935C	W. A. Julian-John W. Snyder	1,350.00
S1-35D	1935D	Georgia Neese Clark-John W. Snyder	1,250.00

UNCUT SHEETS OF SILVER CERTIFICATES ONE DOLLAR, 18 subjects

No.	Series	Treasurer-Secretary	Valuation
S1-35D	1935D	Georgia Neese Clark-John W. Snyder	1,650.00
S1-35E	1935E	Ivy Baker Priest-George M. Humphrey	1,450.00

*No sheets verified

ONE DOLLAR SILVER CERTIFICATES

Face Design $1.00, Series 1934

No.	Series	Treasurer-Secretary	Printed	VF	EF	Unc.
S1-34	1934	Julian-Morgenthau	682,176,000	4.50	6.00	14.00

Face Design $1.00, Series 1935 to 1957B

No.	Series	Treasurer-Secretary	Printed	EF	Unc.
S1-35	1935	Julian-Morgenthau	1,681,552,000	9.50	16.00
S1-35A	1935A	Julian-Morgenthau	6,111,832,000	4.00	7.00
S1-35B	1935B	Julian-Vinson	806,612,000	7.50	14.00
S1-35C	1935C	Julian-Snyder	3,088,108,000	5.00	7.00

$1 SILVER CERTIFICATE
12-subject Sheet

Series	Sec'y. & Treas.	First Serial Number Printed	Last Serial Number Printed	Deliveries First Note	Deliveries Last Note	Total Notes
1934	Morgenthau-Julian	A00 000 001A	G82 176 000A	6-29-35	6-18-36	682,176,000
1935	Morgenthau-Julian	A00 000 001A	R81 552 000A	11-25-35	9- 9-38	1,681,552,000
1935A	Morgenthau-Julian	R81 552 001A	C93 384 000D	9- 9-38	7-27-45	6,111,832,000
1935B	Vinson-Julian	C93 384 001D	K99 996 000D	7-26-45	7- 1-46	806,612,000
1935C	Snyder-Julian	K99 996 001D	R88 104 000E	6-25-46	7-11-49	3,088,108,000

ONE DOLLAR SILVER CERTIFICATES

$1.00 Back Design (wide)

$1.00 Back Design (narrow)

Illustration being reduced does not show the difference too clearly, best seen by comparing backgrounds below words "One Dollar" at bottom.

No.	Series	Treasurer-Secretary	Printed	EF	Unc.
S1-35DW	1935D	Clark-Snyder	4,656,968,000	4.00	6.50
S1-35DN	1935D	Clark-Snyder	146,944,000	4.00	6.50

There are two varieties on the back of 1935D, known as wide and narrow designs, the wide design about 1/16 inch wider, and with back plate number 5015 or less. The wide design was also used on series 1935 to 1935C.

The narrow back design continued to be used on all subsequent issues of $1. certificates, 1935D through 1935H.

Series 1935D was printed in sheets of 12 and 18. Sheets of 12 were made up with both the wide and narrow design. 4,510,024,000 notes were printed in sheets of 12.

Sheets of 18, comprising 745,072,000 notes series 1935D all had the narrow design with back plate numbers starting with 5017.

No.	Series	Treasurer-Secretary	Printed	EF	Unc.
S1-35E	1935E	Priest-Humphrey	5,134,056,000	3.50	5.50

ONE DOLLAR SILVER CERTIFICATES

$1.00 Motto added. Back Design

No.	Series	Treasurer-Secretary	Printed	EF	Unc.
†S1-57	1957	Priest-Anderson	2,609,600,000	—	3.50
S1-35F	1935F	Priest-Anderson	1,173,360,000	—	4.50
†S1-57A	1957A	Smith-Dillon	1,594,080,000	—	3.50
S1-35G	1935G	Smith-Dillon	194,600,000	—	5.00
†S1-35G	1935G	Smith-Dillon	31,320,000	—	6.50
†S1-57B	1957B	Granahan-Dillon	718,400,000	—	3.50
†S1-35H	1935H	Granahan-Dillon	30,520,000	—	4.00

†With Motto "In God We Trust"

$1 SILVER CERTIFICATES
12-subject Sheet

Series	Sec'y. & Treas.	First Serial Number Printed	Last Serial Number Printed	Deliveries First Note	Last Note	Total Notes
1935D	Snyder-Clark	R88 104 001E	F99 999 999G	7-11-49	8- 5-52	3,911,896,000
1935D	Snyder-Clark	H00 000 001G	M98 128 000G	8- 5-52	10-16-53	598,128,000

Serial numbers not used: Four groups of serial numbers, namely J55 796 001B through W99 999 999B, X10 728 001B through X99 999 999B, and Y10 248 001B through Y99 999 999G. Z10 248 001B through Z99 999 999B, for the 1928 series, and M98 128 001G through M99 999 999G, for the 1935 series, were assigned but never used on $1 silver certificates.

18-subject Sheet

Series	Sec'y. & Treas.	First Serial	Last Serial	First Note	Last Note	Total Notes
1935D	Snyder-Clark	G00 000 001G	G99 999 999G	11-20-52	1-14-53	100,000,000
1935D	Snyder-Clark	N00 000 001G	N46 944 000G	1-14-53	2- 4-53	46,944,000
1935E	Humphrey-Priest	N46 944 001G	P81 000 000 I	1-30-53	23-31-57	5,134,056,000
1935F	Anderson-Priest	P81 000 001 I	B54 000 000J	12-31-57	7- 5-61	1,173,000,000
1935F	Anderson-Priest	B71 640 001J	B72 000 000J	7- 4-61	7- 5-61	360,000
1935G	Dillon-Smith	B54 000 001J	B71 640 000J	6- 9-61	7- 5-61	17,640,000
1935G	Dillon-Smith	B72 000 001J	D48 960 000J	7- 5-61	3-12-62	176,960,000
*1935G	Dillon-Smith	D43 960 001J	D80 280 000J	4- 2-62	11-30-62	31,320,000
*1935H	Dillon-Granahan	D80 280 001J	E10 800 000J	6-10-63	10- 4-63	30,520,000

32-subject Sheet

Series	Sec'y. & Treas.	First Serial	Last Serial	First Note	Last Note	Total Notes
*1957	Anderson-Priest	A00 000 001A	B09 600 000B	9- 9-57	3- 3-61	2,600,000
*1957A	Dillon-Smith	A00 000 001A	Q94 080 000A	1-27-61	2- 7-63	1,594,080,000
*1957B	Dillon-Granahan	Q94 080 001A	Y12 480 000A	1-17-63	11- 6-63	718,400,000

*These notes were printed with the Inscription "In God We Trust" on the reverse.

FIVE DOLLAR SILVER CERTIFICATES

Face Design $5.00, Series 1934 to 1934D

No.	Series	Treasurer-Secretary	Printed	VF	EF	Unc.
S5-35	1934	Julian-Morgenthau	350,352,000	8.00	12.00	30.00
S5-34A	1934A	Julian-Morgenthau	740,128,000	7.00	10.00	20.00
S5-34B	1934B	Julian-Vinson	60,328,000	14.00	25.00	45.00
S5-34C	1934C	Julian-Snyder	372,328,000	8.50	12.50	25.00
S5-34D	1934D	Clark-Snyder	491,660,000	8.00	10.00	22.50

A very minor difference exists in the back design of some notes in 1934-D series. To date this has been too minor to create any collector interest or demand.

		$5 SILVER CERTIFICATE 12-subject Sheet				
Series	Sec'y. & Treas.	First Serial Number Printed	Last Serial Number Printed	Deliveries First Note	Last Note	Total Notes
1934	Morgenthau-Julian	A00 000 001A	D50 352 000A	7-20-34	1-26-38	350,352,000
1934A	Morgenthau-Julian	D50 352 001A	K90 480 000A	1-27-38	2- 6-46	740,128,000
1934B	Vinson-Julian	K90 480 001A	L50 808 000A	2- 6-46	12-16-46	60,328,000
1934C	Synder-Julian	L50 808 001A	O23 136 000A	12-19-46	10-24-49	372,328,000
1934D	Snyder-Clark	O23 136 001A	V14 796 000A	10-25-49	10- 1-53	491,660,000

FIVE DOLLAR SILVER CERTIFICATES

Face Design $5.00, Series 1953 to 1953C

No.	Series	Treasurer-Secretary	Printed	VF	EF	Unc.
S5-53	1953	Priest-Humphrey	339,600,000	8.00	12.00	20.00
S5-53A	1953A	Priest-Anderson	232,400,000	8.00	10.00	17.50
S5-53B	1953B	Smith-Dillon	14,196,000	7.50	9.00	20.00

(73,000,000 notes printed only. Only 14,196,000 released.)

S5-53C 1953C Granahan-Dillon. Printed 90,640,000. None released due to discontinuance of Silver Certificates.

$5 SILVER CERTIFICATE
18-subject Sheet

Series	Sec'y. & Treas.	First Serial Number Printed	Last Serial Number Printed	Deliveries First Note	Last Note	Total Notes
1953	Humphrey-Priest	A00 000 001A	D39 600 000A	5-12-53	8-21-57	339,600,000
1953A	Anderson-Priest	D39 600 001A	F72 000 000A	12- 9-57	3-17-61	232,400,000
1953B	Dillon-Smith	F72 000 001A	G45 000 000A	3-28-61	4-25-62	73,000,000
1953C	Dillon-Granahan	G45 000 001A	H35 640 000A	11-12-63		Not released

UNCUT SHEETS
FIVE DOLLARS, 12 subjects

No.	Series	Treasurer-Secretary	Valuation
S5-34	1934	W. A. Julian-Henry Morgenthau, Jr.	2,750.00
S5-34A	1934A	W. A. Julian-Henry Morgenthau, Jr.	Very Rare*
S5-34B	1934B	W. A. Julian-Fred M. Vinson	2,900.00
S5-34C	1934C	W. A. Julian-John W. Snyder	1,750.00
S5-34D	1934D	Georgia Neese Clark-John W. Snyder	1,750.00

FIVE DOLLARS, 18 subjects

S5-53	1953	Ivy Baker Priest-George M. Humphrey, Jr.	2,750.00

*No sheets verified

TEN DOLLAR SILVER CERTIFICATES

Face Design $10.00, Series 1933

No.	Series	Treasurer-Secretary	Printed	VF	EF	Unc.
S10-33	1933	Julian-Morgenthau		650.00	1,250.00	3,250.00

Above values are for notes with higher serial numbers of four and five digits, A0000xxxxA etc.

With the issuance of 1933 certificates, old time avid collectors George Blake and Colonel Green obtained many low and interesting serial numbers. In addition to A00000001A shown above, the following interesting serial numbers have been reported.

02	33	111	666	1111
13	44	333	777	2000
25	55	444	888	3000
29	99	555	1000	33333

Intervening interesting serial numbers, such as 66, 77, 88, 222, etc. are believed to exist.

Only 156,000 series 1933 and 28,000 series 1933A were released. The balance of these notes were destroyed in November 1935. Existence of series 1933A has never been reported. Chuck O'Donnell reports a $10. 1933A star note has been found.

No.	Series	Treasurer-Secretary	Printed	VF	EF	Unc.
S10-34	1934	Julian-Morgenthau	9,132,000	20.00	32.50	50.00
S10-34A	1934A	Julian-Morgenthau	106,300,000	20.00	32.50	50.00
S10-34B	1934B	Julian-Vinson	1,416,000	125.00	275.00	750.00
S10-34C	1934C	Julian-Snyder	21,718,000	15.00	20.00	35.00
S10-34D	1934D	Clark-Snyder	11,630,000	14.00	17.50	32.50

$10 SILVER CERTIFICATE
12-subject Sheet

Series	Sec'y. & Treas.	First Serial Number Printed	Last Serial Number Printed	Deliveries First Note	Last Note	Total Notes
1933	Woodin-Julian	A00 000 001A	A00 216 000A	1- 5-34	2-27-34	216,000
1933A	Morgenthau-Julian	A00 216 001A	A00 552 000A	2-27-34	4- 2-34	336,000
1934	Morgenthau-Julian	A00 000 001A	A09 132 000A	4-17-34	4- 1-35	9,132,000
1934A	Morgenthau-Julian	A09 132 001A	B15 432 000A	4- 2-35	9- 4-46	106,300,000
1934B	Vinson-Morgenthau	B15 432 001A	B16 848 000A	9- 4-46	8- 5-47	1,416,000
1934C	Snyder-Julian	B16 848 001A	B38 566 000A	8- 5-47	7-12-50	21,718,000
1934D	Snyder-Clark	B38 566 001A	B50 196 000A	7-12-50	4-14-53	11,630,000

TEN DOLLAR SILVER CERTIFICATES

Face Design $10.00, Series 1934 to 1934D

Face Design $10.00, Series 1953 to 1953B

No.	Series	Treasurer-Secretary	Printed	VF	EF	Unc.
S10-53	1953	Priest-Humphrey	10,440,000	20.00	25.00	45.00
S10-53A	1953A	Priest-Anderson	10,080,000	15.00	22.50	40.00
S10-53B	1953B	Smith-Dillon	720,000	20.00	25.00	55.00

TEN DOLLAR SILVER CERTIFICATES

Back Design $10.00 used on Silver Certificates, Federal Reserve Notes and Gold Certificates

$10 SILVER CERTIFICATE
18-subject Sheet

Series	Sec'y. & Treas.	First Serial Number Printed	Last Serial Number Printed	Deliveries First Note	Last Note	Total Notes
1953	Humphrey-Priest	A00 000 001A	A10 440 000A	5-12-53	8-27-57	10,440,000
1953A	Anderson-Priest	A10 440 001A	A11 520 000A	2-13-58	2-17-58	1,080,000
1953B	Dillon-Smith	A11 520 001A	A12 240 000A	2- 2-62	3-14-62	720,000
1953C	Dillon-Granahan	None printed				

UNCUT SHEETS

TEN DOLLARS, 12 subjects

No.	Series	Treasurer-Secretary	Valuation
S10-33	1933	W. A. Julian-W. H. Woodin	Very Rare
S10-34	1934	W. A. Julian-Henry Morgenthau, Jr.	3,000.00
S10-34A	1934A	W. A. Julian-Henry Morgenthau, Jr.	Very Rare*
S10-34B	1934B	W. A. Julian-Fred M. Vinson	Very Rare*
S10-34C	1934C	W. A. Julian-John W. Snyder	Very Rare*
S10-34D	1934D	Georgia Neese Clark-John W. Snyder	Very Rare*

TEN DOLLARS, 18 subjects

| S10-53 | 1953 | Ivy Baker Priest-George M. Humphrey | 3,500.00 |

1929 SERIES NATIONAL BANK NOTES

Brown Seals — Issued 1929 to 1935

All notes of this series bear the signatures of the bank president and cashier, as well as the signatures of E. E. Jones, Register of the Treasury and W. O. Woods, United States Treasurer.

The design of this series is the same as used on all current size notes of like denomination. The brown seal is at right of note. The inscription at top of note reads: "National Currency secured by United States Bonds deposited with the Treasurer of the United States."

The obligation to pay at right of note reads: "Redeemable in Lawful Money of the United States at United States Treasury or at the bank of issue." To the left of note is the name of issuing bank, underlined with the words: "Will pay to the Bearer on Demand."

This series which had a life span of only six years affords a real chase for the collector not content with a type note of each denomination. There are countless ways to collect National Bank Notes, the first and most obvious being to obtain a collection of notes from one's own state, or possibly one note from all fifty states and the District of Columbia.

Some collectors seek notes from birthplaces of famous Americans, or places with odd names, or banks with industrial or commercial titles; also low charter numbers, and low or attractive serial numbers. There is plenty in this series to intrigue the collector with a little imagination. It is not impossible to obtain a note from every state including Alaska and Hawaii, although these two will be a little more difficult to acquire. Obtaining the same denomination from every state may also prove a little more difficult. Uncirculated National Bank Notes are becoming very scarce. No star numbers were printed for this series.

VALUATIONS

There are two varieties of this interesting series. Type One, July 1929 to May 1933, and Type Two from May 1933 to 1935. Type One has two charter numbers in black. Type Two in addition to the two black charter numbers also has two in brown of a smaller type size.

The numbering of uncut sheets of these two types is also different. Type One notes in uncut sheets all have the same serial number with changes in prefix letters denoting the position of the note on the sheet. Type Two notes in uncut sheets are numbered consecutively with the prefix letter "A" on all notes. Both types were delivered to banks in uncut sheets of six notes.

Type Two is decidedly the scarcer of the two types, much more so than previously recognized, even in previous editions. Earlier catalogs of other publishers did not emphasize any difference in the relative scarcity of the two types. The Donlon catalog was the first to designate the two issues as Type One and Type Two, and to point out that there should be a difference in valuation.

Valuations of National Currency is effected by many factors, some of which have little bearing on actual rarity such as the popularity of odd names. Notes from one or more cities or banks in a state may be relatively plentiful while most of the notes of other banks of that state are scarce or rare. Small towns are usually scarcer than large cities.

The Rarity Table indicates rarity "as a state only." Pennsylvania as a state is the most common but there are numerous Pennsylvania rarities. The tables, giving the number of banks issuing various denominations and the number known, will help specialists further evaluate rarities. It will be noted that the "commonest state," Pennsylvania has $5 of 450 different banks with only 244 different known to be in collections, which is near the average of all the large states. Some of the smaller states have a much higher ratio of issued to known. Example: $5 New Mexico 8 issued, 6 known; Rhode Island 11 issued, 9 known.

Rarity "as a state" is weighed in some instances by the availability of one bank in each state. This particularly applies to District of Columbia, Hawaii, Kansas and Oregon where one note is plentiful, thereby lowering the rating "as a state."

Thanks to M. O. Warns for his help in compiling this particular section.

RARITY 1
Illinois (617)
New York (541)
Ohio (431)
Pennsylvania (1205)
Texas (562)
( ) indicates number of different notes reported.

RARITY 2
California (254)
Indiana (268)
Iowa (305)
Michigan (239)
Minnesota (344)
Nebraska (230)
New Jersey (348)
Oklahoma (276)
Wisconsin (265)

RARITY 3
Kansas (288)
Kentucky (143)
Maryland (130)
Massachusetts (171)
Missouri (170)
Virginia (167)
West Virginia (130)

RARITY 4
Alabama (135)
Colorado (120)
Connecticut (98)
Dist. of Columbia (22)
Maine (92)
North Carolina (103)
North Dakota (118)
Tennessee (112)

RARITY 5
Arkansas (73)
Florida (117)
Georgia (82)
Louisiana (76)
Oregon (85)
South Carolina (44)
South Dakota (88)
Vermont (70)
Washington (110)

RARITY 6
Mississippi (60)
Montana (81)
New Hampshire (75)
*Rhode Island (30)
Utah (33)
Wyoming (37)
*There is one common note.

RARITY 7
Arizona (16)
Delaware (24)
Hawaii (4)
Idaho (42)
New Mexico (34)

RARITY 8
Nevada (26)

RARITY 9
Alaska (6)

$50.00 and $100.00 notes were not issued by banks in Alabama, Alaska, Arizona, Arkansas, District of Columbia, Georgia, Maine, New Mexico and South Carolina.

For a listing of 1929 National Bank Notes by Charter No., State, City and denomination, see the Hewitt publication, "National Bank Note Issues" authored and sponsored by Society of Paper Money Collectors.

Alabama	No. Issuing Banks	No. Banks Reported in Collections
$5..	65	34
$10..	95	59
$20..	81	42

Alaska		
$5..	2	1
$10..	3	3
$20..	3	2

Arizona		
$5..	5	3
$10..	10	7
$20..	10	6

Arkansas		
$5..	47	18
$10..	58	29
$20..	47	26

California		
$5..	112	76
$10..	157	92
$20..	143	77
$50..	14	6
$100..	14	3

Colorado		
$5..	38	18
$10..	86	54
$20..	79	39
$50..	8	5
$100..	9	4

Connecticut		
$5..	42	28
$10..	56	39
$20..	47	30
$50..	3	1
$100..	3	0

Delaware		
$5..	7	4
$10..	16	11
$20..	14	8
$50..	1	1
$100..	1	0

District of Columbia		
$5..	6	4
$10..	11	9
$20..	11	9

Florida		
$5..	42	32
$10..	50	46
$20..	40	36
$50..	2	2
$100..	3	1

Georgia	No. Issuing Banks	No. Banks Reported in Collections
$5..	50	16
$10..	75	36
$20..	67	30

Hawaii		
$5..	1	1
$10..	1	1
$50..	1	1
$100..	1	1

Idaho		
$5..	18	3
$10..	27	22
$20..	24	14
$50..	3	2
$100..	3	1

Illinois		
$5..	198	84
$10..	421	256
$20..	387	248
$50..	32	16
$100..	29	13

Indiana		
$5..	114	52
$10..	207	112
$20..		189
$50..	15	4
$100..	14	2

Iowa		
$5..	85	41
$10..	232	132
$20..	216	121
$50..	13	6
$100..	12	5

Kansas		
$5..	88	35
$10..	195	127
$20..	184	118
$50..	12	6
$100..	12	2

Kentucky		
$5..	55	19
$10..	131	63
$20..	123	59
$50..	4	1
$100..	5	1

Louisiana		
$5..	23	19
$10..	35	26
$20..	28	26
$50..	3	3
$100..	3	2

Maine	No. Issuing Banks	No. Banks Reported in Collections
$5..	34	27
$10..	56	38
$20..	48	27

Maryland		
$5..	49	28
$10..	82	51
$20..	80	44
$50..	8	4
$100..	8	3

Massachusetts		
$5..	125	61
$10..	127	65
$20..	113	40
$50..	7	3
$100..	7	2

Michigan		
$5..	88	45
$10..	132	93
$20..	120	92
$50..	9	5
$100..	8	4
	98	

Minnesota		
$5..	118	55
$10..	224	159
$20..	210	125
$50..	6	2
$100..	6	3

Mississippi		
$5..	24	20
$10..	32	19
$20..	25	21
$50..	1	0
$100..	1	0

Missouri		
$5..	67	37
$10..	110	70
$20..	101	58
$50..	4	3
$100..	4	2

Montana		
$5..	21	15
$10..	41	33
$20..	35	31
$50..	1	1
$100..	1	1

Nebraska

	No. Issuing Banks	No. Banks Reported In Collections
$5..	52	25
$10..	145	110
$20..	138	90
$50..	6	4
$100..	5	1

Nevada

$5..	7	5
$10..	9	9
$20..	10	10
$50..	1	1
$100..	1	1

New Hampshire

$5..	41	19
$10..	58	36
$20..	50	20
$50..	2	0
$100..	2	0

New Jersey

$5..	183	104
$10..	225	132
$20..	197	101
$50..	12	7
$100..	11	4

New Mexico

$5..	8	6
$10..	21	15
$20..	20	13

New York

$5..	331	160
$10..	469	221
$20..	410	151
$50..	19	6
$100..	16	3

North Carolina

$5..	45	24
$10..	61	53
$20..	48	26
$50..	1	0
$100..	1	0

North Dakota

$5..	34	16
$10..	105	61
$20..	98	40
$50..	1	0
$100..	1	1

Ohio

	No. Issuing Banks	No. Banks Reported In Collections
$5..	145	78
$10..	313	190
$20..	300	151
$50..	17	9
$100..	16	3

Oklahoma

$5..	64	27
$10..	207	128
$20..	196	116
$50..	8	3
$100..	6	2

Oregon

$5..	37	19
$10..	75	38
$20..	69	27
$50..	3	1
$100..	2	0

Pennsylvania

$5..	450	244
$10..	838	500
$20..	795	437
$50..	32	15
$100..	31	9

Rhode Island

$5..	11	9
$10..	11	9
$20..	11	10
$50..	3	1
$100..	3	1

South Carolina

$5..	31	13
$10..	38	15
$20..	30	16

South Dakota

$5..	24	11
$10..	67	43
$20..	60	32
$50..	2	1
$100..	2	1

Tennessee

$5..	56	19
$10..	100	45
$20..	83	41
$50..	6	3
$100..	6	4

Texas

	No. Issuing Banks	No. Banks Reported In Collections
$5..	218	99
$10..	475	225
$20..	447	212
$50..	37	15
$100..	36	11

Utah

$5..	9	6
$10..	17	14
$20..	16	12
$50..	1	1

Vermont

$5..	32	20
$10..	45	27
$20..	38	21
$50..	4	2
$100..	4	0

Virginia

$5..	80	31
$10..	139	76
$20..	129	60
$50..	1	0
$100..	2	0

Washington

$5..	38	16
$10..	80	45
$20..	74	44
$50..	3	1
$100..	2	1

West Virginia

$5..	78	34
$10..	127	53
$20..	117	43
$50..	1	0
$100..	1	0

Wisconsin

$5..	87	55
$10..	139	113
$20..	125	88
$50..	6	5
$100..	6	4

Wyoming

$5..	7	3
$10..	23	19
$20..	22	14
$50..	1	1
$100..	1	0

UNCUT SHEETS 1929 NATIONAL CURRENCY

Six subjects each sheet

Values given are for uncut sheets of Type One. Uncut sheets of Type Two are very much scarcer with a conservative valuation of 50% to 100% higher.

On Type One, all notes have the same serial number, but different prefix letters. Type Two sheets are numbered consecutively with prefix A, and no suffix letter.

Arranged in Rarity Groups. See Rarity Table, Page 51.

	1 and 2	3 and 4	— 5 —	— 6 —	— 7 —	— 8 —	— 9 —
5.00...	500.00	700.00	1200.00	1600.00	2400.00	3500.00	*
10.00...	500.00	700.00	1300.00	1700.00	2500.00	3500.00	*
20.00...	500.00	700.00	1200.00	1600.00	2800.00	4000.00	*
50.00...	1200.00	1400.00	1600.00	2000.00	—	—	*

A hoard of 30 sheets of $5 Cassopolis, Mich. was sold in Rarcoa's 1971 Central States Society Sale making it probably the commonest 1929 national sheet and the one most likely to be offered at discount from catalog.

Rarity of notes in sheet form does not necessarily follow the exact pattern of single note rarity groups. In sheet form there are more different known of New York, second is Texas, followed by Pennsylvania, California, Ohio and Michigan. Approximately 16% of the reported sheets are on New York banks and about 12% Texas.

*No sheets are reported for Alaska and Hawaii. The least number known are: Arizona, Delaware, District of Columbia, and Wyoming with just one sheet known for each state.

Prior to 1970 it was generally believed that the only $100.00 uncut sheet in existence was Tennessee Charter #13349. That sheet was sold as lot No. 1910 in the 1970 ANA convention auction bringing $1400.00. That sheet is illustrated in "The National Bank Note Issues of 1929-1935," published November 1970 by Hewitt Brothers. A chapter on uncut sheets, authored by Peter Huntoon, Johnny O. Bass, Louis Van Belkum and M. Owen Warns, contains valuable charts and material on 541 different uncut sheets.

In February, 1971, Lester Merkin sold, at public auction, the largest group of 1929 uncut sheets ever offered at one time. It comprised 166 sheets covering 107 towns in 17 states and included three previously unrecorded $100 sheets: Charter #10357 Bakersfield, Calif., sold for $1350.00; Charter #13648 Shreveport, La., brought $1450.00, and Charter #10152 Houston, Texas, $1300.00. (The fifth known $100 sheet is Charter #10527 Detroit, Mich.)

Only five $50 sheets are known. They are:
#13648 Shreveport, La.
#9547 Lancaster, Ohio
#10152 Houston, Texas
#10527 Detroit, Michigan
#6370 Miami, Florida

NATIONAL BANK NOTES
TYPE ONE, AND TYPE TWO, FIVE DOLLARS
Lincoln in Center

Face Design $5, Type 1

Face Design $5, Type 2

Prices quoted are for the commonest banks of a rarity group. Current dealer list may offer R-1 $5 uncirculated as low as $20.00 and some other $5 of same state at $75.

	TYPE ONE			TYPE TWO		
Rarity	V. Fine	Ex. Fine	Unc.	V. Fine	Ex. Fine	Unc.
1	20.00	25.00	50.00	30.00	40.00	65.00
2	20.00	25.00	60.00	30.00	50.00	75.00
3	30.00	50.00	70.00	45.00	75.00	100.00
4	35.00	50.00	125.00	50.00	70.00	150.00
5	55.00	80.00	175.00	40.00	70.00	200.00
6	60.00	85.00	250.00	50.00	80.00	250.00
7	75.00	100.00	450.00	70.00	125.00	450.00
8	225.00	425.00	950.00	225.00	450.00	975.00
9	1100.00	1600.00	2500.00	1100.00	1700.00	2500.00

NATIONAL BANK NOTES
TYPE ONE, AND TYPE TWO, TEN DOLLARS
Hamilton in Center

Face Design $10, Type 1

Face Design $10, Type 2

Rarity	TYPE ONE			TYPE TWO		
	V. Fine	Ex. Fine	Unc.	V. Fine	Ex. Fine	Unc.
1	30.00	40.00	55.00	40.00	50.00	75.00
2	30.00	45.00	65.00	40.00	55.00	95.00
3	40.00	55.00	80.00	45.00	90.00	125.00
4	50.00	60.00	130.00	50.00	90.00	175.00
5	70.00	100.00	175.00	75.00	130.00	225.00
6	90.00	125.00	225.00	120.00	200.00	300.00
7	150.00	200.00	350.00	175.00	220.00	400.00
8	225.00	450.00	850.00	225.00	400.00	1000.00
9	1000.00	1500.00	2500.00	1200.00	1650.00	2600.00

NATIONAL BANK NOTES
TYPE ONE, AND TYPE TWO, TWENTY DOLLARS
Jackson in Center

Face Design $20, Type 1

Face Design $20, Type 2

Rarity	TYPE ONE			TYPE TWO		
	V. Fine	Ex. Fine	Unc.	V. Fine	Ex. Fine	Unc.
1	40.00	55.00	65.00	50.00	65.00	85.00
2	40.00	55.00	75.00	50.00	70.00	100.00
3	50.00	65.00	100.00	50.00	70.00	125.00
4	60.00	85.00	130.00	60.00	100.00	150.00
5	90.00	120.00	175.00	90.00	125.00	225.00
6	130.00	180.00	250.00	140.00	190.00	275.00
7	160.00	250.00	450.00	175.00	275.00	475.00
8	375.00	700.00	1100.00	450.00	800.00	1150.00
9	900.00	1200.00	2500.00	1000.00	1300.00	2600.00

NATIONAL BANK NOTES
TYPE ONE AND TYPE TWO, FIFTY DOLLARS
Grant in Center

Face Design $50, Type 1

Back Design $50

Rarity	TYPE ONE			TYPE TWO		
	V. Fine	Ex. Fine	Unc.	V. Fine	Ex. Fine	Unc.
1	80.00	90.00	150.00	120.00	150.00	300.00
2	80.00	90.00	175.00	150.00	200.00	325.00
3	80.00	95.00	200.00	140.00	250.00	350.00
4	100.00	120.00	225.00	150.00	225.00	400.00
5	110.00	125.00	250.00	200.00	350.00	500.00
6	125.00	140.00	300.00	300.00	650.00	1100.00
7	375.00	500.00	1000.00	None reported		
8	525.00	750.00	1200.00	None reported		

NATIONAL BANK NOTES
TYPE ONE AND TYPE TWO, ONE HUNDRED DOLLARS
Franklin in Center

Face Design $100, Type 1

Back Design $100
(also used on Federal Reserve Bank Notes, Federal Reserve Notes and Gold Certificates)

Rarity	TYPE ONE			TYPE TWO		
	V. Fine	Ex. Fine	Unc.	V. Fine	Ex. Fine	Unc.
1	130.00	155.00	200.00	140.00	175.00	300.00
2	130.00	165.00	225.00	150.00	200.00	350.00
3	140.00	175.00	250.00	200.00	250.00	400.00
4	160.00	200.00	275.00	225.00	275.00	450.00
5	160.00	240.00	300.00	225.00	300.00	500.00
6	180.00	275.00	325.00	325.00	525.00	700.00
7	225.00	425.00	700.00	None reported		
8	400.00	600.00	900.00	None reported		

FEDERAL RESERVE BANK NOTES

1929 series. Brown seals and serial numbers.

Issued in $5.00, $10.00, $20.00, $50.00 and $100.00 denominations.

This series bears a marked resemblance to the 1929 National Currency issued by Chartered Banks. Examination of the face of these notes reveals several differences. The Federal Reserve Bank Notes of 1929 bear no charter number, but instead have the designating letter of the Federal Reserve Bank in four places. The brown seal is slightly larger than the seal on the National Bank notes of 1929. The inscription "or by like deposit of other securities" has been added to the obligation. Serial numbers on National currency contained 6 digits while Federal Reserve Banks contain 8 digits.

Unlike the green seal issues, Federal Reserve notes, the letter designating the issuing bank does not appear in a seal, but in four places on the face of the notes, two on each half of the note. These letters are in black, and are in addition to the numeral prefix letter, which also designates bank of issue.

Replacing the signatures of the Bank President and Cashier, are the signatures of the Federal Reserve Bank's Cashier and Governor, with three exceptions. Instead of the Cashier's signature, that of the Deputy Governor appears on New York District notes, that of the Assistant Deputy Governor on Chicago notes, and the signature of the Controller on the St. Louis District notes. All notes of this series have the signatures of E. E. Jones, Register, and W. O. Woods, Treasurer.

This series was authorized by act of Congress March 9, 1933, to permit Federal Reserve Banks to issue currency equal to 100 percent of the face value of United States bonds, or 90% of the estimated value of commercial paper, used as collateral. This made it possible for the banks to issue a larger quantity of paper money than with the former requirement of 40% gold reserve.

The design of the 1929 National Currency was used and the series was dated 1929 although the first notes were not issued until March 11, 1933. Last delivery was on December 21 of the same year. Numbering for each Federal Reserve Bank started with 00000001, preceded by District letters A to L, and with suffix letter "A." The issue being very small never required using suffix letter "B."

Federal Reserve Bank Notes are much scarcer than realized, especially in new condition. The price section of catalog shows the number of notes printed, but it is estimated that less than half of this number ever reached circulation. Collectors endeavoring to collect complete sets of all Federal Reserve Banks, in any denomination, are finding it is not a simple matter. Assembling complete sets in the future will be still more difficult due to the increasing number of currency collectors.

FIVE DOLLAR FEDERAL RESERVE BANK NOTES

Face Design $5

No.	District	Printed	Fine	Ex. Fine	Unc.
FB5-29	A-Boston	3,180,000	20.00	35.00	70.00
FB5-29	B-New York	2,100,000	20.00	35.00	70.00
FB5-29	C-Philadelphia	3,096,000	20.00	32.50	70.00
FB5-29	D-Cleveland	4,236,000	20.00	30.00	70.00
FB5-29	E-Richmond	No record	—	—	—
FB5-29	F-Atlanta	1,884,000	25.00	45.00	90.00
FB5-29	G-Chicago	5,988,000	20.00	30.00	60.00
FB5-29	H-St. Louis	276,000	50.00	150.00	250.00
FB5-29	I - Minneapolis	684,000	30.00	65.00	140.00
FB5-29	J-Kansas City	2,460,000	20.00	30.00	80.00
FB5-29	K-Dallas	996,000	30.00	45.00	90.00
FB5-29	L-San Francisco	360,000	100.00	225.00	1000.00

FEDERAL RESERVE BANK NOTES (NATIONAL CURRENCY)—1929
ALL 12 SUBJECT. Treasurer: Woods — Register: Jones
$5.00 NOTES

Federal Reserve District	First Serial Number Printed	Last Serial Number Printed	First Note Delivered	Last Note Delivered
Boston	A00 000 001A	A03 180 000A	3-11-33	8-11-33
New York	B00 000 001A	B02 100 000A	3-28-33	8-19-33
Philadelphia	C00 000 001A	C03 096 000A	3-11-33	12-21-33
Cleveland	D00 000 001A	D04 236 000A	3-11-33	11-22-33
Richmond	No record	No record	No record	No record
Atlanta	F00 000 001A	F01 884 000A	3-17-33	3-30-33
Chicago	G00 000 001A	G05 988 000A	3 16-33	10- 9-33
St. Louis	H00 000 001A	H00 276 000A	3-22-33	3-30-33
Minneapolis	I 00 000 001A	I 00 684 000A	3-23-33	3-28-33
Kansas City	J00 000 001A	J02 460 000A	3-28-33	1-11-34
Dallas	K00 000 001A	K00 996 000A	3-18-33	3-30-33
San Francisco	L00 000 001A	L00 360 000A	3-30-33	3-30-33

TEN DOLLAR FEDERAL RESERVE BANK NOTES

Face Design $10

No.	District	Printed	Fine	Ex. Fine	Unc.
FB10-29	A-Boston	1,680,000	22.50	35.00	65.00
FB10-29	B-New York	5,556,000	20.00	32.50	55.00
FB10-29	C-Philadelphia	1,416,000	22.50	35.00	70.00
FB10-29	D-Cleveland	2,412,000	22.50	32.50	70.00
FB19-29	E-Richmond	1,356,000	25.00	35.00	75.00
FB10-29	F-Atlanta	1,056,000	27.50	35.00	80.00
FB10-29	G-Chicago	3,156,000	22.50	30.00	65.00
FB10-29	H-St. Louis	1,584,000	27.50	35.00	75.00
FB10-29	I-Minneapolis	588,000	30.00	40.00	80.00
FB10-29	J-Kansas City	1,284,000	27.50	35.00	70.00
FB10-29	K-Dallas	504,000	30.00	40.00	85.00
FB10-29	L-San Francisco	1,080,000	22.50	35.00	75.00

FEDERAL RESERVE BANK NOTES (NATIONAL CURRENCY)—1929
ALL 12 SUBJECT. Treasurer: Woods — Register: Jones
$10.00 NOTES

Federal Reserve District	First Serial Number Printed	Last Serial Number Printed	First Note Delivered	Last Note Delivered
Boston	A00 000 001A	A01 680 000A	3-22-33	7-12-33
New York	B00 000 001A	B05 556 000A	3-10-33	10-14-33
Philadelphia	C00 000 001A	C01 416 000A	3-28-33	11-18-33
Cleveland	D00 000 001A	D02 412 000A	3-12-33	11- 4-33
Richmond	E00 000 001A	E01 356 000A	3-17-33	3-30-33
Atlanta	F00 000 001A	F01 056 000A	3-11-33	8-26-33
Chicago	G00 000 001A	G03 156 000A	3-13-33	8-26-33
St. Louis	H00 000 001A	H01 584 000A	3-16-33	3-30-33
Minneapolis	I 00 000 001A	I 00 588 000A	3-22-33	3-29-33
Kansas City	J00 000 001A	J01 284 000A	3-13-33	3-30-33
Dallas	K00 000 001A	K00 504 000A	3-29-33	3-30-33
San Francisco	L00 000 001A	L01 080 000A	3-11-33	3-30-33

A sheet of twelve $10.00 series 1929 Federal Reseve Bank Notes, New York Federal Reserve Bank (410B), was listed in the Grinnell sale held Nov. 30, 1946 in Syracuse, N.Y., under catalog lot #5998. The description stated that "As far as is known, this is the only uncut sheet of this series."

The Grinnell sheet was numbered B73A to B84A. Two other uncut sheets have been reported bearing serial Nos. B85A to B96A and B97A to B108A.

TWENTY DOLLAR FEDERAL RESERVE BANK NOTES

Face Design $20

No.	District	Printed	Fine	Ex. Fine	Unc.
FB20-29	A-Boston	972,000	35.00	50.00	75.00
FB20-29	B-New York	2,568,000	30.00	45.00	70.00
FB20-29	C-Philadelphia	1,008,000	35.00	45.00	75.00
FB20-29	D-Cleveland	1,020,000	35.00	45.00	75.00
FB20-29	E-Richmond	1,632,000	32.50	4500	7500
FB20-29	F-Atlanta	960,000	35.00	45.00	75.00
FB20-29	G-Chicago	2,028,000	30.00	42.50	70.00
FB20-29	H-St. Louis	444,000	40.00	60.00	100.00
FB20-29	I - Minneapolis	864,000	35.00	45.00	75.00
FB20-29	J-Kansas City	612,000	35.00	45.00	75.00
FB20-29	K-Dallas	468,000	40.00	50.00	90.00
FB20-29	L-San Francisco	888,000	35.00	45.00	75.00

FEDERAL RESERVE BANK NOTES (NATIONAL CURRENCY)—1929
ALL 12 SUBJECT. Treasurer: Woods — Register: Jones
$20.00 NOTES

Federal Reserve District	First Serial Number Printed	Last Serial Number Printed	First Note Delivered	Last Note Delivered
Boston	A00 000 001A	A00 972 000A	3-18-33	3-29-33
New York	B00 000 001A	B02 568 000A	3-14-33	9-22-33
Philadelphia	C00 000 001A	C01 008 000A	3-16-33	3-29-33
Cleveland	D00 000 001A	D01 020 000A	3-21-33	3-29-33
Richmond	E00 000 001A	E01 632 000A	3-14-33	3.27-33
Atlanta	F00 000 001A	F00 960 000A	4-18-33	4-22-33
Chicago	G00 000 001A	G02 028 000A	3-13-33	9-28-33
St. Louis	I100 000 001A	H00 444 000A	3-13-33	3-30-33
Minneapolis	I 00 000 001A	I 00 864 000A	3-11-33	3-21-33
Kansas City	J00 000 001A	J00 612 000A	3-30-33	12-22-34
Dallas	K00 000 001A	K00 468 000A	3-15-33	3-16-33
San Francisco	L00 000 001A	L00 888 000A	3-20-33	3-26-33

FIFTY DOLLAR FEDERAL RESERVE BANK NOTES

Face Design $50

No.	District	Printed	Fine	Ex. Fine	Unc.
FB50-29	A-Boston	No record	—	—	—
FB50-29	B-New York	636,000	85.00	125.00	200.00
FB50-29	C-Philadelphia	No record	—	—	—
FB50-29	D-Cleveland	684,000	85.00	125.00	200.00
FB50-29	E-Richmond	No record	—	—	—
FB50-29	F-Atlanta	No record	—	—	—
FB50-29	G-Chicago	300,000	90.00	125.50	240.00
FB50-29	H-St. Louis	No record	—	—	—
FB50-29	I - Minneapolis	132,000	110.00	190.00	300.00
FB50-29	J-Kansas City	276,000	90.00	150.00	250.00
FB50-29	K-Dallas	168,000	90.00	160.00	275.00
FB50-29	L-San Francisco	576,000	80.00	125.00	200.00

FEDERAL RESERVE BANK NOTES (NATIONAL CURRENCY)—1929
ALL 12 SUBJECT. Treasurer: Woods — Register: Jones
$50.00 NOTES

Federal Reserve District	First Serial Number Printed	Last Serial Number Printed	First Note Delivered	Last Note Delivered
Boston	A00 000 001A	No record	No record	No record
New York	B00 000 001A	B00 636 000A	3-16-33	3-29-33
Philadelphia	C00 000 001A	No record	No record	No record
Cleveland	D00 000 001A	D00 684 000A	3-17-33	3-29-33
Richmond	E00 000 001A	No record	No record	No record
Atlanta	F00 000 001A	No record	No record	No record
Chicago	G00 000 001A	G00 300 000A	8-29-33	8-30-33
St. Louis	H00 000 001A	No record	No record	No record
Minneapolis	I 00 000 001A	I 00 132 000A	3-28-33	3-29-33
Kansas City	J00 000 001A	J00 276 000A	3-23-33	3-30-34
Dallas	K00 000 001A	K00 168 000A	3-11-33	3-17-33
San Francisco	L00 000 001A	L00 576 000A	3-17-33	3-25-33

ONE HUNDRED DOLLAR FEDERAL RESERVE BANK NOTES

Face Design $100

No.	District	Printed	Fine	Ex. Fine	Unc.
FB100-29 A-Boston		No record	—	—	—
FB100-29 B-New York		480,000	120.00	165.00	250.00
FB100-29 C-Philadelphia		No record	—	—	—
FB100-29 D-Cleveland		276,000	120.00	175.00	350.00
FB100-29 E-Richmond		192,000	125.00	190.00	300.00
FB100-29 F-Atlanta		No record	—	—	—
FB100-29 G-Chicago		384,000	120.00	165.00	300.00
FB100-29 H-St. Louis		No record	—	—	—
FB100-29 I - Minneapolis		144,000	125.00	190.00	325.00
FB100-29 J-Kansas City		96,000	140.00	200.00	340.00
FB100-29 K-Dallas		36,000	160.00	240.00	400.00
FB100-29 L-San Francisco		No record	—	—	—

Note: This is little demand for $100 notes in less than extra fine condition.

FEDERAL RESERVE BANK NOTES (NATIONAL CURRENCY)—1929
ALL 12 SUBJECT. Treasurer: Woods — Register: Jones
$100.00 NOTES

Federal Reserve District	First Serial Number Printed	Last Serial Number Printed	First Note Delivered	Last Note Delivered
Boston	A00 000 001A	No record	No record	No record
New York	B00 000 001A	B00 480 000A	3-20-33	3-30-33
Philadelphia	C00 000 001A	No record	No record	No record
Cleveland	D00 000 001A	D00 276 000A	3-16-33	3-30-33
Richmond	E00 000 001A	F00 192 000A	3-11-33	3-17-33
Atlanta	F00 000 001A	No record	No record	No record
Chicago	G00 000 001A	G00 384 000A	3-15-33	3-29-33
St. Louis	H00 000 001A	No record	No record	No record
Minneapolis	I 00 000 001A	I 00 144 000A	3-23-33	3-29-33
Kansas City	J00 000 001A	J00 096 000A	3-24-33	3-30-34
Dallas	K00 000 001A	K00 036 000A	3-30-33	3-30-33
San Francisco	L00 000 001A	No record	No record	No record

FEDERAL RESERVE NOTES

GREEN TREASURY SEALS AND SERIAL NUMBERS
BLACK BANK SEALS

Previously issued in denominations of $5 to $10,000, with the $1 denomination added in the 1963 series. All denominations higher than $100 have now been discontinued. Due to the wording in the redemption inscription on all Federal Reserve notes, 1928 through 1928D series, many collectors and the uninformed public, mistake the early issues for Gold Certificates. The clause reads: "Redeemable in gold on demand at the United States Treasury or in gold or lawful money at any Federal Reserve Bank." This clause was changed by Act of Dec. 28, 1933, due to the removal of gold coins from circulation.

Collectors endeavor to obtain a complete series in the $1 and $5 denominations. Some include the $10 notes, and a few reach for the $20, $50 or $100. These issues were not preserved in any quantity and completing a series of the early issues, offers quite a challenge. With the issuance of the $1 1963 series, collector interest was aroused in some of the higher denominations of the "green seals" resulting in a greatly increased demand. Values will continue to accelerate as collectors seek the early and hard to find issues.

FACE DESIGNS FEDERAL RESERVE NOTES

The first face design appears on series 1928 and 1928A of the $5.00, $10.00, and $20.00 denomination, and on the 1928 series only of the $50.00 and $100.00 denominations. This design has a large black numeral in black bank seal at left, indicating the Federal Reserve Bank of issue. The green Treasury seal is at right of note.

The second design brings only a minor change with the large numeral in the Federal Reserve Seal being replaced by a black letter. This design appears on all issues of $5.00, $10.00 and $20.00 denominations in series 1928B-C and D, and on series 1928A of the $50.00 and $100.00 notes.

The design of the 1934 series is the same as the preceding notes, but the inscription is changed. See description next page.

The third design occurs on series 1950, A-B-C-D and E of all denominations. The Federal Reserve Seal is small with a smaller letter indicating bank of issue. The green Treasury seal is also smaller. The series date has been removed from upper left and is used in lower right only, with the word "of" removed. The inscription reading the same as series 1934 is in micro letters.

The 1963 series brought a radical change in the inscription and in the obligation to pay as described on next page. Otherwise the basic face design is the same. On the $1.00 notes added to this series, the basic design of the $1.00 Silver Certificates, was used with a new border design which eliminates the small word "ONE" used eight times in the border design of the $1.00 United States notes and Silver Certificates. The plate number and letters are also a little higher on the right side of note.

The 1969 series introduced the new Treasury Seal, and also brought into full use the engraving of the "series designation" and signatures of the Treasurer of the United States, and Secretary of the Treasury onto the face plates (and not printed during the overprinting operation). (Note: this engraving of formerly overprinted portions enable the issuance of the Series 1963B notes in such a short time.)

BACK DESIGNS FEDERAL RESERVE NOTES

The back design of all series is the same as used on other issues of the same denomination. During the printing of the $20.00 1934C series of Federal Reserve notes and continuing thereafter on all issues of this denomination, a change occurred in the back design of the $20.00 notes. Due to the "face-lifing" work on the White House, a new design was engraved. Comparison of two designs shows the difference. "White House" was changed to "The White House."

The back design of all denominations, starting with the 1963 series, have the motto, "In God We Trust."

OBLIGATIONS FEDERAL RESERVE NOTES

On all series and denominations of Federal Reserve notes, 1928 through 1950E, the obligation to pay reads: "The United States of America will pay to the bearer on demand (amount)."

Starting with the 1963 series, all denominations issued, the words: "will pay to the bearer on demand" have been removed. The wording in the design at bottom of note simply states the denomination.

INSCRIPTIONS FEDERAL RESERVE NOTES

On all series through 1950E the inscription reads: "The note is legal Tender for all debts, public and private, and is redeemable in lawful money of the United States at the United States Treasury, or at any Federal Reserve Bank." Starting with the 1950 series, this clause is set in much smaller type.

Commencing with series 1963, all denominations, inscription, like the obligation to pay, has been greatly abbreviated and now reads: "This note is legal tender for all debts, public and private."

SERIAL NUMBERING OF $1 FEDERAL RESERVE NOTES

Numbering machines at the Bureau of Engraving & Printing are customarily reset to 00000001 only with a change of design or series year. Silver certificate numbering began with A00000001A on series 1928, 1934, 1935 and 1957. $1 Federal Reserve notes, series 1963 and 1969, also began with 00000001 for each District.

Numbering of $1 1963A series of Federals was not continuous from series 1963. Numbering machines were reset to No. 1 for all Districts. This was done with good planning by the Bureau, as a heavy run of 1963A series might have exhausted the 25 possible suffix letters, requiring a new suffix of AA, or other type of indicator.

The Series 1963B continued the Serial numbers of Series 1963A for the districts printed. Series 1969 started back at No. 1, and Series 1969A continued (for most districts) where the former series ended (see serials in the proper charts). Series 1969B, however, started back at No. 1. The next series, 1969C, continued the serials, as it did not have extremely large runs. Series 1969D started back at No. 1. Series 1974 started back at No. 1, for $1 only.

COPE overprinting commenced during the early printing of Series 1969B. See front of Catalog for complete listing of these notes, which started with $1 denomination and is now extended to all denominations printed. (Note: to date no star notes have been produced on COPE.)

SERIAL NUMBERING OF $5.00 AND HIGHER

Serial numbers continued consecutively during all Series, and started back at No. 1 when a new Series commenced. However, with new Series 1974, the serials continued from the last serial of Series 1969C ($5, 10, 20, 50, 100).

ONE DOLLAR FEDERAL RESERVE NOTES
Series 1963, Granahan-Dillon

	PLAIN NUMBERS				STAR NUMBERS		
No.	District	No. Printed	Unc.	No.	District	No. Printed	Unc.
F1-63	A-Boston	87,680,000	3.75	F1*-63	A-Boston	6,400,000	4.75
F1-63	B-N.Y.	219,200,000	3.50	F1*-63	B-N.Y.	15,360,000	4.50
F1-63	C-Phila.	123,680,000	3.75	F1*-63	C-Phila.	10,880,000	4.50
F1-63	D-Cleve.	108,320,000	3.75	F1*-63	D-Cleve.	8,320,000	4.50
F1-63	E-Richm'd	159,520,000	3.75	F1*-63	E-Richm'd	12,160,000	4.50
F1-63	F-Atlanta	221,120,000	3.50	F1*-63	F-Atlanta	19,200,000	4.25
F1-63	G-Chicago	279,360,000	3.50	F1*-63	G-Chicago	19,840,000	4.25
F1-63	H-St. Louis	99,840,000	3.75	F1*-63	H-St. Louis	9,600,000	4.50
F1-63	I-Minn.	44,800,000	3.50	F1*-63	I-Minn.	5,120,000	4.75
F1-63	J-Kan. City	88,960,000	3.50	F1*-63	J-Kan. City	8,960,000	4.50
F1-63	K-Dallas	85,760,000	3.50	F1*-63	K-Dallas	8,960,000	4.50
F1-63	L-San F.	200,000,000	3.50	F1*-63	L-San F.	14,720,000	4.25

See page 12 for "Block Letter" listing and pricing.

$1 FEDERAL RESERVE NOTES—SERIES 1963 (32 Subject)
Secretary-Treasurer: Dillon-Granahan

Federal Reserve District	First Serial Number Printed	Last Serial Number Printed	First Note Delivered	Last Note Delivered
Boston	A00 000 001A	A87 680 000A	11-19-63	4-20-65
New York	B00 000 001A	B19 200 000C	11-15-63	5-14-65
Philadelphia	C00 000 001A	C23 680 000B	11-15-63	6-30-65
Cleveland	D00 000 001A	D08 320 000B	11-14-63	7- 2-65
Richmond	E00 000 001A	E59 520 000B	11-18-63	4-23-65
Atlanta	F00 000 001A	F21 120 000C	11-12-63	6-15-65
Chicago	G00 000 001A	G79 360 000C	11- 7-63	4-28-65
St. Louis	H00 000 001A	H99 840 000A	11-13-63	7-27-65
Minneapolis	I 00 000 001A	I 44 800 000A	11-18-63	7-19-65
Kansas City	J00 000 001A	J88 960 000A	11- 8-63	7-23-65
Dallas	K00 000 001A	K85 760 000A	11- 6-63	6-28-65
San Francisco	L00 000 001A	L99 999 999B	11- 6-63	5-12-65

Face Design $1.00, Series 1963

ONE DOLLAR FEDERAL RESERVE NOTES

Series 1963A, Granahan-Fowler

PLAIN NUMBERS				STAR NUMBERS			
No.	District	No. Printed	Unc.	No.	District	No. Printed	Unc.
F1-63A	A-Boston	319,840,000	3.50	F1*-63A	A-Boston	19,840,000	4.50
F1-63A	B-N.Y.	657,600,000	3.50	F1*-63A	B-N.Y.	48,640,000	4.50
F1-63A	C-Phila.	375,520,000	3.50	F1*-63A	C-Phila.	26,240,000	4.50
F1-63A	D-Cleve.	337,120,000	3.50	F1*-63A	D-Cleve.	21,120,000	4.50
F1-63A	E-Richm'd	532,000,000	3.50	F1*-63A	E-Richm'd	41,600,000	4.50
F1-63A	F-Atlanta	636,480,000	3.50	F1*-63A	F-Atlanta	40,960,000	4.50
F1-63A	G-Chgo	784,480,000	3.50	F1*-63A	G-Chgo	52,480,000	4.50
F1-63A	H-St. L.	264,000,000	3.50	F1*-63A	H-St. L.	17,920,000	4.50
F1-63A	I-Minn.	112,160,000	3.50	F1*-63A	I-Minn.	7,040,000	4.50
F1-63A	J-K. C.	219,200,000	3.50	F1*-63A	J-K. C.	14,720,000	4.50
F1-63A	K-Dallas	288,960,000	3.50	F1*-63A	K-Dallas	19,184,000	4.50
F1-63A	L-San F.	576,800,000	3.50	F1*-63A	L-San F.	42,880,000	4.50

See page 12 for "Block Letter" listing and pricing.

$1 FEDERAL RESERVE NOTES—SERIES 1963A (32 Subject)
Secretary-Treasurer: Granahan-Fowler

Federal Reserve District	First Serial Number Printed	Last Serial Number Printed	First Note Delivered	Last Note Delivered
Boston	A00 000 001A	A19 840 000D	7- 8-65	6-23-69
New York	B00 000 001A	B57 600 000G	5-14-65	1-28-69
Philadelphia	C00 000 001A	C75 520 000D	8- 2-65	7-23-69
Cleveland	D00 000 001A	D37 120 000D	7- 2-65	7-24-69
Richmond	E00 000 001A	E32 000 000F	4-19-65	1-16-69
Atlanta	F00 000 001A	F36 480 000G	8-30-65	6-23-69
Chicago	G00 000 001A	G84 480 000H	5-12-65	1-29-69
St. Louis	H00 000 001A	H64 000 000C	7-28-65	6-23-69
Minneapolis	I 00 000 001A	I 12 160 000B	9-22-65	6- 9-69
Kansas City	J00 000 001A	J19 200 000C	8-17-65	2-24-69
Dallas	K00 000 001A	K88 960 000C	7- 6-65	8- 7-69
San Francisco	L00 000 001A	L76 800 000F	5-12-65	1-31-69

Joseph W. Barr's appointment as Secretary of the Treasury, by former Pres. Johnson, to serve for only 20 days, created considerable excitement among collectors. News writers also noted the very short term of Secy. Barr, and many articles were written which created a demand for the Barr notes from non-collectors as well as collectors.

Although Secy. Barr held office only 20 days, notes with this signature continued to be printed until after the appointment in May of 1969 of Dorothy Andrews Elston, Treasurer and David M. Kennedy, Secretary.

Series 1963B, Granahan-Barr

PLAIN NUMBERS				STAR NUMBERS			
No.	District	No. Printed	Unc.	No.	District	No. Printed	Unc.
F1-63B	B-N.Y.	123,040,000	3.50	F1*-63B	B-N.Y.	3,680,000	5.00
F1-63B	E-Richm'd	93,600,000	3.50	F1*-63B	E-Richm'd	3,200,000	6.50
F1-63B	G-Chgo	91,040,000	3.50	F1*-63B	G-Chgo	2,400,000	5.00
F1-63B	J-K. C.	44,800,000	4.50	F1*-63B	J-K. C.	None printed	
F1-63B	L-San F.	30,880,000	4.00	F1*-63B	L-San F.	3,040,000	5.00

See page 12 for "Block Letter" listing and pricing.

ONE DOLLAR FEDERAL RESERVE NOTES

$1 FEDERAL RESERVE NOTES—SERIES 1963B (32 Subject)
Secretary-Treasurer: Granahan-Barr

Federal Reserve District	First Serial Number Printed	Last Serial Number Printed	First Note Delivered	Last Note Delivered
New York	B57 600 001G	B80 640 000H	1-27-69	11-12-69
Richmond	E32 000 001F	E25 600 000G	1-16-69	10-31-69
Chicago	G84 480 001H	G75 520 000 I	1-23-69	9- 8-69
Kansas City	J19 200 001C	J64 000 000C	3- 6-69	10-15-69
San Francisco	L76 800 001F	L83 200 000G	1-22-69	10- 8-69

$1 FEDERAL RESERVE NOTES—SERIES 1963B (32 Subject)

Federal Reserve District	First Serial Number Printed	Last Serial Number Printed
New York	B48 800 001*	B52 480 000*
Richmond	E41 600 001*	E44 800 000*
Chicago	G52 640 001*	G55 040 000*
Kansas City	(None)	(None)
San Francisco	L43 040 001*	L46 080 000*

Face Design with Dorothy Andrews Elston and David M. Kennedy signatures

Series 1969, Elston-Kennedy

PLAIN NUMBERS				STAR NUMBERS			
No.	District	No. Printed	Unc.	No.	District	No. Printed	Unc.
F1-69	A-Boston	99,200,000	3.00	F1*-69	A-Boston	5,120,000	4.00
F1-69	B-N.Y.	69,120,000	3.00	F1*-69	B-N.Y.	14,080,000	4.00
F1-69	C-Phila.	68,480,000	3.00	F1*-69	C-Phila.	3,200,000	4.50
F1-69	D-Cleve.	20,480,000	3.00	F1*-69	D-Cleve.	5,760,000	4.00
F1-69	E-Richm'd	50,560,000	3.00	F1*-69	E-Richm'd	10,880,000	4.00
F1-69	F-Atlanta	85,120,000	3.00	F1*-69	F-Atlanta	7,680,000	4.00
F1-69	G-Chicago	59,520,000	3.00	F1*-69	G-Chicago	12,160,000	4.25
F1-69	H-St. Louis	74,880,000	3.00	F1*-69	H-St. Louis	3,840,000	4.50
F1-69	I-Minn.	48,000,000	3.00	F1*-69	I-Minn.	1,920,000	5.50
F1-69	J-Kan. City	95,360,000	3.00	F1*-69	J-Kan. City	5,760,000	4.00
F1-69	K-Dallas	13,440,000	3.00	F1*-69	K-Dallas	5,120,000	4.00
F1-69	L-San F.	26,240,000	3.00	F1*-69	L-San F.	9,600,000	4.00

See page 12 for "Block Letter" listing and pricing.

ONE DOLLAR FEDERAL RESERVE NOTES

$1 FEDERAL RESERVE NOTES—SERIES 1969 (32 Subject)

Federal Reserve District	First Serial Number Printed	Last Serial Number Printed	First Note Delivered	Last Note Delivered
Boston	A00 000 001A	A99 200 000A	7-21-69	3-29-71
New York	B00 000 001A	B69 120 000C	7- 7-69	2- 3-71
Philadelphia	C00 000 001A	C68 480 000A	8-12-69	4- 7-71
Cleveland	D00 000 001A	D20 480 000B	8-11-69	3- 8-71
Richmond	E00 000 001A	E50 560 000C	7- 7-69	3- 5-71
Atlanta	F00 000 001A	F85 120 000B	8-19-69	2-25-71
Chicago	G00 000 001A	G59 520 000D	7- 7-69	2- 8-71
St. Louis	H00 000 001A	H74 880 000A	8- 8-69	12- 8-71
Minneapolis	I 00 000 001A	I 48 000 000A	7- 7-69	12- 9-70
Kansas City	J00 000 001A	J95 360 000A	7- 7-69	2- 3-71
Dallas	K00 000 001A	K13 440 000B	8-21-69	12- 8-70
San Francisco	L00 000 001A	L26 240 000C	7- 7-69	2- 8-71

$1 FEDERAL RESERVE STAR NOTES—SERIES 1963 (32 Subject)

Federal Reserve District	First Serial Number Printed	Last Serial Number Printed
Boston	A00 000 001*	A05 120 000*
New York	B00 000 001*	B14 080 000*
Philadelphia	C05 120 001*	C05 753 000*
Cleveland	D00 000 001*	D05 760 000*
Richmond	E00 000 001*	E10 880 000*
Atlanta	F00 000 001*	F07 680 000*
Chicago	G00 000 001*	G12 160 000*
St. Louis	H00 000 001*	H03 840 000*
Minneapolis	I 00 000 001*	I 01 920 000*
Kansas City	J00 000 001*	J05 760 000*
Dallas	K00 000 001*	K05 120 000*
San Francisco	L00 000 001*	L09 600 000*

Series 1969A, Kabis-Kennedy

F1-69A—The first notes of this new series were printed on October 26, 1970. Over 550 million printed. This series is a first in U.S. paper money history being created by the marriage of the Treasurer.

PLAIN NUMBERS

No.	District	No. Printed	Unc.
F1-69A	A-Boston	40,480,000	3.00
F1-69A	B-N.Y.	122,520,000	3.00
F1-69A	C-Phila.	44,960,000	3.00
F1-69A	D-Cleve.	30,080,000	3.00
F1-69A	E-Richm'd	66,080,000	3.00
F1-69A	F-Atlanta	70,560,000	3.00
F1-69A	G-Chgo	75,680,000	3.00
F1-69A	H-St. L.	41,120,000	3.00
F1-69A	I-Minn.	21,760,000	3.50
F1-69A	J-K. C.	40,480,000	3.00
F1-69A	K-Dallas	27,520,000	3.50
F1-69A	L-San F.	51,840,000	3.00

STAR NUMBERS

No.	District	No. Printed	Unc.
F1*-69A	A-Boston	1,120,000	3.50
F1*-69A	B-N.Y.	6,240,000	3.00
F1*-69A	C-Phila.	1,760,000	3.50
F1*-69A	D-Cleve.	1,280,000	3.50
F1*-69A	E-Richm'd	3,200,000	3.00
F1*-69A	F-Atlanta	2,400,000	3.00
F1*-69A	G-Chgo	4,480,000	3.00
F1*-69A	H-St. L.	1,280,000	3.50
F1*-69A	I-Minn.	640,000	6.00
F1*-69A	J-K. C.	1,120,000	3.50
F1*-69A	K-Dallas	None	
F1*-69A	L-San F.	3,840,000	3.00

See page 12 for "Block Letter" listing and pricing.

ONE DOLLAR FEDERAL RESERVE NOTES

$1 FEDERAL RESERVE NOTES—SERIES 1969A (32 Subject)

Federal Reserve District	First Serial Number Printed	Last Serial Number Printed	First Note Delivered	Last Note Delivered
Boston	A99 200 001A	A39 680 000B	1- 4-71	6-16-71
New York	B69 120 001C	B91 520 000D	1-26-71	5-18-71
Philadelphia	C68 480 001A	C13 440 000B	1- 5-71	5-26-71
Cleveland	D20 480 001B	D50 560 000B	1- 4-71	7- 6-71
Richmond	E50 560 001C	E16 640 000D	12- 4-70	5-21-71
Atlanta	F85 120 001B	F55 680 000C	1- 4-71	6-10-71
Chicago	G59 520 001D	G35 200 000E	1- 4-71	6- 1-71
St. Louis	H74 880 001A	H16 000 000B	1-19-71	7-19-71
Minneapolis	I 48 000 001A	I 69 760 000A	1-20-71	6-23-71
Kansas City	J95 360 001A	J35 840 000B	1- 6-71	6-29-71
Dallas	K13 440 001B	K40 960 000B	1-26-71	4-27-71
San Francisco	L26 240 001C	L78 080 000C	1- 4-71	5-19-71

$1 FEDERAL RESERVE STAR NOTES—SERIES 1969A (32 Subject)

Federal Reserve District	First Serial Number Printed	Last Serial Number Printed
Boston	A05 280 001*	A06 400 000*
New York	B14 240 001*	B20 480 000*
Philadelphia	C03 360 001*	C05 120 000*
Cleveland	D05 760 001*	D07 040 000*
Richmond	E10 880 001*	E14 080 000*
Atlanta	F07 840 001*	F10 240 000*
Chicago	G12 160 001*	G16 640 000*
St. Louis	H03 840 001*	H05 120 000*
Minneapolis	I 01 920 001*	I 02 560 000*
Kansas City	J05 920 001*	J07 040 000*
Dallas	None Printed	
San Francisco	L09 600 001*	L13 440 000*

Series 1969B, Kabis-Connally

John B. Connally, sworn in as Secretary on Feb. 11, 1971. Printing of $1 began on April 20, 1971. First notes printed were Dallas, which were first released in Washington, D.C. (a month later they were released in Texas district). This series was short-lived due to the death of Mrs. Kabis on July 3, 1971.

PLAIN NUMBERS

No.	District	No. Printed	Unc.
F1-69B	A-Boston	94,720,000	3.00
F1-69B	B-N.Y.	329,440,000	3.00
F1-69B	C-Phila.	133,280,000	3.00
F1-69B	D-Cleve.	91,520,000	3.00
F1-69B	E-Richm'd	180,000,000	3.00
F1-69B	F-Atlanta	170,400,000	3.00
F1-69B	G-Chgo	204,480,000	3.00
F1-69B	H-St. L.	59,520,000	3.00
F1-69B	I-Minn.	33,920,000	3.00
F1-69B	J-K. C.	67,200,000	3.00
F1-69B	K-Dallas	116,640,000	3.00
F1-69B	L-San F.	208,960,000	3.00

STAR NUMBERS

No.	District	No. Printed	Unc.
F1*-69B	A-Boston	1,920,000	3.50
F1*-69B	B-N.Y.	7,040,000	3.00
F1*-69B	C-Phila.	3,200,000	3.00
F1*-69B	D-Cleve.	4,480,000	3.50
F1*-69B	E-Richm'd	3,840,000	3.00
F1*-69B	F-Atlanta	3,840,000	3.00
F1*-69B	G-Chgo	4,480,000	3.00
F1*-69B	H-St. L.	1,920,000	3.50
F1*-69B	I-Minn.	640,000	3.50
F1*-69B	J-K. C.	2,560,000	3.00
F1*-69B	K-Dallas	5,120,000	3.00
F1*-69B	L-San F.	5,760,000	3.00

ONE DOLLAR FEDERAL RESERVE NOTES

$1 FEDERAL RESERVE NOTES—SERIES 1969B (32 Subject)

Federal Reserve District	First Serial Number Printed	Last Serial Number Printed	First Note Delivered	Last Note Delivered
Boston	A00 000 001A	A94 720 000B	5-24-71	9-13-72
New York	B00 000 001A	B29 440 000D	5- 5-71	7-19-72
Philadelphia	C00 000 001A	C33 280 000B	5-20-71	9-12-72
Cleveland	D00 000 001A	D91 520 000A	6-30-71	6-26-72
Richmond	E00 000 001A	E80 000 000B	5- 7-71	5-16-72
Atlanta	F00 000 001A	F70 400 000B	5-25-71	5-25-72
Chicago	G00 000 001A	G04 480 000C	6- 2-71	5- 8-72
St. Louis	H00 000 001A	H59 520 000A	7-29-71	7-15-72
Minneapolis	I 00 000 001A	I 33 920 000A	7- 7-71	6-21-72
Kansas City	J00 000 001A	J67 200 000A	7- 6-71	5-25-72
Dallas	K00 000 001B	K16 640 000B	5- 5-71	8- 1-72
San Francisco	L00 000 001A	L08 960 000C	5- 5-71	5-16-72

$1 FEDERAL RESERVE STAR NOTES—SERIES 1969B (32 Subject)

Federal Reserve District	First Serial Number Printed	Last Serial Number Printed
Boston	A00 000 001*	A01 920 000*
New York	B00 000 001*	B07 040 000*
Philadephia	C00 000 001*	C03 200 000*
Cleveland	D00 000 001*	D04 840 000*
Richmond	E00 000 001*	E03 840 000*
Atlanta	F00 000 001*	F03 840 000*
Chicago	G00 000 001*	G04 480 000*
St. Louis	H00 000 001*	H01 920 000*
Minneapolis	I 02 560 001*	I 03 200 000*
Kansas City	J00 000 001*	J02 560 000*
Dallas	K00 000 001*	K05 120 000*
San Francisco	L00 000 001*	L05 760 000*

Series 1969C, Banuelos-Connally

PLAIN NUMBERS

No.	District	No. Printed	Unc.
F1-69C	A-Boston	None	
F1-69C	B-N.Y.	46,720,000	2.50
F1-69C	C-Phila.	None	
F1-69C	D-Cleve.	15,520,000	2.50
F1-69C	E-Richm'd	61,600,000	2.50
F1-69C	F-Atlanta	60,960,000	2.50
F1-69C	G-Chgo	137,120,000	2.50
F1-69C	H-St. L.	23,680,000	2.50
F1-69C	I-Minn.	25,600,000	2.50
F1-69C	J-K. C.	38,560,000	2.50
F1-69C	K-Dallas	29,440,000	2.50
F1-69C	L-San F.	101,280,000	2.50

STAR NUMBERS

No.	District	No. Printed	Unc.
F1*-69C	A-Boston	None	
F1*-69C	B-N.Y.	None	
F1*-69C	C-Phila.	None	
F1*-69C	D-Cleve.	480,000	5.00
F1*-69C	E-Richm'd	480,000	5.00
F1*-69C	F-Atlanta	3,680,000	3.50
F1*-69C	G-Chgo	1,748,000	3.50
F1*-69C	H-St. L.	640,000	5.00
F1*-69C	I-Minn.	640,000	5.00
F1*-69C	J-K. C.	480,000	3.50
F1*-69C	K-Dallas	640,000	4.50
F1*-69C	L-San F.	2,400,000	7.50

ONE DOLLAR FEDERAL RESERVE NOTES

$1 FEDERAL RESERVE NOTES—SERIES 1969C (32 Subject)

Federal Reserve District	First Serial Number Printed	Last Serial Number Printed	First Note Delivered	Last Note Delivered
Boston	None Printed			
New York	B29 440 001D	B79 360 000D	7-19-72	9-12-72
Philadelphia	None Printed			
Cleveland	D91 520 001A	D07 040 000B	6-26-72	9-14-72
Richmond	E80 000 001B	E41 600 000C	5- 1-72	9- 5-72
Atlanta	F70 400 001B	F31 360 000B	5-25-72	10- 3-72
Chicago	G04 480 001C	G41 600 000D	5- 8-72	9-18-72
St. Louis	H59 520 001A	H83 200 000A	6-15-72	9-12-72
Minneapolis	I 33 920 001A	I 59 520 000A	8- 8-72	3-21-72
Kansas City	J67 200 001A	J05 760 000B	5-25-72	10- 4-72
Dallas	K16 640 001B	K46 080 000B	8- 1-72	11- 7-72
San Francisco	L08 960 001C	L10 240 000D	5-16-72	11- 8-72

$1 FEDERAL RESERVE STAR NOTES—SERIES 1969C (32 Subject)

Federal Reserve District	First Serial Number Printed	Last Serial Number Printed
Boston	None Printed	
New York	None Printed	
Philadelphia	None Printed	
Cleveland	D04 640 001*	D05 120 000*
Richmond	E04 000 001*	E04 480 000*
Atlanta	F04 000 001*	F07 680 000*
Chicago	G04 640 001*	G06 388 000*
St. Louis	H01 920 001*	H02 560 000*
Minneapolis	I 03 200 001*	I 03 840 000*
Kansas City	J02 720 001*	J03 200 000*
Dallas	K05 120 001*	K05 760 000*
San Francisco	L05 760 001*	L07 040 000*
San Francisco	L07 200 001*	L08 320 000*

(NOTE: Stars from San Francisco 07 040 001 through 07 199 999 were not used. Therefore, there are two runs of numbers.)

Series 1969D, Banuelos-Shultz

PLAIN NUMBERS			STAR NUMBERS		
No.	District	Unc.	No.	District No. Printed	Unc.
F1-69D	A-Boston	2.00	F1*-69D	A-Boston	3.50
F1-69D	B-New York	2.00	F1*-69D	B-New York	3.00
F1-69D	C-Philadelphia	2.00	F1*-69D	C-Philadelphia	3.00
F1-69D	D-Cleveland	2.00	F1*-69D	D-Cleveland	3.00
F1-69D	E-Richmond	2.00	F1*-69D	E-Richmond	3.00
F1-69D	F-Atlanta	2.00	F1*-69D	F-Atlanta	3.00
F1-69D	G-Chicago	2.00	F1*-69D	G-Chicago	3.00
F1-69D	H-St. Louis	2.00	F1*-69D	H-St. Louis	3.00
F1-69D	I-Minneapolis	2.00	F1*-69D	I-Minneapolis	3.00
F1-69D	J-Kansas City	2.00	F1*-69D	J-Kansas City	3.00
F1-69D	K-Dallas	2.00	F1*-69D	K-Dallas	3.00
F1-69D	L-San Francisco	2.00	F1*-69D	L-San Francisco	3.00

ONE DOLLAR FEDERAL RESERVE NOTES

$1 FEDERAL RESERVE NOTES—SERIES 1969D (32 Subject)

Federal Reserve District	First Serial Number Printed	Last Serial Number Printed	First Note Delivered	Last Note Delivered
Boston	A00 000 001A	A87 040 000B	9-13-72	10-29-74
New York	B00 000 001A	B68 480 000E	9-12-72	7-29-74
Philadelphia	C00 000 001A	C18 560 000C	9-12-72	9-24-74
Cleveland	D00 000 001A	D61 440 000B	9-21-72	9-10-74
Richmond	E00 000 001A	E74 240 000D	8- 7-72	9- 3-74
Atlanta	F00 000 001A	F77 440 000D	10- 3-72	9-17-74
Chicago	G00 000 001A	G78 080 000D	9-18-72	10-29-74
St. Louis	H00 000 001A	H68 840 000B	10-26-72	10-17-74
Minneapolis	I 00 000 001A	I 83 200 000A	12-15-72	10- 9-74
Kansas City	J00 000 001A	J85 760 000B	10- 4-72	10- 9-74
Dallas	K00 000 001A	K58 240 000B	11- 7-72	8-27-74
San Francisco	L00 000 001A	L00 640 000E	11- 8-72	10-11-74

Series 1974, Neff-Simon

PLAIN NUMBERS			STAR NUMBERS		
No.	District	Unc.	No.	District	Unc.
F1-74	A-Boston	1.75	F1*-74	A-Boston	2.50
F1-74	B-New York	1.75	F1*-74	B-New York	2.00
F1-74	C-Philadelphia	1.75	F1*-74	C-Philadelphia	2.50
F1-74	D-Cleveland	1.75	F1*-74	D-Cleveland	2.50
F1-74	E-Richmond	1.75	F1*-74	E-Richmond	2.00
F1-74	F-Atlanta	1.75	F1*-74	F-Atlanta	2.00
F1-74	G-Chicago	1.75	F1*-74	G-Chicago	2.00
F1-74	H-St. Louis	1.75	F1*-74	H-St. Louis	2.00
F1-74	I-Minneapolis	1.75	F1*-74	I-Minneapolis	3.50
F1-74	J-Kansas City	1.75	F1*-74	J-Kansas City	2.00
F1-74	K-Dallas	1.75	F1*-74	K-Dallas	2.50
F1-74	L-San Francisco	1.75	F1*-74	L-San Francisco	2.00

$1 FEDERAL RESERVE NOTES—SERIES 1974 (32 Subject)

Federal Reserve District	First Serial Number Printed	Last Serial Number Printed	First Note Delivered
Boston	A00 000 001A	A69 760 000C	10-29-74
New York	B00 000 001A	B40 320 000H	7-29-74
Philadelphia	C00 000 001A	C08 960 000D	9-24-74
Cleveland	D00 000 001A	D40 960 000C	9-10-74
Richmond	E00 000 001A	E44 160 000G	8-30-74
Atlanta	F00 000 001A	F99 840 000F	9-17-74
Chicago	G00 000 001A	G73 600 000E	10-29-74
St. Louis	H00 000 001A	H91 520 000C	10-17-74
Minneapolis	I 00 000 001A	I 44 160 000B	10- 9-74
Kansas City	J00 000 001A	J23 680 000C	9-26-74
Dallas	K00 000 001A	K30 720 000D	8-27-74
San Francisco	L00 000 001A	L37 120 000H	10-11-74

ONE DOLLAR FEDERAL RESERVE NOTES

$1 FEDERAL RESERVE STAR NOTES—SERIES 1974 (32 Subject)

Federal Reserve Bank	First Serial Number Printed	Last Serial Number Printed
Boston	A00 160 001*	A02 560 000*
New York	B00 160 001*	B08 960 000*
Philadelphia	C00 160 001*	C01 920 000*
Cleveland	D00 000 001*	D01 280 000*
Richmond	E00 160 001*	E05 760 000*
Atlanta	F00 160 001*	F07 680 000*
Chicago	G00 160 001*	G07 040 000*
St. Louis	H00 000 001*	H03 200 000*
Minneapolis	I 00 000 001*	I 00 640 000*
Kansas City	J00 000 001*	J03 200 000*
Dallas	K00 000 001*	K01 920 000*
San Francisco	L00 160 001*	L04 480 000*

NOTE: All Districts started at 00 160 001 for Star notes, except Kansas City which started at 01*. There are many gaps in the Star Serial numbers, but these have little real significance (except for the very specialized collector.)

Series 1977, currently being released, all started with 00 000 001. (First printed in September 1977 for Atlanta district).

TWO DOLLAR FEDERAL RESERVE NOTES

Federal reserve notes in this denomination were first released on April 13, 1976 on the anniversary of Jefferson's birthday. For the first time, the United States Postal Service allowed the cancellation of first class postage rate on the note, to denote "first day of issue." This cancellation was also allowed on July 4, 1976, the 200th birthday of our country. The interest caused by the new note, with a beautiful "Signing of the Declaration of Independence" vignette on the reverse, plus the first day cancellation brought a shortage of notes in many areas, with local sell-outs within hours. Most of the $2 notes have been overprinted COPE, though some press runs and all star notes were conventional.

It is still too early to say whether the release of this $2 note was highly successful, or whether the public as a whole is accepting it in normal commerce. Time alone will tell this story, but it is hoped that this denomination will circulate normally along with the other denominations. This will help conserve large numbers of notes that must be printed to supply demand. Cropping of the Trumbull painting which omitted some of the personages, created some furor by states left out — and the possibility exists that a revised design may be made.

TWO DOLLAR FEDERAL RESERVE NOTES

Face Design $2.00, Series 1976

Back Design $2.00, Series 1976

Star notes have been printed for all districts, and reported. All of the star printings did not start back at 00000001, and many districts had no notes with lower serial numbers than 00. All were conventionally overprinted, and only a few of the districts have appeared in large numbers.

Series 1976, Neff-Simon

No.	PLAIN NUMBERS District		Unc.	No.	STAR NUMBERS District		Unc.
F2-76	A-Boston	A00 000 001A	4.50	F2*-76	A-Boston	A00 000 001*	5.50
F2-76	B-N.Y...	B00 000 001A	4.50	F2*-76	B-N.Y...	B00 000 001*	5.50
F2-76	C-Phila..	C00 000 001A	4.50	F2*-76	C-Phila..	C00 000 001*	5.50
F2-76	D-Cleve..	D00 000 001A	4.50	F2*-76	D-Cleve.	D00 000 001*	5.50
F2-76	E-Rich...	E00 000 001A	4.50	F2*-76	E-Rich...	E00 000 001*	5.50
F2-76	F-Atlanta	F00 000 001A	4.50	F2*-76	F-Atlanta	F00 000 001*	5.50
F2-76	G-Chgo .	G00 000 001A	4.50	F2*-76	G-Chgo .	G00 000 001*	10.00
F2-76	H-St. L...	H00 000 001A	4.50	F2*-76	H-St. L. .	H00 000 001*	5.50
F2-76	I-Minn...	I 00 000 001A	4.50	F2*-76	I-Minn...	I 00 000 001*	5.50
F2-76	J-K. C....	J00 000 001A	4.50	F2*-76	J-K. C...	J00 000 001*	5.50
F2-76	K-Dallas .	K00 000 001A	4.50	F3*-76	K-Dallas	K00 000 001*	5.50
F2-76	L-San F..	L00 000 001A	3.50	F2*-76	L-San F..	L00 000 001*	8.50

FIVE DOLLAR FEDERAL RESERVE NOTES

Star notes were printed for almost every denomination and series of the Federal Reserve notes from $5 up. In the early series (1928 and 1934) Star notes are quite scarce, and should be saved in all conditions. From Series 1950 to the present, there are more star notes to be found, but they are still worth saving.

Face Design $5.00, Series 1928 and 1928A

Series 1928, Tate-Mellon

Large numeral in seal indicating Federal Reserve District.

No.	District	Ex.Fine	Unc.
F5-28	A-Boston	20.00	40.00
F5-28	B-New York	17.00	35.00
F5-28	C-Philadelphia	17.00	35.00
F5-28	D-Cleveland	17.00	40.00
F5-28	E-Richmond	20.00	47.50
F5-28	F-Atlanta	20.00	45.00
F5-28	G-Chicago	15.00	45.00
F5-28	H-St. Louis	20.00	50.00
F5-28	I-Minneapolis	22.50	55.00
F5-28	J-Kansas City	20.00	50.00
F5-28	K-Dallas	20.00	50.00
F5-28	L-San Fran.	17.00	45.00

Series 1928A, Woods-Mellon

Large numeral in seal as in 1928 series.

No.	District	Ex.Fine	Unc.
F5-28A	A-Boston	18.00	40.00
F5-28A	B-New York	15.00	35.00
F5-28A	C-Philadelphia	16.00	35.00
F5-28A	D-Cleveland	16.00	35.00
F5-28A	E-Richmond	20.00	45.00
F5-28A	F-Atlanta	16.00	40.00
F5-28A	G-Chicago	15.00	32.50
F5-28A	H-St. Louis	16.00	40.00
F5-28A	I-Minneapolis	20.00	45.00
F5-28A	J-Kansas City	17.00	45.00
F5-28A	K-Dallas	17.50	45.00
F5-28A	L-San Fran.	16.00	37.50

FIVE DOLLAR FEDERAL RESERVE NOTES

The Bureau of Engraving & Printing records show the total number of notes issued for the combined series of 1928, 1928A, 1928B and 1928C with no beginning or closing number for the separate series. These totals as given are as follows:

District	Quantity	District	Quantity
Boston	43,056,000	Chicago	64,812,000
New York	103,260,000	St. Louis	28,008,000
Philadelphia	46,560,000	Minneapolis	11,436,000
Cleveland	42,348,000	Kansas City	18,036,000
Richmond	22,224,000	Dallas	13,752,000
Atlanta	30,024,000	San Francisco	43,728,000

Face Design $5.00, Series 1928B, C and D

Series 1928B, Woods-Mellon. Large letter in seal replaces numeral.

No.	District	Ex.Fine	Unc.	No.	District	Ex.Fine	Unc.
F5-28B	A-Boston	17.00	35.00	F5-28B	G-Chicago	15.00	35.00
F5-28B	B-New York	17.00	32.50	F5-28B	H-St. Louis	17.00	37.50
F5-28B	C-Philadelphia	17.00	30.00	F5-28B	I-Minneapolis	16.00	45.00
F5-28B	D-Cleveland	15.00	37.50	F5-28B	J-Kansas City	14.00	37.50
F5-28B	E-Richmond	18.00	42.50	F5-28B	K-Dallas	16.00	40.00
F5-28B	F-Atlanta	17.00	35.00	F5-28B	L-San Fran.	14.00	32.50

Series 1928C. Woods-Mills. Large letter in seal.

No.	District	Ex.Fine	Unc.	No.	District	Ex.Fine	Unc.
F5-28C	D-Cleveland	165.00	300.00	F5-28C	L-San Fran.	175.00	375.00
F5-28C	F-Atlanta	165.00	300.00				

Series 1928D, Woods-Woodin. Large letter in seal.

No.	District	V.F.	Ex.Fine	Unc.
F5-28D	F-Atlanta	225.00	300.00	725.00

FIVE DOLLAR FEDERAL RESERVE NOTES

Although Bureau records indicate that no series 1928D notes were issued for any District, Atlanta notes do exist and are very rare. There is a span of over two million numbers between the oldest and highest serial numbers reported. However series 1928B and series 1928C notes have also been reported within this same span of numbers. Therefore previous reported estimates of over two million series 1928D Atlanta notes having been printed, needs revising.

$5 FEDERAL RESERVE NOTES—SERIES 1928, 1928A, 1928B, 1928C & 1928D (12 Subject)

Federal Reserve District	First Serial Number Printed	Last Serial Number Printed	First Note Delivered	Last Note Delivered
Boston	A00 000 001A	A43 056 000A	1-21-29	1-10-34
New York	B00 000 001A	B03 260 000B	2- 6-29	10-13-34
Philadelphia	C00 000 001A	C46 560 000A	2- 7-29	11- 1-33
Cleveland	D00 000 001A	D42 348 000A	2-11-29	1-11-34
Richmond	E00 000 001A	E22 224 000A	2-15-29	10-13-32
Atlanta	F00 000 001A	F30 024 000A	2-16-29	5-28-35
Chicago	G00 000 001A	G64 812 000A	1-22-29	12- 1-34
St. Louis	H00 000 001A	H28 008 000A	2-25-29	10- 4-34
Minneapolis	I 00 000 001A	I 11 436 000A	2-27-29	10- 5-34
Kansas City	J00 000 001A	J18 036 000A	2- 1-29	10- 7-33
Dallas	K00 000 001A	K13 752 000A	3- 2-29	8-13-35
San Francisco	L00 000 001A	L43 728 000A	1-30-29	10- 9-35

Remarks: Several appointments (as indicated in table below) normally requiring a change to be made on all plates; also the replacement of the number centered in the Seal by a letter to designate the location of banks, were indicated by the records examined. These records, however, did not specify dates and beginning or ending serial numbers for each of the series designations within the entire 1928 Series of $5 Federal Reserve Notes. Records indicate there were no 1928D Series Notes delivered. The following table indicates the dates which would govern changes that normally should have been made during the period over which the 1928, 1928A, 1928B, 1928C and 1928D Notes were delivered.

Secretary	Treasurer	Series	Combination Began	Ended
Mellon	Tate	1928	April 30, 1928	January 17, 1929
Mellon	Woods	1928A&B	January 18, 1929	February 12, 1932
Mills	Woods	1928C	February 13, 1932	March 3, 1933
Woodin	Woods	1928D	March 5, 1933	May 31, 1933

Replacement of Number by a Letter in Seal designating bank 9-23-29.
The reason for change to Series 1928 was introduction of smaller size currency.

FIVE DOLLAR FEDERAL RESERVE NOTES

Face Design $5.00, Series 1934, A, B, C and D

Series 1934, Julian-Morgenthau

	Darker Green Seal				Lighter Green Seal		
No.	District	Ex.Fine	Unc.	No.	District	Ex.Fine	Unc.
F5-34	A-Boston	14.00	32.50	F5-34I	A-Boston	16.00	37.50
F5-34	B-New York	12.50	30.00	F5-34I	B-New York	16.00	35.00
F5-34	C-Philadelphia	12.50	30.00	F5-34I	C-Philadelphia	16.00	35.00
F5-34	D-Cleveland	14.00	30.00	F5-34I	D-Cleveland	16.00	32.50
F5-34	E-Richmond	15.00	30.00	F5-34I	E-Richmond	18.00	35.00
F5-34	F-Atlanta	14.00	32.50	F5-34I	F-Atlanta	18.00	35.00
F5-34	G-Chicago	12.50	30.00	F5-34I	G-Chicago	16.00	35.00
F5-34	H-St. Louis	14.00	30.00	F5-34I	H-St. Louis	19.00	37.50
F5-34	I-Minneapolis	15.00	37.50	F5-34I	I-Minneapolis	19.00	40.00
F5-34	J-Kansas City	14.00	35.00	F5-34I	J-Kansas City	19.00	40.00
F5-34	K-Dallas	14.00	35.00	F5-34I	K-Dallas	19.00	40.00
F5-34	L-San Francisco	14.00	35.00	F5-34I	L-San Francisco	16.00	37.50

Suffix letter "I" is used to catalog numbering to indicate lighter Green Seal.

The Bureau of Engraving and Printing records do not give the separate total number of notes issued in series 1934 and 1934A. The combined totals as given by the Bureau are as follows:

District	Quantity	District	Quantity
Boston	50,040,000	Chicago	111,736,000
New York	173,476,000	St. Louis	53,052,000
Philadelphia	70,704,000	Minneapolis	15,468,000
Cleveland	57,660,000	Kansas City	30,984,000
Richmond	66,060,000	Dallas	31,560,000
Atlanta	67,776,000	*San Francisco	94,536,000

*Total for San Francisco includes Hawaii overprint series 1934 and 1934A.

Starting number for each of the above Districts was 00000001A on series 1934, prefix letter indicating issuing Bank. Numbering was consecutive through series 1934D.

FIVE DOLLAR FEDERAL RESERVE NOTES

Series 1934A, Julian-Morgenthau

No.	District	Ex.Fine	Unc.	No.	District	Ex.Fine	Unc.
F5-34A	A-Boston	12.00	30.00	F5-34A	G-Chicago	12.00	25.00
F5-34A	B-New York	11.00	25.00	F5-34A	H-St. Louis	14.00	32.50
F5-34A	C-Philadelphia	12.00	30.00	F5-34A	I-Minneapolis	None	—
F5-34A	D-Cleveland	12.00	35.00	F5-34A	J-Kansas City	None	—
F5-34A	E-Richmond	13.00	35.00	F5-34A	K-Dallas	None	—
F5-34A	F-Atlanta	13.00	27.50	F5-34A	L-San Fran.	12.00	25.00

$5 FEDERAL RESERVE NOTES—SERIES 1934 & 1934A (12 Subject)
Secretary-Treasurer: Morgenthau-Julian

Federal Reserve District	First Serial Number Printed	Last Serial Number Printed	First Note Delivered	Last Note Delivered
Boston	A00 000 001A	A50 040 000A	12-13-35	1- 4-46
New York	B00 000 001A	B73 476 000B	12- 6-34	11-16-45
Philadelphia	C00 000 001A	C70 704 000A	1-30-35	11-23-45
Cleveland	D00 000 001A	D57 660 000A	12-13-35	11-27-45
Richmond	E00 000 001A	E66 060 000A	12-13-35	1-15-46
Atlanta	F00 000 001A	F67 776 000A	6- 7-35	11-19-45
Chicago	G00 000 001A	G11 736 000B	1-23-35	12-21-45
St. Louis	H00 000 001A	H53 052 000A	11- 2-34	3- 6-46
Minneapolis	I 00 000 001A	I 15 468 000A	11-12-34	9-11-44
Kansas City	J00 000 001A	J30 984 000A	12-13-35	9-28-45
Dallas	K00 000 001A	K31 560 000A	8-12-35	4- 2-47
San Francisco	L00 000 001A	L94 536 000A	10-10-35	3- 7-46

Series 1934B, Julian-Vinson

No.	District	Printed	Ex.Fine	Unc.
F5-34B	A-Boston	4,548,000	15.00	32.00
F5-34B	B-New York	21,072,000	12.50	28.00
F5-34B	C-Philadelphia	9,720,000	12.50	32.00
F5-34B	D-Cleveland	9,816,000	12.50	30.00
F5-34B	E-Richmond	4,968,000	15.00	30.00
F5-34B	F-Atlanta	5,280,000	15.00	35.00
F5-34B	G-Chicago	10,584,000	12.50	32.50
F5-34B	H-St. Louis	3,120,000	20.00	37.50
F5-34B	I-Minneapolis	2,688,000	20.00	40.00
F5-34B	J-Kansas City	755,000	30.00	50.00
F5-34B	K-Dallas	None	—	—
F5-34B	L-San Francisco	10,108,000	12.50	35.00

$5 FEDERAL RESERVE NOTES—SERIES 1934B (12 Subject)
Secretary-Treasurer: Vinson-Julian

Federal Reserve District	First Serial Number Printed	Last Serial Number Printed	First Note Delivered	Last Note Delivered
Boston	A50 040 001A	A54 588 000A	1- 5-46	11- 4-46
New York	B73 476 001B	C80 424 000A	12- 4-45	10-23-46
Philadelphia	C70 704 001A	B94 548 000B	11-19-45	11- 5-46
Cleveland	D57 660 001A	D67 476 000A	11-28-45	1-16-47
Richmond	E66 060 001A	E71 028 000A	1-25-46	11-14-46
Atlanta	F67 776 001A	F73 056 000A	11-28-45	12-31-46
Chicago	G11 736 001A	G22 320 000B	12-26-45	11- 4-46
St. Louis	H53 052 001A	H56 172 000A	3- 7-46	9-17-46
Minneapolis	I 15 468 001A	I 18 156 000A	5- 2-46	4- 1-47
Kansas City	J30 984 001A	J31 728 000A	2-11-47	2-21-47
Dallas	None Printed	None Printed		
San Francisco	L94 536 001A	L04 644 000B	3- 7-46	11-19-46

FIVE DOLLAR FEDERAL RESERVE NOTES
Series 1934C, Julian-Snyder

No.	District	Printed	Ex.Fine	Unc.
F5-34C	A-Boston	13,788,000	10.00	22.50
F5-34C	B-New York	63,232,000	10.00	25.00
F5-34C	C-Philadelphia	21,844,000	10.00	22.50
F5-34C	D-Cleveland	20,412,000	10.00	20.00
F5-34C	E-Richmond	22,968,000	10.00	20.00
F5-34C	F-Atlanta	21,720,000	10.00	20.00
F5-34C	G-Chicago	57,744,000	10.00	20.00
F5-34C	H-St. Louis	19,824,000	10.00	22.00
F5-34C	I-Minneapolis	4,824,000	12.50	27.50
F5-34C	J-Kansas City	6,384,000	10.00	25.00
F5-34C	K-Dallas	4,776,000	12.50	27.50
F5-34C	L-San Francisco	7,848,000	10.00	25.00

$5 FEDERAL RESERVE NOTES—SERIES 1934C (12 Subject)
Secretary-Treasurer: Snyder-Julian

Federal Reserve District	First Serial Number Printed	Last Serial Number Printed	First Note Delivered	Last Note Delivered
Boston	A54 588 001A	A68 376 000A	11- 5-46	9-20-49
New York	B94 548 001B	B57 780 000C	11- 5-46	12-30-49
Philadelphia	C80 424 001A	C02 268 000B	11- 6-46	12-28-49
Cleveland	D67 476 001A	D87 888 000A	1-20-47	12-28-49
Richmond	E71 028 001A	E93 996 000A	11-27-46	10-24-49
Atlanta	F73 056 001A	F94 776 000A	3-12-47	12-16-49
Chicago	G22 320 001A	G80 064 000B	11- 4-46	12-30-49
St. Louis	H56 172 001A	H75 996 000A	9-30-46	12-14-49
Minneapolis	I 18 156 001A	I 22 980 000A	4-17-47	3- 3-50
Kansas City	J31 728 001A	J38 112 000A	2-27-47	5- 1-50
Dallas	K31 560 001A	K36 336 000A	4-11-47	7- 3-50
San Francisco	L04 644 001A	L12 492 000A	11-19-46	11-28-49

Series 1934D, Clark-Snyder

No.	District	Printed	Ex.Fine	Unc.
F5-34D	A-Boston	12,178,000	10.00	17.50
F5-34D	B-New York	54,924,000	10.00	15.00
F5-34D	C-Philadelphia	12,796,000	10.00	20.00
F5-34D	D-Cleveland	10,420,000	10.00	20.00
F5-34D	E-Richmond	13,180,000	10.00	18.00
F5-34D	F-Atlanta	10,036,000	10.00	18.00
F5-34D	G-Chicago	36,576,000	10.00	20.00
F5-34D	H-St. Louis	7,796,000	10.00	20.00
F5-34D	I-Minneapolis	3,648,000	12.00	27.50
F5-34D	J-Kansas City	6,812,000	10.00	20.00
F5-34D	K-Dallas	1,944,000	14.00	25.00
F5-34D	L-San Francisco	11,284,000	10.00	20.00

$5 FEDERAL RESERVE NOTES—SERIES 1934D (12 Subject)
Secretary-Treasurer: Snyder-Clark

Federal Reserve District	First Serial Number Printed	Last Serial Number Printed	First Note Delivered	Last Note Delivered
Boston	A68 376 001A	A80 554 000A	1-10-50	1-25-51
New York	B57 780 001C	B12 704 000D	1- 3-50	1-25-51
Philadelphia	C02 268 001B	C15 064 000B	1-16-50	1-24-51
Cleveland	D87 888 001B	D98 308 000B	1- 5-50	1-24-51
Richmond	E93 996 001A	E07 176 000B	1-10-50	1-30-51
Atlanta	F94 776 001A	F04 812 000B	1- 6-50	1-30-51
Chicago	G80 064 001B	G16 640 000C	1-12-50	1-18-51
St. Louis	H75 996 001A	H83 792 000A	2- 1-50	1-24-51
Minneapolis	I 22 980 001A	I 26 628 000A	3-13-50	1-15-51
Kansas City	J38 112 001A	J44 924 000A	5- 5-50	1-25-51
Dallas	K36 336 001A	K38 280 000A	7-13-50	9-19-50
San Francisco	L12 492 001B	L23 776 000B	2- 1-50	1-31-51

FIVE DOLLAR FEDERAL RESERVE NOTES

Face Design $5.00, Series 1950 to 1950E

Series 1950. Clark-Snyder. Serial numbers and Treasury seal smaller. Signatures printed instead of engraved. Starting number for each District was 00000001A with prefix letter indicating issuing Bank. Numbering was consecutive through series 1950E.

No.	District	Printed	Ex.Fine	Unc.
F5-50	A-Boston	30,672,000	8.00	15.00
F5-50	B-New York	106,768,000	8.00	12.00
F5-50	C-Philadelphia	44,784,000	8.50	15.00
F5-50	D-Cleveland	54,000,000	8.50	15.00
F5-50	E-Richmond	47,088,000	8.50	15.00
F5-50	F-Atlanta	52,416,000	8.50	15.00
F5-50	G-Chicago	85,104,000	7.50	15.00
F5-50	H-St. Louis	36,864,000	8.50	17.50
F5-50	I-Minneapolis	11,796,000	10.00	20.00
F5-50	J-Kansas City	25,428,000	8.00	15.00
F5-50	K-Dallas	22,848,000	8.50	16.00
F5-50	L-San Francisco	55,048,000	8.00	14.00

$5 FEDERAL RESERVE NOTES—SERIES 1950 (12 Subject)
Secretary-Treasurer: Snyder-Clark

Federal Reserve District	First Serial Number Printed	Last Serial Number Printed	First Note Delivered	Last Note Delivered
Boston	A00 000 001A	A30 672 000A	2- 7-51	7-28-53
New York	B00 000 001A	B06 768 000B	2- 2-51	7- 6-53
Philadelphia	C00 000 001A	C44 784 000A	2-28-51	6-23-53
Cleveland	D00 000 001A	D54 000 000A	2- 5-51	7-20-53
Richmond	E00 000 001A	E47 088 000A	11- 7-50	7-14-53
Atlanta	F00 000 001A	F52 416 000A	2-21-51	7-14-53
Chicago	G00 000 001A	G85 104 000A	2- 7-51	7- 6-53
St. Louis	H00 000 001A	H36 864 000A	2-21-51	7- 6-53
Minneapolis	I 00 000 001A	I 11 796 000A*	4-16-51	9- 1-53
Kansas City	J00 000 001A	J25 428 000A*	4-16-51	9- 1-53
Dallas	K00 000 001A	K22 848 000A*	4-20-51	8-28-53
San Francisco	L00 000 001A	L55 008 000A	2- 6-51	7- 6-53

Serial Nos. I 11 796 001A through I 11 808 000A, J25 428 001A through J25 488 000A and K22 848 001A through K22 896 000A were assigned for the Minneapolis, Kansas City and Dallas notes but were never used.

FIVE DOLLAR FEDERAL RESERVE NOTES

Series 1950A, Priest-Humphrey

No.	District	Printed	Ex.Fine	Unc.
F5-50A	A-Boston	53,568,000	7.50	13.00
F5-50A	B-New York	186,472,000	7.50	13.00
F5-50A	C-Philadelphia	69,616,000	7.50	13.00
F5-50A	D-Cleveland	45,360,000	7.50	13.00
F5-50A	E-Richmond	76,672,000	7.50	13.00
F5-50A	F-Atlanta	86,464,000	7.50	13.00
F5-50A	G-Chicago	129,296,000	7.00	13.00
F5-50A	H-St. Louis	54,936,000	7.50	14.00
F5-50A	I-Minneapolis	11,232,000	9.00	15.00
F5-50A	J-Kansas City	29,952,000	7.50	14.00
F5-50A	K-Dallas	24,984,000	7.50	14.00
F5-50A	L-San Francisco	90,712,000	7.50	13.00

$5 FEDERAL RESERVE NOTES—SERIES 1950A (18 Subject)
Secretary-Treasurer: Humphrey-Priest

Federal Reserve District	First Serial Number Printed	Last Serial Number Printed	First Note Delivered	Last Note Delivered
Boston	A30 672 001A	A84 240 000A	7-31-53	8-27-57
New York	B06 768 001B	B93 240 000C	7-20-53	7-30-57
Philadelphia	C44 784 001A	C14 400 000B	7-31-53	8-27-57
Cleveland	D54 000 001A	D99 360 000A	7-30-53	2-15-57
Richmond	E47 088 001A	E23 760 000B	7-27-53	8-12-57
Atlanta	F52 416 001A	F38 880 000B	7-16-53	9-13-57
Chicago	G85 104 001A	G14 400 000C	7-21-53	8- 7-57
St. Louis	H36 864 001A	H91 800 000A	7- 6-53	9-10-57
Minneapolis	I 11 808 001A	I 23 040 000A	9-25-53	7-16-55
Kansas City	J25 488 001A	J55 440 000A	9- 4-53	8-10-56
Dallas	K22 898 001A	K47 880 000A	8-31-53	8-29-57
San Francisco	L55 008 001A	L45 720 000B	7-14-53	7- 8-57

Series 1950B, Priest-Anderson

No.	District	Printed	Ex.Fine	Unc.
F5-50B	A-Boston	30,880,000	7.00	14.00
F5-50B	B-New York	85,960,000	7.00	13.00
F5-50B	C-Philadelphia	43,560,000	7.00	13.00
F5-50B	D-Cleveland	38,800,000	7.00	13.00
F5-50B	E-Richmond	52,920,000	7.00	13.00
F5-50B	F-Atlanta	80,560,000	7.00	13.00
F5-50B	G-Chicago	104,320,000	7.00	13.00
F5-50B	H-St. Louis	25,840,000	7.00	15.00
F5-50B	I-Minneapolis	20,880,000	7.00	17.50
F5-50B	J-Kansas City	32,400,000	7.00	14.00
F5-50B	K-Dallas	52,120,000	7.00	13.00
F5-50B	L-San Francisco	56,080,000	7.00	13.00

$5 FEDERAL RESERVE NOTES—SERIES 1950B (18 Subject)
Secretary-Treasurer: Anderson-Priest

Federal Reserve District	First Serial Number Printed	Last Serial Number Printed	First Note Delivered	Last Note Delivered
Boston	A84 240 001A	A15 120 000B	9-25-57	5-29-61
New York	B93 240 001C	B79 200 000D	9-25-57	9-30-60
Philadelphia	C14 400 001B	C57 960 000B	9-25-57	3-23-61
Cleveland	D99 360 001A	D38 160 000B	5-25-57	1-31-61
Richmond	E23 760 001B	E76 680 000B	9-25-57	6-14-61
Atlanta	F38 880 001B	F19 440 000C	9-25-57	4-19-61
Chicago	G14 400 001C	G18 720 000D	9-25-57	3-31-61
St. Louis	H91 800 001A	H17 640 000B	9-25-57	4-14-61
Minneapolis	I 23 040 001A	I 43 920 000A	9-25-57	3-21-60
Kansas City	J55 440 001A	J87 840 000A	9-25-57	8-16-60
Dallas	K47 880 001A	K99 999 999A	9-25-57	5-12-61
San Francisco	L45 720 001B	L01 800 000C	9-25-57	3-28-61

FIVE DOLLAR FEDERAL RESERVE NOTES
Series 1950C, Smith-Dillon

No.	District	Printed	Ex.Fine	Unc.
F5-50C	A-Boston	20,880,000	7.00	12.00
F5-50C	B-New York	47,440,000	7.00	13.00
F5-50C	C-Philadelphia	29,520,000	7.00	13.00
F5-50C	D-Cleveland	33,840,000	7.00	13.00
F5-50C	E-Richmond	33,400,000	7.00	13.00
F5-50C	F-Atlanta	54,360,000	7.00	13.00
F5-50C	G-Chicago	56,880,000	7.00	14.00
F5-50C	H-St. Louis	22,680,000	7.00	13.00
F5-50C	I-Minneapolis	12,960,000	7.00	15.00
F5-50C	J-Kansas City	24,760,000	7.00	13.00
F5-50C	K-Dallas	3,960,000	8.50	18.00
F5-50C	L-San Francisco	25,920,000	7.00	13.00

$5 FEDERAL RESERVE NOTES—SERIES 1950C (18 Subject)
Secretary-Treasurer: Dillon-Smith

Federal Reserve District	First Serial Number Printed	Last Serial Number Printed	First Note Delivered	Last Note Delivered
Boston	A15 120 001B	A36 000 000B	8-16-61	2- 1-63
New York	B79 200 001D	B26 640 000E	3- 3-61	12-17-62
Philadelphia	C57 960 001B	C87 480 000B	3-27-61	11- 7-62
Cleveland	D38 160 001B	D72 000 000B	5- 4-61	2- 4-63
Richmond	E76 680 001B	E10 080 000C	7-18-61	3- 1-63
Atlanta	F19 440 001C	F73 800 000C	5-12-61	3-11-63
Chicago	G18 720 001D	G75 600 000D	4- 3-61	2- 7-63
St. Louis	H17 640 001B	H40 320 000B	7-18-61	3- 5-63
Minneapolis	I 43 920 001A	I 56 880 000A	8-18-61	10- 2-62
Kansas City	J87 840 001A	J12 600 000B	8-18-61	3-11-63
Dallas	K00 000 001B	K03 960 000B	5-12-61	1- 2-63
San Francisco	L01 800 001C	L27 720 000C	7-28-61	2-15-63

Series 1950D, Granahan-Dillon

No.	District	Printed	Ex.Fine	Unc.
F5-50D	A-Boston	25,200,000	7.00	12.00
F5-50D	B-New York	102,160,000	7.00	11.00
F5-50D	C-Philadelphia	21,520,000	7.00	12.00
F5-50D	D-Cleveland	23,400,000	7.00	12.00
F5-50D	E-Richmond	42,480,000	7.00	11.00
F5-50D	F-Atlanta	35,200,000	7.00	12.00
F5-50D	G-Chicago	67,240,000	7.00	11.00
F5-50D	H-St. Louis	20,160,000	7.00	11.50
F5-50D	I-Minneapolis	7,920,000	7.00	12.50
F5-50D	J-Kansas City	11,160,000	7.00	11.00
F5-50D	K-Dallas	7,200,000	7.00	12.50
F5-50D	L-San Francisco	53,280,000	7.00	12.00

$5 FEDERAL RESERVE NOTES—SERIES 1950D (18 Subject)
Secretary-Treasurer: Dillon-Granahan

Federal Reserve District	First Serial Number Printed	Last Serial Number Printed	First Note Delivered	Last Note Delivered
Boston	A36 000 001B	A61 200 000B	2- 3-63	8-31-65
New York	B26 640 001E	B28 800 000F	12-19-62	1-27-65
Philadelphia	C87 480 001B	C09 000 000C	11- 9-62	10-25-63
Cleveland	D72 000 001B	D95 400 000B	2- 6-63	8-12-65
Richmond	E10 080 001C	E52 560 000C	3- 3-63	7- 2-65
Atlanta	F73 800 001C	F09 000 000D	3-13-63	7- 2-65
Chicago	G75 600 001D	G42 840 000E	2- 9-63	8-19-65
St. Louis	H40 320 001B	H60 480 000B	3- 7-63	7-26-65
Minneapolis	I 56 880 001A	I 64 800 000A	10- 5-63	9-23-64
Kansas City	J12 600 001B	J23 760 000B	3-14-63	2-23-65
Dallas	K03 960 001B	K11 160 000B	1- 5-63	2- 5-65
San Francisco	L27 720 001C	L81 000 000C	2-17-63	6- 7-65

FIVE DOLLAR FEDERAL RESERVE NOTES

Series 1950E, Granahan-Fowler. Printed for three Districts only.

No.	District	Printed	Ex.Fine	Unc.
F5-50E	B-New York	82,000,000	—	12.00
F5-50E	G-Chicago	14,760,000	—	15.00
F5-50E	L-San Francisco	34,400,000	—	12.00

The above series was released after Series 1963. These are the last notes printed on flat presses.

$5 FEDERAL RESERVE NOTES—SERIES 1950E (18 Subject)

Federal Reserve District	First Serial Number Printed	Last Serial Number Printed	First Note Delivered	Last Note Delivered
New York	B28 800 001F	B10 800 000G	9- 9-65	7-26-67
Chicago	G42 840 001E	G57 600 000E	9-17-65	6- 6-66
San Francisco	L81 800 001C	L05 400 000D	9-29-65	6-29-66

$5.00 Motto added. Back Design, introduced in Series 1963

Series 1963, Granahan-Dillon

No.	District	Printed	Ex.Fine	Unc.
F5-63	A-Boston	4,480,000	—	14.00
F5-63	B-New York	12,160,000	—	13.00
F5-63	C-Philadelphia	8,320,000	—	12.00
F5-63	D-Cleveland	10,240,000	—	13.00
F5-63	E-Richmond	None Printed	—	—
F5-63	F-Atlanta	17,920,000	—	13.00
F5-63	G-Chicago	22,400,000	—	13.00
F5-63	H-St. Louis	14,080,000	—	13.00
F5-63	I-Minneapolis	None Printed	—	—
F5-63	J-Kansas City	19,200,000	—	15.00
F5-63	K-Dallas	8,960,000	—	14.00
F5-63	L-San Francisco	18,560,000	—	13.00

Starting number for above series was 00000001A with prefix indicating bank of issue. Numbering was consecutive through series 1963A.

FIVE DOLLAR FEDERAL RESERVE NOTES

$5 FEDERAL RESERVE NOTES—SERIES 1963 (32 Subject)
Secretary-Treasurer: Granahan-Dillon

Federal Reserve District	First Serial Number Printed	Last Serial Number Printed	First Note Delivered	Last Note Delivered
Boston	A00 000 001A	A04 480 000A	1-12-65	7- 2-65
New York	B00 000 001A	B12 160 000A	3- 4-65	5-11-65
Philadelphia	C00 000 001A	C08 320 000A	9-16-64	3-30-65
Cleveland	D00 000 001A	D10 240 000A	6-10-65	6-25-65
Richmond	None Printed			
Atlanta	F00 000 001A	F17 920 000A	2-24-65	7- 2-65
Chicago	G00 000 001A	G22 400 000A	9-21-65	7-15-65
St. Louis	H00 000 001A	H14 080 000A	2- 2-65	7-15-65
Minneapolis	None Printed			
Kansas City	J00 000 001A	J01 920 000A	5-28-65	7- 2-65
Dallas	K00 000 001A	K05 760 000A	4-29-65	6-24-65
San Francisco	L00 000 001A	L18 650 000A	1-18-65	4-29-65

Series 1963A, Granahan-Fowler

No.	District	No. Printed	Unc.
F5-63A	A-Boston	77,440,00	11.00
F5-63A	B-N.Y.	98,080,000	13.00
F5-63A	C-Phila.	106,400,000	11.00
F5-63A	D-Clevel'd	83,840,000	11.00
F5-63A	E-Rich.	None Printed	—
F5-63A	F-Atl'ta	117,920,000	11.00
F5-63A	G-Chgo	213,440,000	11.00
F5-63A	H-St. L.	56,960,000	11.00
F5-63A	I-Minn.	None Printed	—
F5-63A	J-K. C.	55,040,000	11.00
F5-63A	K-Dallas	64,000,000	11.00
F5-63A	L-San F.	128,800,000	11.00

$5 FEDERAL RESERVE NOTES—SERIES 1932A (32 Subject)
Secretary-Treasurer: Fowler-Granahan

Federal Reserve District	First Serial Number Printed	Last Serial Number Printed	First Note Delivered	Last Note Delivered
Boston	A04 480 001A	A81 920 000A	7-29-65	5- 5-69
New York	B12 160 001A	B10 240 000B	6-22-65	1-17-69
Philadelphia	C08 320 001A	C14 720 000B	8-23-65	4-28-69
Cleveland	D10 240 001A	D94 080 000A	9-30-65	7-10-69
Richmond	E00 000 001A	E18 560 000B	4-30-65	6-25-68
Atlanta	F17 920 001A	F35 840 000B	8-12-65	5-27-69
Chicago	G22 400 001A	G35 840 000C	6- 7-65	4-30-69
St. Louis	H14 080 001A	H71 040 000A	1-28-66	8- 4-69
Minneapolis	I 00 000 001A	I 32 640 000A	7-23-65	7-25-68
Kansas City	J01 920 001A	J56 960 000A	8- 5-65	2-28-69
Dallas	K05 760 001A	K69 760 000A	7-30-65	8- 5-69
San Francisco	L18 560 001A	L47 360 000B	6-22-65	9- 9-69

Series 1969, Elston-Kennedy

No.	District	No. Printed	Unc.
F5-69	A-Boston	51,200,00	9.50
F5-69	B-N.Y.	198,560,000	9.50
F5-69	C-Phila.	69,120,000	9.50
F5-69	D-Clevel'd	56,320,000	9.50
F5-69	E-Rich.	84,480,000	9.50
F5-69	F-Atlanta	84,480,000	9.50
F5-69	G-Chgo	125,600,000	9.50
F5-69	H-St. L.	27,520,000	9.50
F5-69	I-Minn.	16,640,000	9.50
F5-69	J-K. C.	48,640,000	9.50
F5-69	K-Dallas	39,680,000	9.50
F5-69	L-San F.	103,840,000	9.50

FIVE DOLLAR FEDERAL RESERVE NOTES

Face Design $5.00, Series 1969, with New Treasury Seal

This is the first $5. note to bear the new Treasury seal. See page 24 for description, and illustration of this new seal.

$5 FEDERAL RESERVE NOTES—SERIES 1969 (32 Subject)
Secretary-Treasurer: Elston-Kennedy

Federal Reserve District	First Serial Number Printed	Last Serial Number Printed	First Note Delivered	Last Note Delivered
Boston	A00 000 001A	A51 200 000A	8-25-69	8-11-71
New York	B00 000 001A	B98 560 000B	8- 4-69	7-15-71
Philadelphia	C00 000 001A	C69 120 000A	8-26-69	8-11-71
Cleveland	D00 000 001A	D56 320 000A	9-15-69	8-16-71
Richmond	E00 000 001A	E84 480 000A	8- 6-69	8-20-71
Atlanta	F00 000 001A	F84 480 000A	8-26-69	7-29-71
Chicago	G00 000 001A	G25 600 000B	8- 4-69	7-20-71
St. Louis	H00 000 001A	H27 520 000A	1-26-70	7- 1-71
Minneapolis	I 00 000 001A	I 16 640 000A	9-17-69	6-23-71
Kansas City	J00 000 001A	J48 640 000A	8-27-69	8-10-71
Dallas	K00 000 001A	K39 680 000A	12- 2-69	6-29-71
San Francisco	L00 000 001A	L03 840 000B	9-10-69	11-10-71

Series 1969A, Kabis-Connally

No.	District	No. Printed	Unc.
F5-69A	A-Boston	23,040,00	8.50
F5-69A	B-N.Y.	62,240,000	8.50
F5-69A	C-Phila.	32,160,000	8.50
F5-69A	D-Clevel'd	21,120,000	8.50
F5-69A	E-Rich.	37,920,000	8.50
F5-69A	F-Atl'ta	25,120,000	8.50
F5-69A	G-Chgo	60,800,000	8.50
F5 69A	H-St. L.	15,360,000	8.50
F5-69A	I-Minn.	8,960,000	8.50
F5-69A	J-K. C.	17,920,000	8.50
F5-69A	K-Dallas	21,920,000	8.50
F5-69A	L-San F.	44,800,000	8.50

FIVE DOLLAR FEDERAL RESERVE NOTES

$5 FEDERAL RESERVE NOTES—SERIES 1969A (32 Subject)
Secretary-Treasurer: Kabis-Connally

Federal Reserve District	First Serial Number Printed	Last Serial Number Printed	First Note Delivered	Last Note Delivered
Boston	A51 200 001A	A74 240 000A	9-29-71	7-17-72
New York	B98 560 001B	B60 800 000C	7-15-71	6-21-72
Philadelphia	C69 120 001A	C01 280 000B	10-27-71	11-13-72
Cleveland	D56 320 001A	D77 440 000A	10-18-71	7-31-72
Richmond	E84 400 001A	E22 400 000B	8-20-71	8- 1-72
Atlanta	F84 480 001A	F09 600 000B	7-29-71	4-12-72
Chicago	G25 600 001B	G86 400 000B	7-20-71	7- 6-72
St. Louis	H27 620 001A	H42 880 000A	9- 2-71	6-20-72
Minneapolis	I 16 640 001A	I 25 600 000A	6-28-71	5- 2-73
Kansas City	J48 640 001A	J66 560 000A	8-10-71	7-18-72
Dallas	K39 680 001A	K60 800 000A	8-10-71	7-25-72
San Francisco	L03 840 001B	L48 640 000B	11-10-71	6- 7-72

Series 1969B, Banuelos-Connally

No.	District	No. Printed	Unc.	No.	District	No. Printed	Unc.
F5-69B	A-Boston	5,760,00	8.50	F5-69B	G-Chgo	27,040,000	8.50
F5-69B	B-N. Y.	34,560,000	8.50	F5-69B	H-St. L.	5,120,000	8.50
F5-69B	C-Phila.	5,120,000	8.50	F5-69B	I-Minn.	8,320,000	8.50
F5-69B	D-Clevel'd	12,160,000	8.50	F5-69B	J-K. C.	8,320,000	8.50
F5-69B	E-Rich.	15,360,000	8.50	F5-69B	K-Dallas	12,160,000	8.50
F5-69B	F-Atl'ta	18,560,000	8.50	F5-69B	L-San F.	23,680,000	8.50

$5 FEDERAL RESERVE NOTES—SERIES 1969B (32 Subject)
Secretary-Treasurer: Banuelos-Connally

Federal Reserve District	First Serial Number Printed	Last Serial Number Printed	First Note Delivered	Last Note Delivered
Boston	A74 240 001A	A80 000 000A	7-17-72	10- 4-72
New York	B60 800 001C	B95 368 000C	6-21-72	10-24-72
Philadelphia	C01 280 001B	C06 400 000B	11-13-72	1-16-73
Cleveland	D77 440 001A	D89 600 000A	7-31-72	1- 2-73
Richmond	E22 400 001B	E37 762 000B	8- 1-72	12-13-72
Atlanta	F09 600 001B	F28 160 000B	5-12-72	10-26-72
Chicago	G86 400 001B	G13 440 000C	7- 6-72	10-31-72
St. Louis	H42 880 001A	H48 000 000A	6-20-72	9-12-72
Minneapolis	I 25 600 001A	I 33 920 000A	5- 2-73	10-17-73
Kansas City	J66 560 001A	J74 880 000A	7-18-72	11-28-72
Dallas	K60 800 001A	K72 960 000A	7-25-72	2-13-73
San Francisco	L48 640 001B	L72 320 000B	6- 7-72	10-25-72

Series 1969C, Banuelos-Shultz

No.	District	Unc.	No.	District	Unc.
F5-69C	A-Boston	8.00	F5-69C	G-Chicago	8.00
F5-69C	B-New York	8.00	F5-69C	H-St. Louis	8.00
F5-69C	C-Philadelphia	8.00	F5-69C	I-Minneapolis	8.00
F5-69C	D-Cleveland	8.00	F5-69C	J-K. C.	8.00
F5-69C	E-Richmond	8.00	F5-69C	K-Dallas	8.00
F5-69C	F-Atlanta	8.00	F5-69C	L-San Francisco	8.00

$5 FEDERAL RESERVE NOTES—SERIES 1969C (32 Subject)
Secretary-Treasurer: Banuelos-Shultz

Federal Reserve District	First Serial Number Printed	Last Serial Number Printed	First Note Delivered	Last Note Delivered
Boston	A80 000 001A	A30 720 000B	11- 6-72	12- 4-74
New York	B95 360 001C	B15 360 000E	10-24-72	10- 2-74
Philadelphia	C06 400 001B	C60 160 000B	1-16-73	11- 6-74
Cleveland	D89 600 001A	D33 280 000B	1- 2-73	10-15-74
Richmond	E37 760 001B	E11 520 000C	11- 2-72	9-27-74
Atlanta	F28 160 001B	F09 600 000C	10-26-72	11-14-74
Chicago	G13 440 001C	G67 840 000C	10-31-72	9-18-74
St. Louis	H48 000 001A	H86 400 000A	11-28-72	8-27-74
Minneapolis	I 33 920 001A	I 45 440 000A	10-17-73	5- 6-74
Kansas City	J74 880 001A	J16 000 000B	11-28-72	
Dallas	K72 960 001A	K14 080 000B	2-13-73	12-10-74
San Francisco	L72 320 001B	L53 120 000C	10-25-73	

FIVE DOLLAR FEDERAL RESERVE NOTES

Series 1974, Neff-Simon

No.	District	Unc.	No.	District	Unc.
F5-74	A-Boston	7.50	F5-74	G-Chicago	7.50
F5-74	B-New York	7.50	F5-74	H-St. Louis	7.50
F5-74	C-Philadelphia	7.50	F5-74	I-Minneapolis	7.50
F5-74	D-Cleveland	7.50	F5-74	J-K. C.	7.50
F5-74	E-Richmond	7.50	F5-74	K-Dallas	7.50
F5-74	F-Atlanta	7.50	F5-74C	L-San Francisco	7.50

$5 FEDERAL RESERVE NOTES—SERIES 1974 (32 Subject)
Secretary-Treasurer: Neff-Simon

Federal Reserve District	First Serial Number Printed	Last Serial Number Printed	First Note Delivered
Boston	A30 720 001B	A88 960 000B	12- 4-74
New York	B15 360 001E	B68 480 000F	10- 2-74
Philadelphia	C60 160 001B	C14 080 000C	11- 6-74
Cleveland	D33 280 001B	D11 520 000C	10-22-74
Richmond	E11 520 001C	E46 720 000D	9-27-74
Atlanta	F09 600 001C	F37 120 000D	12- 5-74
Chicago	G67 840 001C	G63 360 000D	11-21-74
St. Louis	H86 400 001A	H51 200 000B	11- 5-74
Minneapolis	I 45 440 001A	I 87 040 000A	11-13-74
Kansas City	J16 000 001B	J58 242 000B	
Dallas	K14 080 001B	K71 680 000B	
San Francisco	L53 120 001C	L92 800 000D	

NOTE: Some of these notes were printed on 4-plate Giorl, some were COPE overprinted.

Series 1977 currently being printed. all started with 00 000 001.

TEN DOLLAR FEDERAL RESERVE NOTES

Face Design, Hamilton Facing Left, Series 1928

Series 1928, Tate-Mellon. Federal Reserve District indicated by number in seal.

No.	District	Ex.Fine	Unc.	No.	District	Ex.Fine	Unc.
F10-28	A-Boston	25.00	50.00	F10-28	G-Chicago	25.00	55.00
F10-28	B-New York	25.00	50.00	F10-28	H-St. Louis	27.50	65.00
F10-28	C-Phila.	25.00	50.00	F10-28	I-Minneapolis	27.50	65.00
F10-28	D-Cleveland	25.00	50.00	F10-28	J-Kansas City	27.50	65.00
F10-28	E-Richmond	27.50	55.00	F10-28	K-Dallas	27.50	65.00
F10-28	F-Atlanta	25.00	55.00	F10-28	L-San Fran.	25.00	55.00

The Bureau of Engraving and Printing records do not separate the total number of notes in each series: 1928, 1928A, 1928B and 1928C. The combined totals as given by the Bureau are as follows:

District	Quantity	District	Quantity
Boston	43,944,000	Chicago	55,104,000
New York	73,944,000	St. Louis	15,360,000
Philadelphia	32,520,000	Minneapolis	9,120,000
Cleveland	32,532,000	Kansas City	11,640,000
Richmond	17,604,000	Dallas	8,712,000
Atlanta	15,576,000	San Francisco	23,448,000

The starting number for each District in the 1928 series was 00000001A with prefix letter to indicate issuing Bank. The numbering was consecutive through series 1928, 1928A, 1928B and 1928C.

TEN DOLLAR FEDERAL RESERVE NOTES

Back Design $10.00, Series 1928 to 1950D

No.	District	Ex.Fine	Unc.
F10-28B	A-Boston	20.00	30.00
F10-28B	B-New York	20.00	30.00
F10-28B	C-Phila.	20.00	30.00
F10-28B	D-Cleveland	20.00	35.00
F10-28B	E-Richmond	20.00	35.00
F10-28B	F-Atlanta	20.00	35.00
F10-28B	G-Chicago	20.00	30.00
F10-28B	H-St. Louis	20.00	40.00
F10-28B	I-Minn.	20.00	40.00
F10-28B	J-Kansas City	20.00	40.00
F10-28B	K-Dallas	22.50	45.00
F10-28B	L-San Fran.	20.00	35.00

Face Design $10.00, Series 1928B and C

Series 1928A, Woods-Mellon. Large number in seal as in 1928 series.

No.	District	Ex.Fine	Unc.
F10-28A	A-Boston	20.00	35.00
F10-28A	B-New York	20.00	30.00
F10-28A	C-Phila.	20.00	40.00
F10-28A	D-Cleveland	20.00	40.00
F10-28A	E-Richmond	20.00	47.50
F10-28A	F-Atlanta	20.00	45.00
F10-28A	G-Chicago	20.00	40.00
F10-28A	H-St. Louis	20.00	70.00
F10-28A	I-Minn.	20.00	90.00
F10-28A	J-Kansas City	20.00	65.00
F10-28A	K-Dallas	20.00	60.00
F10-28A	L-San Fran.	20.00	45.00

TEN DOLLAR FEDERAL RESERVE NOTES

Series 1928C, Woods-Mills. Issued by only five Federal Reserve Banks.

No.	District	Ex.Fine	Unc.	No.	District	Ex.Fine	Unc.
F10-28C	B-New York	30.00	50.00	F10-28C	F-Atlanta	32.50	65.00
F10-28C	D-Cleveland	25.00	45.00	F10-28C	G-Chicago	20.00	50.00
F10-28C	E-Rich.	35.00	85.00				

$10 FEDERAL RESERVE NOTES—SERIES 1928, 1928A, 1928B and 1928C (12 Subject)

Federal Reserve District	First Serial Number Printed	Last Serial Number Printed	First Note Delivered	Last Note Delivered
Boston	A00 000 001A	A48 944 000A	2-19-29	10- 6-34
New York	B00 000 001A	B73 944 000A	3- 1-29	8-16-34
Philadelphia	C00 000 001A	C32 520 000A	3- 8-29	11- 1-34
Cleveland	D00 000 001A	D32 532 000A	3-22-29	1- 4-35
Richmond	E00 000 001A	E17 604 000A	3-28-29	10- 5-34
Atlanta	F00 000 001A	F15 576 000A	4- 3-29	8-19-35
Chicago	G00 000 001A	G55 104 000A	4- 6-29	10-22-34
St. Louis	H00 000 001A	H15 860 000A	4- 8-29	11- 1-34
Minneapolis	I 00 000 001A	I 09 120 000A	4-13-29	10- 2-34
Kansas City	J00 000 001A	J11 640 000A	3- 9-29	12- 5-34
Dallas	K00 000 001A	K08 712 000A	4- 9-29	5-24-32
San Francisco	L00 000 001A	L23 448 000A	4-17-29	9-19-35

Remarks: 1. 1928 Series—Introduction of small size Currency Notes. 2. 1928A—New Treasurer appointed. 3. 1928B—A letter used in lieu of a number to designate geographical location of bank. 4. 1928C—New Secretary appointed.

No records were found indicating serial numbers of the first notes of Series 1928A, 1928B and 1928C or Serial number of last note of Series 1928, 1928A and 1928B for any of the Federal Reserve Banks. No dates or serial numbers were found other than those listed on this record. The table of office terms (listed below) will indicate approximately the time of the various changes for the series covered by this record.

Secretary	Treasurer	Series	Combination Began	Ended
Mellon	Tate	1928	April 30, 1928	January 17, 1929
Mellon	Woods	1928A&B	January 18, 1929	February 12, 1932
Mills	Woods	1928C	February 13, 1932	March 3, 1933

Face Design, $10.00, Series 1934 to 1934D

TEN DOLLAR FEDERAL RESERVE NOTES

The Bureau of Engraving and Printing records do not give the separate total number of notes issued in series 1934 and 1934A. The combined totals as given by the Bureau are as follows:

District	Quantity	District	Quantity
Boston	138,292,000	Chicago	231,344,000
New York	371,688,000	St. Louis	69,528,000
Philadelphia	123,172,000	Minneapolis	31,392,000
*Cleveland-Estimated	117,328,000	Kansas City	50,556,000
Richmond	110,992,000	Dallas	44,688,000
Atlanta	98,652,000	**San Francisco	153,892,000

**Includes notes overprinted "Hawaii" series 1934A.

* While there is no record of the exact number of notes issued to Cleveland Federal Reserve Bank for series 1934, 1934A or 1934B, the closing serial number for the 1934B series is given as D17,328,000B. The D-A series, totaling 100,000,000 notes was completed, and 17,328,000 notes were issued in the D-B serial numbers. Therefore, the total issue for Cleveland in these three series would appear to be 117,328,000.

Series 1934, Julian-Morgenthau

Serial numbers for each District start with 00000001A, with bank letter as prefix. Numbering was consecutive through series 1934D.

Darker Green Seal				**Lighter Green Seal**			
No.	District	Ex.Fine	Unc.	No.	District	Ex.Fine	Unc.
F10-34	A-Boston	20.00	30.00	F10-34I	A-Boston	25.00	35.00
F10-34	B-New York	15.00	27.50	F10-34I	B-New York	25.00	35.00
F10-34	C-Phila.	17.50	30.00	F10-34I	C-Phila.	20.00	32.50
F10-34	D-Cleveland	17.50	30.00	F10-34I	D-Cleveland	25.00	40.00
F10-34	E-Richmond	20.00	35.00	F10-34I	E-Richmond	20.00	37.50
F10-34	F-Atlanta	20.00	35.00	F10-34I	F-Atlanta	20.00	40.00
F10-34	G-Chicago	15.00	30.00	F10-34I	G-Chicago	20.00	30.00
F10-34	H-St. Louis	20.00	38.00	F10-34I	H-St. Louis	25.00	40.00
F10-34	I-Minn.	20.00	38.00	F10-34I	I-Minn.	20.00	40.00
F10-34	J-Kansas City	20.00	40.00	F10-34I	J-Kansas City	25.00	45.00
F10-34	K-Dallas	20.00	40.00	F10-34I	K-Dallas	25.00	40.00
F10-34	L-San Fran.	20.00	30.00	F10-34I	L-San Fran.	25.00	32.50

Suffix letter "I" is used in catalog numbering to indicate lighter Green Seal.

$10 FEDERAL RESERVE NOTES—SERIES 1934 (12 Subject)
Secretary-Treasurer: Morgenthau-Julian

Federal Reserve District	First Serial Number Printed	Last Serial Number Printed	First Note Delivered	Last Note Delivered
Boston	A00 000 001A	No record	11-9-34	No record
New York	B00 000 001A	No record	10-17-34	No record
Philadelphia	C00 000 001A	No record	11-30-34	No record
Cleveland	D00 000 001A	No record	2-16-35	No record
Richmond	E00 000 001A	No record	1-23-35	No record
Atlanta	F00 000 001A	No record	8-20-35	No record
Chicago	G00 000 001A	No record	11-9-34	No record
St. Louis	H00 000 001A	No record	11-30-34	No record
Minneapolis	I00 000 001A	No record	12-10-34	No record
Kansas City	J00 000 001A	No record	2-15-35	No record
Dallas	K00 000 001A	No record	12-13-35	No record
San Francisco	L00 000 001A	No record	9-19-35	No record

TEN DOLLAR FEDERAL RESERVE NOTES

Series 1934A, Julian-Morgenthau

No.	District	Ex.Fine	Unc.	No.	District	Ex.Fine	Unc.
F10-34A	A-Boston	15.00	25.00	F10-34A	G-Chicago	15.00	22.50
F10-34A	B-New York	15.00	25.00	F10-34A	H-St. Louis	15.00	32.50
F10-34A	C-Phila.	15.00	25.00	F10-34A	I-Minn.	20.00	35.00
F10-34A	D-Cleveland	15.00	27.50	F10-34A	J-Kansas City	15.00	27.50
F10-34A	E-Richmond	15.00	28.00	F10-34A	K-Dallas	15.00	27.50
F10-34A	F-Atlanta	15.00	28.00	F10-34A	L-San Fran.	25.00	60.00

$10 FEDERAL RESERVE NOTES—SERIES 1934A (12 Subject)
Secretary-Treasurer: Morgenthau-Julian

Federal Reserve District	First Serial Number Printed	Last Serial Number Printed	First Note Delivered	Last Note Delivered
Boston	No record	A38 292 000B	No record	2- 1-46
New York	No record	B71 688 000D	No record	11-21-45
Philadelphia	No record	C23 172 000B	No record	2-19-46
Cleveland	No record	No record	No record	No record
Richmond	No record	E10 992 000B	No record	2-21-46
Atlanta	No record	F98 652 000A	No record	1-30-46
Chicago	No record	G31 344 000C	No record	12- 5-45
St. Louis	No record	H69 528 000A	No record	1-22-46
Minneapolis	No record	I 31 392 000A	No record	8-12-46
Kansas City	No record	J50 556 000A	No record	2- 6-46
Dallas	No record	K44 688 000A	No record	11-27-45
San Francisco	No record	L53 892 000B	No record	2-15-46

Series 1934B, Julian-Vinson

No.	District	Printed	Ex.Fine	Unc.
F10-34B	A-Boston	6,480,000	15.00	25.00
F10-34B	B-New York	42,616,000	15.00	22.50
F10-34B	C-Philadelphia	10,332,000	15.00	25.00
F10-34B	D-Cleveland Printed	No record	15.00	30.00
F10-34B	E-Richmond	6,912,000	15.00	30.00
F10-34B	F-Atlanta	6,700,000	15.00	30.00
F10-34B	G-Chicago	17,664,000	15.00	25.00
F10-34B	H-St. Louis	5,568,000	15.00	30.00
F10-34B	I-Minneapolis	2,412,000	15.00	30.00
F10-34B	J-Kansas City	4,356,000	15.00	30.00
F10-34B	K-Dallas	5,304,000	15.00	30.00
F10-34B	L-San Francisco	9,240,000	15.00	25.00

$10 FEDERAL RESERVE NOTES—SERIES 1934B (12 Subject)
Secretary-Treasurer: Vinson-Julian

Federal Reserve District	First Serial Number Printed	Last Serial Number Printed	First Note Delivered	Last Note Delivered
Boston	A38 292 001B	A44 772 000B	2- 8-46	11-13-46
New York	B71 688 001D	B14 304 000E	11-29-45	11- 4-46
Philadelphia	C23 172 001B	C33 504 000B	2-19-46	10-16-46
Cleveland	No record	D17 328 000B	No record	1-17-47
Richmond	E10 992 001B	E17 904 000B	2-21-46	12- 4-46
Atlanta	F98 652 001A	F05 352 000B	3-22-46	12-19-46
Chicago	G31 344 001C	G49 008 000C	12- 5-45	10-30-46
St. Louis	H69 528 001A	H75 096 000A	2- 6-46	10-10-46
Minneapolis	I 31 392 001A	I 33 804 000A	8-12-46	4- 2-47
Kansas City	J50 556 001A	J54 912 000A	2-18-46	1-19-50
Dallas	K44 688 001A	K49 992 000A	11-28-45	6- 3-47
San Francisco	L53 892 001B	L63 132 000B	2-15-46	10-22-46

TEN DOLLAR FEDERAL RESERVE NOTES

Series 1934C, Julian-Snyder

No.	District	Printed	Ex.Fine	Unc.
F10-34C	A-Boston	43,980,000	14.00	25.00
F10-34C	B-New York	108,532,000	14.00	22.50
F10-34C	C-Philadelphia	42,072,000	14.00	22.50
F10-34C	D-Cleveland	43,152,000	35.00	85.00
F10-34C	E-Richmond	34,452,000	14.00	25.00
F10-34C	F-Atlanta	44,352,000	14.00	25.00
F10-34C	G-Chicago	97,456,000	14.00	22.50
F10-34C	H-St. Louis	33,520,000	14.00	25.00
F10-34C	I-Minneapolis	9,936,000	18.50	30.00
F10-34C	J-Kansas City	19,836,000	14.00	25.00
F10-34C	K-Dallas	23,040,000	14.00	25.00
F10-34C	L-San Francisco	41,092,000	14.00	22.50

$10 FEDERAL RESERVE NOTES—SERIES 1934C (12 Subject)
Secretary-Treasurer: Snyder-Julian

Federal Reserve District	First Serial Number Printed	Last Serial Number Printed	First Note Delivered	Last Note Delivered
Boston	A44 772 001B	A88 752 000B	11-13-46	11- 1-49
New York	B14 304 001E	B22 836 000F	11- 4-46	9-28-49
Philadelphia	C33 504 001B	C75 576 000B	10-16-46	10-14-49
Cleveland	D17 328 001B	D60 480 000B	1-17-47	10-27-49
Richmond	E17 904 001B	E52 356 000B	12- 4-46	10-19-49
Atlanta	F05 352 001B	F49 704 000B	12-11-46	12-20-49
Chicago	G49 008 001C	G46 464 000D	10-30-46	10-12-49
St. Louis	H75 096 001A	H08 616 000B	10-24-46	10-27-49
Minneapolis	I 33 804 001A	I 43 740 000A	4-14-47	10-21-49
Kansas City	J54 912 001A	J74 748 000A	1- 9-47	1-19-50
Dallas	K49 992 001A	K73 032 000A	8- 6-47	12-20-49
San Francisco	L63 132 001B	L04 224 000C	10-22-46	10- 3-49

Series 1934D, Clark-Snyder

Note: Due to flourish at the end of Mrs. Clark's signature the name appears to be Clarke, however, Clark is correct spelling.

No.	District	Printed	Ex.Fine	Unc.
F10-34D	A-Boston	19,972,000	13.00	25.00
F10-34D	B-New York	60,452,000	13.00	25.00
F10-34D	C-Philadelphia	19,194,000	13.00	25.00
F10-34D	D-Cleveland	20,220,000	13.00	27.50
F10-34D	E-Richmond	18,664,000	13.00	25.00
F10-34D	F-Atlanta	17,180,000	13.00	25.00
F10-34D	G-Chicago	55,692,000	13.00	25.00
F10-34D	H-St. Louis	13,796,000	13.00	25.00
F10-34D	I-Minneapolis	5,292,000	13.00	30.00
F10-34D	J-Kansas City	7,992,000	13.00	32.50
F10-34D	K-Dallas	7,680,000	13.00	30.00
F10-34D	L-San Francisco	24,312,000	13.00	25.00

TEN DOLLAR FEDERAL RESERVE NOTES

$10 FEDERAL RESERVE NOTES—SERIES 1934D (12 Subject)
Secretary-Treasurer: Snyder-Clark

Federal Reserve District	First Serial Number Printed	Last Serial Number Printed	First Note Delivered	Last Note Delivered
Boston	A88 752 001B	A08 724 000C	11- 1-49	1-30-51
New York	B22 836 001F	B83 288 000F	9-28-49	1-31-51
Philadelphia	C75 576 001B	C94 760 000B	10-14-49	1-22-51
Cleveland	D60 480 001B	D80 700 000B	10-27-49	1-30-51
Richmond	E52 356 001B	E71 000 000B	10-19-49	1-24-51
Atlanta	F49 704 001B	F66 884 000B	12-20-49	1-24-51
Chicago	G46 464 001D	G02 156 000E	10-13-49	1-29-51
St. Louis	H08 616 001B	H22 412 000B	10-27-49	1-16-51
Minneapolis	I 43 740 001A	I 49 132 000A	11- 7-49	1-25-51
Kansas City	J74 748 001A	J82 740 000A	3-14-50	1-25-51
Dallas	K73 032 001A	K80 712 000A	2- 9-50	1-25-51
San Francisco	L04 224 001C	L28 536 000C	10-17-49	1-26-51

Face Design $10, Series 1950 to 1950D

Series 1950, Clark-Snyder

Serial numbers and Treasury seal smaller. Series number for each District start with No. 00000001A, with Bank letter as prefix. Numbering is consecutive through series 1950E.

No.	District	Printed	Ex.Fine	Unc.
F10-50	A-Boston	70,992,000	15.00	25.00
F10-50	B-New York	218,576,000	15.00	25.00
F10-50	C-Philadelphia	76,320,000	15.00	25.00
F10-50	D-Cleveland	76,032,000	15.00	25.00
F10-50	E-Richmond	61,776,000	15.00	25.00
F10-50	F-Atlanta	63,792,000	15.00	25.00
F10-50	G-Chicago	161,056,000	15.00	25.00
F10-50	H-St. Louis	47,808,000	15.00	25.00
F10-50	I -Minneapolis	18,864,000	15.00	25.00
F10-50	J-Kansas City	36,332,000	15.00	25.00
F10-50	K-Dallas	33,264,000	15.00	25.00
F10-50	L-San Francisco	76,896,000	15.00	25.00

TEN DOLLAR FEDERAL RESERVE NOTES

$10 FEDERAL RESERVE NOTES—SERIES 1950 (12 Subject)
Secretary-Treasurer: Snyder-Clark

Federal Reserve District	First Serial Number Printed	Last Serial Number Printed	First Note Delivered	Last Note Delivered
Boston	A00 000 001A	A70 992 000A	7-14-51	5-20-53
New York	B00 000 001A	B18 576 000C	2- 8-51	4- 1-53
Philadelphia	C00 000 001A	C76 320 000A	2-21-51	6- 5-53
Cleveland	D00 000 001A	D76 032 000A	2- 7-51	5- 6-53
Richmond	E00 000 001A	E61 776 000A	11- 7-50	5- 7-53
Atlanta	F00 000 001A	F63 792 000A	2-20-51	6-12-53
Chicago	G00 000 001A	G61 056 000B	2- 1-51	5- 5-53
St. Louis	H00 000 001A	H47 808 000A	3-19-51	6- 5-53
Minneapolis	I 00 000 001A	I 18 864 000A	2-27-51	10- 1-53
Kansas City	J00 000 001A	J36 332 000A*	2-27-51	10- 1-53
Dallas	K00 000 001A	K33 264 000A	2-28-51	10- 1-53
San Francisco	L00 000 001A	L76 896 000A	2- 6-51	5-13-53

Serial Nos. J 36 332 001A through J 36 432 000A were assigned for the 1950 Series for the Kansas City Notes but were never used.

Series 1950A, Priest-Humphrey

No.	District	Printed	Ex.Fine	Unc.
F10-50A	A-Boston	104,248,000	15.00	25.00
F10-50A	B-New York	356,664,000	15.00	25.00
F10-50A	C-Philadelphia	71,920,000	15.00	25.00
F10-50A	D-Cleveland	75,088,000	15.00	25.00
F10-50A	E-Richmond	82,144,000	15.00	25.00
F10-50A	F-Atlanta	73,288,000	15.00	25.00
F10-50A	G-Chicago	235,064,000	15.00	25.00
F10-50A	H-St. Louis	46,512,000	15.00	25.00
F10-50A	I-Minneapolis	8,136,000	15.00	25.00
F10-50A	J-Kansas City	25,488,000	15.00	25.00
F10-50A	K-Dallas	21,816,000	15.00	25.00
F10-50A	L-San Francisco	101,584,000	15.00	25.00

$10 FEDERAL RESERVE NOTES—SERIES 1950A (18 Subject)
Secretary-Treasurer: Humphrey-Priest

Federal Reserve District	First Serial Number Printed	Last Serial Number Printed	First Note Delivered	Last Note Delivered
Boston	A70 992 001A	A75 240 000B	5-27-53	8-15-57
New York	B18 576 001C	B75 240 000F	4- 3-53	8-23-57
Philadelphia	C76 240 001A	C48 240 000B	6-18-53	4-30-57
Cleveland	D76 032 001A	D51 120 000B	5-22-53	9- 9-57
Richmond	E61 776 001A	E43 920 000B	5-22-53	8-21-57
Atlanta	F63 792 001A	F37 080 000B	6-29-53	6-18-57
Chicago	G61 056 001B	G96 120 000D	5- 5-53	9-12-57
St. Louis	H47 808 001A	H94 320 000A	6-29-53	3-18-57
Minneapolis	I 18 864 001A	I 27 720 000A	10- 1-53	6-30-55
Kansas City	J36 432 001A	J61 920 000A	10-28-53	8- 7-56
Dallas	K33 264 001A	K55 080 000A	10- 5-53	9- 3-57
San Francisco	L76 896 001A	L78 480 000B	5-15-53	5-15-57

TEN DOLLARS FEDERAL RESERVE NOTES
Series 1950B, Priest-Anderson

No.	District	Printed	Unc.
F10-50B	A-Boston	49,240,000	20.00
F10-50B	B-New York	170,840,000	20.00
F10-50B	C-Philadelphia	66,880,000	20.00
F10-50B	D-Cleveland	55,360,000	20.00
F10-50B	E-Richmond	51,120,000	20.00
F10-50B	F-Atlanta	66,520,000	20.00
F10-50B	G-Chicago	165,080,000	20.00
F10-50B	H-St. Louis	33,040,000	20.00
F10-50B	I-Minneapolis	13,320,000	22.50
F10-50B	J-Kansas City	33,480,000	20.00
F10-50B	K-Dallas	26,280,000	20.00
F10-50B	L-San Francisco	55,000,000	20.00

$10 FEDERAL RESERVE NOTES—SERIES 1950B (18 Subject)
Secretary-Treasurer: Anderson-Priest

Federal Reserve District	First Serial Number Printed	Last Serial Number Printed	First Note Delivered	Last Note Delivered
Boston	A75 240 001B	A24 480 000C	1-14-58	5-15-61
New York	B75 240 001F	B46 080 000H	9-25-57	2-10-61
Philadelphia	C48 240 001B	C15 120 000C	12-12-58	4-17-61
Cleveland	D51 120 001B	D06 480 000C	9-25-57	2-28-61
Richmond	E43 920 001B	E95 040 000B	12-18-57	5- 4-61
Atlanta	F37 080 001B	F03 600 000C	9- 3-58	4- 5-61
Chicago	G96 120 001D	G61 200 000F	9-25-57	4- 4-61
St. Louis	H94 320 001A	H27 360 000B	10- 1-58	4-19-61
Minneapolis	I 27 000 001A	I 40 320 000A	7-23-58	3- 4-60
Kansas City	J61 920 001A	J95 400 000A	9-26-61	3- 8-63
Dallas	K55 080 001A	K81 360 000A	9-25-57	1-11-61
San Francisco	L78 480 001B	L33 480 000C	7-11-58	1-10-61

Series 1950C, Smith-Dillon

No.	District	Printed	Unc.
F10-50C	A-Boston	51,120,000	18.00
F10-50C	B-New York	126,520,000	18.00
F10-50C	C-Philadelphia	25,200,000	18.00
F10-50C	D-Cleveland	33,120,000	18.00
F10-50C	E-Richmond	45,640,000	18.00
F10-50C	F-Atlanta	38,880,000	18.00
F10-50C	G-Chicago	69,400,000	18.00
F10-50C	H-St. Louis	23,040,000	18.00
F10-50C	I-Minneapolis	9,000,000	18.00
F10-50C	J-Kansas City	23,320,000	18.00
F10-50C	K-Dallas	17,640,000	18.00
F10-50C	L-San Francisco	35,640,000	18.00

$10 FEDERAL RESERVE NOTES—SERIES 1950C (18 Subject)
Secretary-Treasurer: Dillon-Smith

Federal Reserve District	First Serial Number Printed	Last Serial Number Printed	First Note Delivered	Last Note Delivered
Boston	A24 480 001C	A75 600 000C	9- 1-61	3-14-63
New York	B46 080 001H	B66 600 000 I	3- 2-61	2-25-63
Philadelphia	C15 120 001C	C40 320 000C	6- 2-61	11-20-62
Cleveland	D06 480 001C	D39 600 000C	7-27-61	2- 4-63
Richmond	E95 040 001B	E40 680 000C	6-19-61	3-14-63
Atlanta	F03 600 001C	F42 480 000C	5-26-61	3- 1-63
Chicago	G61 200 001F	G30 600 000G	4- 5-61	2-18-63
St. Louis	H27 360 001B	H50 400 000B	7-15-59	3-11-63
Minneapolis	I 40 320 001A	I 49 320 000A	11- 4-60	10- 3-62
Kansas City	J95 400 001A	J18 720 000A	9-26-61	3- 8-63
Dallas	K81 360 001A	K99 000 000A	10-23-59	1- 2-63
San Francisco	L33 480 001C	L69 120 000C	9- 8-61	2-19-63

TEN DOLLAR FEDERAL RESERVE NOTES

Series 1950D, Granahan-Dillon

No.	District	Printed	Unc.
F10-50D	A-Boston	38,800,000	18.00
F10-50D	B-New York	150,320,000	18.00
F10-50D	C-Philadelphia	19,080,000	18.00
F10-50D	D-Cleveland	24,120,000	18.00
F10-50D	E-Richmond	33,840,000	18.00
F10-50D	F-Atlanta	36,000,000	18.00
F10-50D	G-Chicago	115,480,000	18.00
F10-50D	H-St. Louis	10,440,000	18.00
F10-50D	I-Minneapolis	None	—
F10-50D	J-Kansas City	15,480,000	18.00
F10-50D	K-Dallas	18,280,000	18.00
F10-50D	L-San Francisco	62,560,000	18.00

$10 FEDERAL RESERVE NOTES—SERIES 1950D (18 Subject)
Secretary-Treasurer: Dillon-Granahan

Federal Reserve District	First Serial Number Printed	Last Serial Number Printed	First Note Delivered	Last Note Delivered
Boston	A75 600 001C	A14 400 000D	7- 5-63	1-13-65
New York	B66 600 001I	B16 920 000K	2- 2-63	7- 2-65
Philadelphia	C40 320 001C	C59 400 000C	4-22-63	7- 2-65
Cleveland	D39 600 001C	D63 720 000C	2-20-63	4-27-65
Richmond	E40 680 001C	E74 520 000C	4-15-63	6-30-65
Atlanta	F42 480 001C	F78 480 000C	4- 8-63	4-25-65
Chicago	G30 600 001G	G46 000 000H	2-19-63	8-27-65
St. Louis	H50 400 001B	H60 840 000B	8-22-63	10-27-64
Minneapolis	None Printed			
Kansas City	J18 720 001B	J34 200 000B	10-25-63	8-30-65
Dallas	K99 000 001A	K17 280 000B	11- 1-63	7-29-65
San Francisco	L69 120 001C	L31 680 000D	3-20-63	6-30-65

See 1963 and 1963A in Catalog Section.

Face Design $10.00, Series 1963 and 1963A

TEN DOLLAR FEDERAL RESERVE NOTES

Series 1950E, Granahan-Fowler

Printed for three Districts only, and released after Series 1963.

No.	District	Printed	Unc.
F10-50E	B-New York	37,800,000	22.00
F10-50E	G-Chicago	65,080,000	22.00
F10-50E	L-San Francisco	17,280,000	25.00

$10 FEDERAL RESERVE NOTES—SERIES 1950E

Federal Reserve District	First Serial Number Printed	Last Serial Number Printed	First Note Delivered	Last Note Delivered
New York	B16 920 001K	B54 720 000K	10-29-65	9-16-68
Chicago	G46 080 001H	G11 160 000 I	9-13-65	10- 3-67
San Francisco	L13 680 001D	L48 960 000D	9-17-65	6- 6-66

$10.00 Motto added. Back Design first used on 1963 Series

Motto "In God We Trust" added to reverse design. Serial numbers for each District start with 00000001A with Bank letter as prefix. Numbering is consecutive through series 1963A.

Series 1963, Granahan-Dillon

No.	District	Printed	Unc.
F10-63	A-Boston	5,760,000	18.00
F10-63	B-New York	24,960,000	17.50
F10-63	C-Philadelphia	6,400,000	17.50
F10-63	D-Cleveland	7,040,000	17.50
F10-63	E-Richmond	4,480,000	18.00
F10-63	F-Atlanta	10,880,000	17.50
F10-63	G-Chicago	35,200,000	17.50
F10-63	H-St. Louis	13,440,000	18.00
F10-63	I -Minneapolis	None	—
F10-63	J-Kansas City	3,840,000	20.00
F10-63	K-Dallas	5,120,000	18.00
F10-63	L-San Francisco	14,080,000	17.50

TEN DOLLAR FEDERAL RESERVE NOTES

$10 FEDERAL RESERVE NOTES—SERIES 1963

Federal Reserve District	First Serial Number Printed	Last Serial Number Printed	First Note Delivered	Last Note Delivered
Boston	A00 000 001A	A05 760 000A	1-13-65	7- 2-65
New York	B00 000 001A	B24 960 000A	4-24-64	5- 6-65
Philadelphia	C00 000 001A	C06 400 000A	3-19-65	3-26-65
Cleveland	D00 000 001A	D07 040 000A	4-28-65	6- 4-65
Richmond	E00 000 001A	E04 480 000A	5- 4-65	5- 6-64
Atlanta	F00 000 001A	F10 880 000A	4-29-65	7- 2-65
Chicago	G00 000 001A	G35 200 000A	4-24-64	5-14-65
St. Louis	H00 000 001A	H13 440 000A	7-22-64	7- 8-65
Minneapolis	None Printed	No record	No record	No record
Kansas City	J00 000 001A	J03 840 000A	5-24-65	7- 2-65
Dallas	K00 000 001A	K05 120 000A	4-28-65	6-29-65
San Francisco	L00 000 001A	L14 080 000A	4-28-64	4-28-65

Series 1963A, Granahan-Fowler

No.	District	Printed	Unc.
F10-63A	A-Boston	131,360,000	18.00
F10-63A	B-New York	199,360,000	18.00
F10-63A	C-Philadelphia	100,000,000	18.00
F10-63A	D-Cleveland	72,960,000	18.00
F10-63A	E-Richmond	114,720,000	18.00
F10-63A	F-Atlanta	80,000,000	18.00
F10-63A	G-Chicago	195,520,000	18.00
F10-63A	H-St. Louis	43,520,000	18.00
F10-63A	I-Minneapolis	16,640,000	18.00
F10-63A	J-Kansas City	31,360,000	18.80
F10-63A	K-Dallas	48,640,000	18.00
F10-63A	L-San Francisco	87,200,000	18.00

$10 FEDERAL RESERVE NOTES—SERIES 1963A

Federal Reserve District	First Serial Number Printed	Last Serial Number Printed	First Note Delivered	Last Note Delivered
Boston	A05 760 001A	A37 120 000B	9- 1-65	6-23-69
New York	B24 960 001A	B24 230 000C	6-24-65	7-23-69
Philadelphia	C06 400 001A	C06 400 000A	8-24-65	6-11-69
Cleveland	D07 040 001A	D80 000 000A	9-30-65	7-28-69
Richmond	E04 480 001A	E19 200 000B	5-12-65	5-26-69
Atlanta	F10 880 001A	F90 880 000A	8-18-65	6-27-69
Chicago	G35 200 001A	G30 720 000B	6- 3-65	4-21-69
St. Louis	H13 440 001A	H56 960 000A	8-31-66	8- 8-69
Minneapolis	I 00 000 001A	I 16 640 000A	7-21-66	10-31-68
Kansas City	J03 840 001A	J35 200 000A	8-12-65	3-11-69
Dallas	K05 120 001A	K53 760 000A	8-18-65	8-22-69
San Francisco	L14 080 001A	L01 280 000B	6-25-65	9- 3-69

Series 1969, Elston-Kennedy

No.	District	Printed	Unc.
F10-69	A-Boston	74,880,000	16.50
F10-69	B-New York	247,360,000	16.50
F10-69	C-Philadephia	56,960,000	16.50
F10-69	D-Cleveland	57,600,000	16.50
F10-69	E-Richmond	56,960,000	16.50
F10-69	F-Atlanta	53,760,000	16.50
F10-69	G-Chicago	142,240,000	16.50
F10-69	H-St. Louis	22,400,000	16.50
F10-69	I-Minneapolis	12,800,000	16.50
F10-69	J-Kansas City	31,260,000	16.50
F10-69	K-Dallas	30,080,00	16.50
F10-69	L-San Francisco	56,320,000	16.50

TEN DOLLAR FEDERAL RESERVE NOTES

Face Design $10.00 with New Treasury Seal

$10 FEDERAL RESERVE NOTES—SERIES 1969

Federal Reserve District	First Serial Number Printed	Last Serial Number Printed	First Note Delivered	Last Note Delivered
Boston	A00 000 001A	A74 880 000A	9- 8-69	8-18-71
New York	B00 000 001A	B47 360 000C	8-20-69	9- 9-71
Philadelphia	C00 000 001A	C56 960 000A	9- 2-69	8-25-71
Cleveland	D00 000 001A	D57 600 000A	9- 2-69	10- 4-71
Richmond	E00 000 001A	E56 960 000A	10-16-69	9-21-71
Atlanta	F00 000 001A	F53 760 000A	8-21-69	9-27-71
Chicago	G00 000 001A	G42 240 000B	8- 4-69	7-19-71
St. Louis	H00 000 001A	H22 400 000A	2-12-70	7- 1-71
Minneapolis	I 00 000 001A	I 12 800 000A	10- 8-69	4- 7-71
Kansas City	J00 000 001A	J31 360 000A	8-27-69	9-16-71
Dallas	K00 000 001A	K30 080 000A	11-18-69	8- 3-71
San Francisco	L00 000 001A	L56 320 000A	11- 6-69	9-22-71

Series 1969A, Kabis-Connally

No.	District	Printed	Unc.
F10-69A	A-Boston	41,120,000	16.50
F10-69A	B-New York	111,840,000	16.50
F10-69A	C-Philadelphia	24,320,000	16.50
F10-69A	D-Cleveland	23,680,000	16.50
F10-69A	E-Richmond	25,600,000	16.50
F10-69A	F-Atlanta	20,480,000	16.50
F10-69A	G-Chicago	80,160,000	16.50
F10-69A	H-St. Louis	15,360,000	16.50
F10-69A	I -Minneapolis	8,320,000	18.00
F10-69A	J-Kansas City	10,880,000	16.50
F10-69A	K-Dallas	20,480,000	16.50
F10-69A	L-San Francisco	27,520,000	16.50

TEN DOLLAR FEDERAL RESERVE NOTES

$10 FEDERAL RESERVE NOTES—SERIES 1969A

Federal Reserve District	First Serial Number Printed	Last Serial Number Printed	First Note Delivered	Last Note Delivered
Boston	A74 880 001A	A16 000 000B	10- 5-71	7-31-72
New York	B47 360 001C	B59 520 000D	9- 9-71	7-12-72
Philadelphia	C56 960 001A	C81 280 000A	10-16-71	7- 3-72
Cleveland	D57 600 001A	D81 280 000A	10- 4-71	6- 5-72
Richmond	E56 960 001A	E82 560 000A	9-21-71	7- 3-72
Atlanta	F53 760 001A	F74 240 000A	9-27-71	6- 6-72
Chicago	G42 240 001B	G22 400 000C	7-19-71	7-12-72
St. Louis	H22 400 001A	H37 760 000A	7-19-71	7-27-72
Minneapolis	I 12 800 001A	I 21 120 000A	11-17-71	4-25-73
Kansas City	J31 360 001A	J42 240 000A	9-16-71	7-20-72
Dallas	K30 080 001A	K50 560 000A	8- 3-71	9-12-72
San Francisco	L56 320 001A	L83 840 000A	9-22-71	7- 5-72

Series 1969B, Banuelos-Connally

No.	District	No. Printed	Unc.	No.	District	No. Printed	Unc.
F10-69B	A-Boston	16,640,00	16.00	F10-69B	G-Chgo	32,640,000	16.00
F10-69B	B-N.Y.	60,320,000	16.00	F10-69B	H-St. L.	8,960,000	16.00
F10-69B	C-Phila.	16,000,000	16.00	F10-69B	I-Minn.	3,200,000	16.00
F10-69B	D-Clevel'd	12,800,000	16.00	F10-69B	J-K. C.	5,120,000	16.00
F10-69B	E-Rich.	12,160,000	16.00	F10-69B	K-Dallas	5,760,000	16.00
F10-69B	F-Atl'ta	13,440,000	16.00	F10-69B	L-San F.	23,840,000	16.00

$10 FEDERAL RESERVE NOTES—SERIES 1969B

Federal Reserve District	First Serial Number Printed	Last Serial Number Printed	First Note Delivered	Last Note Delivered
Boston	A16 000 001B	A32 640 000B	7-31-72	1- 3-73
New York	B59 520 001D	B19 840 000E	7-12-72	11- 6-72
Philadelphia	C81 280 001A	C97 280 000A	7- 3-72	11-13-72
Cleveland	D81 280 001A	D94 080 000A	6- 5-72	12-12-72
Richmond	E82 560 001A	E94 720 000A	7- 3-72	11-17-72
Atlanta	F74 240 001A	F87 680 000A	6- 6-72	2-22-73
Chicago	G22 400 001C	G55 040 000C	7-26-72	11-15-72
St. Louis	H37 760 001A	H46 720 000A	7-27-72	2-27-73
Minneapolis	I 21 120 001A	I 24 320 000A	4-25-73	9- 5-73
Kansas City	J42 240 001A	J47 360 000A	7-20-72	1-18-73
Dallas	K50 560 001A	K56 320 000A	9-12-72	2- 6-73
San Francisco	L83 840 001A	L07 680 000B	7- 5-72	11-22-72

Series 1969C, Banuelos-Shultz

No.	District	Unc.	No.	District	Unc.
F10-69C	A-Boston	15.00	F10-69C	G-Chgo	15.00
F10-69C	B-New York	15.00	F10-69C	H-St. Louis	15.00
F10-69C	C-Philadelphia	15.00	F10-69C	I-Minneapolis	15.00
F10-69C	D-Cleveland	15.00	F10-69C	J-Kansas City	15.00
F10-69C	E-Richmond	15.00	F10-69C	K-Dallas	15.00
F10-69C	F-Atlanta	15.00	F10-69C	L-San Francisco	15.00

$10 FEDERAL RESERVE NOTES—SERIES 1969C (32 Subject)

Federal Reserve District	First Serial Number Printed	Last Serial Number Printed	First Note Delivered	Last Note Delivered
Boston	A32 640 001B	A77 440 000B	2- 3-73	9- 9-74
New York	B19 840 001E	B23 040 000G	11- 6-72	9- 3-74
Philadelphia	C97 280 001A	C67 200 000B	11-13-72	9-19-74
Cleveland	D94 080 001A	D40 960 000B	12-12-72	9-26-74
Richmond	E94 720 001A	E40 320 000B	11- 2-72	9-21-74
Atlanta	F87 680 001A	F33 920 000B	3- 1-73	9- 9-74
Chicago	G55 040 001C	G10 240 000D	1- 3-73	
St. Louis	H46 720 001A	H76 520 000A	2-27-73	
Minneapolis	I 24 320 001A	I 35 840 000A	9- 5-73	7-10-74
Kansas City	J47 360 001A	J70 400 000A	1-18-73	
Dallas	K56 320 001A	K81 280 000A	2- 6-73	12-10-74
San Francisco	L07 680 001B	L64 640 000B	11-22-72	

TEN DOLLAR FEDERAL RESERVE NOTES

Series 1974, Neff-Simon

No.	District	Unc.	No.	District	Unc.
F10-74	A-Boston	13.50	F10-74	G-Chicago	13.50
F10-74	B-New York	13.50	F10-74	H-St. Louis	13.50
F10-74	C-Philadelphia	13.50	F10-74	I-Minneapolis	13.50
F10-74	D-Cleveland	13.50	F10-74	J-Kansas City	13.50
F10-74	E-Richmond	13.50	F10-74	K-Dallas	13.50
F10-74	F-Atlanta	13.50	F10-74	L-San Francisco	13.50

$10 FEDERAL RESERVE NOTES—SERIES 1974 (32 Subject)

Federal Reserve District	First Serial Number Printed	Last Serial Number Printed	First Note Delivered
Boston	A77 440 001B	A81 920 000C	9-25-74
New York	B23 040 001G	B62 080 000I	9- 3-74
Philadelphia	C67 200 001B	C36 480 000C	10- 8-74
Cleveland	D40 960 001B	D98 560 000C	10-15-74
Richmond	E40 320 001B	E46 080 000C	9-21-74
Atlanta	F33 920 001B	F09 600 000C	9-11-74
Chicago	G10 240 001D	G14 720 000F	
St. Louis	H76 520 001A	H21 760 000B	
Minneapolis	I 35 840 001A	I 63 360 000A	12-11-74
Kansas City	J70 400 001A	J94 720 000A	
Dallas	K81 280 001A	K21 120 000B	
San Francisco	L64 640 001B	L35 200 000C	

Series 1977 currently being printed all started with 00 000 001.

TWENTY DOLLAR FEDERAL RESERVE NOTES

Face Design. Head of Jackson. $20.00, Series 1928 and 1928A

Series 1928, Tate-Mellon
Large numeral in seal indicating Federal Reserve District.

No.	District	Ex.Fine	Unc.	No.	District	Ex.Fine	Unc.
F20-28	A-Boston	32.50	65.00	F20-28	G-Chicago	30.00	55.00
F20-28	B-New York	30.00	60.00	F20-28	H-St. Louis	32.50	75.00
F20-28	C-Phila.	32.50	65.00	F20-28	I-Minneapolis	32.50	75.00
F20-28	D-Cleveland	30.00	65.00	F20-28	J-Kansas City	32.50	75.00
F20-28	E-Richmond	35.00	75.00	F20-28	K-Dallas	35.00	75.00
F20-28	F-Atlanta	32.50	65.00	F20-28	L-San Fran.	32.50	70.00

Series 1928A, Woods-Mellon.
Large number in seal as in 1928 series.

No.	District	Ex.Fine	Unc.	No.	District	Ex.Fine	Unc.
F20-28A	A-Boston	35.00	65.00	F20-28A	G-Chicago	32.50	75.00
F20-28A	B-New York	32.50	75.00	F20-28A	H-St. Louis	35.00	70.00
F20-28A	C-Phila.	32.50	65.00	F20-28A	I-Minn.	None Issued	
F20-28A	D-Cleveland	35.00	70.00	F20-28A	J-Kansas City	40.00	95.00
F20-28A	E-Richmond	32.50	75.00	F20-28A	K-Dallas	32.50	70.00
F20-28A	F-Atlanta	32.50	70.00	F20-28A	L-San Fran.	None Issued	

The Bureau of Engraving and Printing records do not separate the total number of notes in each series: 1928, 1928A, 1928B and 1928C. The combined totals as given by the Bureau are as follows:

District	Quantity	District	Quanity
Boston	12,168,000	Chicago	31,020,000
New York	31,500,000	St. Louis	6,852,000
Philadelphia	13,440,000	Minneapolis	5,844,000
Cleveland	22,416,000	Kansas City	7,440,000
Richmond	9,660,000	Dallas	4,380,000
Atlanta	7,416,000	San Francisco	17,183,000

The starting number for each of the Districts, in the 1928 series, was 00000001A, with prefix letter indicating issuing Bank. Numbering was consecutive through series 1928C.

TWENTY DOLLAR FEDERAL RESERVE NOTES

Face Design $20.00, Series 1928B and C

Series 1928B, Woods-Mellon. Large letter replaces number in seal.

No.	District	Ex.Fine	Unc.
F20-28B	A-Boston	35.00	55.00
F20-28B	B-New York	30.00	55.00
F20-28B	C-Phila.	35.00	55.00
F20-28B	D-Cleveland	35.00	55.00
F20-28B	E-Richmond	27.50	55.00
F20-28B	F-Atlanta	30.00	60.00
F20-28B	G-Chicago	30.00	55.00
F20-28B	H-St. Louis	40.00	65.00
F20-28B	I-Minn.	32.50	60.00
F20-28B	J-Kansas City	27.50	60.00
F20-28B	K-Dallas	35.00	70.00
F20-28B	L-San Fran.	30.00	55.00

Series 1928C, Woods-Mills. Issued only by Chicago and San Francisco.

No.	District	Ex.Fine	Unc.
F20-28C	G-Chicago	75.00	125.00
F20-28C	F-San Fran.	80.00	140.00

$20 FEDERAL RESERVE NOTES—SERIES 1928, 1928A, 1928B, 1928C (12 Subject)
Secretary-Treasurer—1928—Mellon-Tate—1928A&B—Mellon-Woods—1928C—Mills-Woods

Federal Reserve District	First Serial Number Printed	Last Serial Number Printed	First Note Delivered	Last Note Delivered
Boston	A00 000 001A	A12 168 000A	4- 5-29	10- 7-35
New York	B00 000 001A	B31 500 000A	4- 9-29	2- 1-35
Philadelphia	C00 000 001A	C13 440 000A	4-16-28	3-20-35
Cleveland	D00 000 001A	D22 416 000A	4-20-29	9-18-35
Richmond	E00 000 001A	E09 660 000A	4-26-29	10-27-34
Atlanta	F00 000 001A	F07 416 000A	4-27-29	10- 9-35
Chicago	G00 000 001A	G31 020 000A	5- 2-29	3-23-35
St. Louis	H00 000 001A	H06 852 000A	5- 3-29	10-31-34
Minneapolis	I 00 000 001A	I 05 844 000A	5- 6-29	5- 1-35
Kansas City	J00 000 001A	J07 440 000A	5- 8-29	8-15-35
Dallas	K00 000 001A	K04 380 000A	5-13-29	10-20-33
San Francisco	L00 000 001A	L17 184 000A	5- 9-29	2-10-34

Remarks: No records were found indicating serial numbers of the first note of Series 1928A, 1928B and 1928C or serial numbers of last note of Series 1928, 1928A and 1928B for any of the Federal Reserve Banks. No dates or serial numbers were found other than those listed on this record.

The table below of office terms will indicate approximately the time of the various changes for the series covered by this record.

Secretary	Treasurer	Series	Combination Began	Ended
Mellon	Tate	1928	April 30, 1928	January 17, 1929
Mellon	Woods	1928A&B	January 18, 1929	February 12, 1932
Mills	Woods	1928C	February 13, 1932	March 3, 1933

The starting number for each of the Districts in the 1934 series was 00000001A with prefix letter indicating Bank. Numbering was consecutive through series 1934D.

TWENTY DOLLAR FEDERAL RESERVE NOTES

Face Design $20, Series 1934 and 1934A

The Bureau of Engraving and Printing records do not separate the total number of notes in each series, 1934 and 1934A. The combined totals for the two series as given by the Bureau are as follows:

District	Quantity	District	Quantity
Boston	38,376,000	Chicago	105,316,000
New York	113,080,000	St. Louis	29,364,000
Philadelphia	45,168,000	Minneapolis	16,296,000
Cleveland	67,164,000	Kansas City	28,812,000
Richmond	72,036,000	Dallas	22,164,000
Atlanta	44,652,000	*San Francisco	111,952,000

*Including "Hawaii" Overprint Series 1934 and 1934A.

Series 1934, Julian-Morgenthau.

Darker Green Seal

No.	District	Ex.Fine	Unc.
F20-34	A-Boston	35.00	55.00
F20-34	B-New York	30.00	50.00
F20-34	C-Phila.	35.00	50.00
F20-34	D-Cleveland	35.00	50.00
F20-34	E-Richmond	35.00	50.00
F20-34	F-Atlanta	35.00	50.00
F20-34	G-Chicago	35.00	50.00
F20-34	H-St. Louis	30.00	50.00
F20-34	I-Minn.	30.00	50.00
F20-34	J-Kansas City	35.00	50.00
F20-34	K-Dallas	35.00	55.00
F20-34	L-San Fran.	35.00	50.00

Lighter Green Seal

No.	District	Ex.Fine	Unc.
F20-34l	A-Boston	35.00	55.00
F20-34l	B-New York	30.00	50.00
F20-34l	C-Phila.	35.00	50.00
F20-34l	D-Cleveland	35.00	50.00
F20-34l	E-Richmond	35.00	50.00
F20-34l	F-Atlanta	35.00	50.00
F20-34l	G-Chicago	30.00	50.00
F20-34l	H-St. Louis	35.00	55.00
F20-34l	I-Minn.	35.00	55.00
F20-34l	J-Kansas City	35.00	55.00
F20-34l	K-Dallas	35.00	55.00
F20-34l	L-San Fran.	30.00	50.00

Suffix letter "l" is used to catalog numbering to indicate lighter Green Seal.

TWENTY DOLLAR FEDERAL RESERVE NOTES

Series 1934A, Julian-Morgenthau

No.	District	Ex.Fine	Unc.	No.	District	Ex.Fine	Unc.
F20-34A	A-Boston	35.00	50.00	F20-34A	G-Chicago	35.00	55.00
F20-34A	B-New York	35.00	50.00	F20-34A	H-St. Louis	35.00	55.00
F20-34A	C-Phila.	35.00	50.00	F20-34A	I-Minn.	35.00	60.00
F20-34A	D-Cleveland	35.00	50.00	F20-34A	J-Kansas City	35.00	50.00
F20-34A	E-Richmond	35.00	50.00	F20-34A	K-Dallas	35.00	50.00
F20-34A	F-Atlanta	35.00	50.00	F20-34A	L-San Fran.	35.00	50.00

$20 FEDERAL RESERVE NOTES—SERIES 1934 & 1934A (12 Subject)
Secretary-Treasurer: Morgenthau-Julian

Federal Reserve District	First Serial Number Printed	Last Serial Number Printed	First Note Delivered	Last Note Delivered
Boston	A00 000 001A	A38 376 000A	10- 7-35	9-27-45
New York	B00 000 001A	B13 080 000B	2- 2-35	11-29-45
Philadelphia	C00 000 001A	C45 168 000A	3-20-35	12-26-45
Cleveland	D00 000 001A	D67 164 000A	9-19-35	8-30-44
Richmond	E00 000 001A	E72 036 000A	2- 2-35	12-29-45
Atlanta	F00 000 001A	F44 652 000A	11-27-35	11-28-45
Chicago	G00 000 001A	G05 316 000B	12- 5-35	2- 4-46
St. Louis	H00 000 001A	H29 364 000A	2- 7-35	1-15-46
Minneapolis	I 00 000 001A	I 16 296 000A	5- 2-35	9-29-44
Kansas City	J00 000 001A	J28 812 000A	8-16-35	12-19-45
Dallas	K00 000 001A	K22 164 000A	12-27-35	11-26-45
San Francisco	L00 000 001A	L11 952 000B	12-20-35	12-11-45

Series 1934B, Julian-Vinson

No.	District	Printed	Ex.Fine	Unc.
F20-34B	A-Boston	3,456,000	35.00	55.00
F20-34B	B-New York	24,900,000	35.00	50.00
F20-34B	C-Philadelphia	5,400,000	35.00	50.00
F20-34B	D-Cleveland	3,960,000	35.00	50.00
F20-34B	E-Richmond	8,994,000	30.00	50.00
F20-34B	F-Atlanta	8,976,000	35.00	45.00
F20-34B	G-Chicago	9,720,000	30.00	45.00
F20-34B	H-St. Louis	5,820,000	35.00	50.00
F20-34B	I-Minneapolis	3,036,000	35.00	55.00
F20-34B	J-Kansas City	4,188,000	35.00	50.00
F20-34B	K-Dallas	2,880,000	35.00	55.00
F20-34B	L-San Francisco	9,720,000	35.00	50.00

$20 FEDERAL RESERVE NOTES—SERIES 1934B (12 Subject)
Secretary-Treasurer: Vinson-Julian

Federal Reserve District	First Serial Number Printed	Last Serial Number Printed	First Note Delivered	Last Note Delivered
Boston	A38 376 001A	A41 832 000A	4-15-46	3- 1-47
New York	B13 080 001B	B37 980 000B	11-29-45	2- 4-47
Philadelphia	C45 168 001A	C50 568 000A	2-18-46	9-20-46
Cleveland	D67 164 001A	D71 124 000A	2- 1-46	3- 5-47
Richmond	E72 036 001A	E81 030 000A	2- 8-46	1-23-47
Atlanta	F44 652 001A	F53 628 000A	11-29-45	11-29-46
Chicago	G05 316 001B	G15 036 000B	2- 4-46	1-10-47
St. Louis	H29 364 001A	H35 184 000A	4- 8-45	2- 3-47
Minneapolis	I 16 296 001A	I 19 332 000A	12-14-45	10-22-47
Kansas City	J28 812 001A	J33 000 000A	2-14-46	4- 9-47
Dallas	K22 164 001A	K25 044 000A	2-27-46	3-10-47
San Francisco	L11 952 001B	L21 672 000B	12-11-45	1-16-47

TWENTY DOLLAR FEDERAL RESERVE NOTES
Type One Back Design

Back Design $20.00 with Small Shrubbery

Type Two Back Design

Back Design $20.00 with Large Shrubbery and Balcony

The above illustrations show the changes in back design which occurred during the printing of the 1934C series. The new design has been used on all subsequent series of the $20.00 denomination.

There are two back designs in series 1934C as shown above. Type Two is believed to be scarcer than Type One.

Series 1934C, Julian-Snyder

No.	District	Printed	Ex.Fine	Uno.
F20-34C	A-Boston	8,202,000	35.00	55.00
F20-34C	B-New York	17,880,000	30.00	50.00
F20-34C	C-Philadelphia	11,988,000	30.00	50.00
F20-34C	D-Cleveland	17,256,000	30.00	50.00
F20-34C	E-Richmond	23,638,000	30.00	50.00
F20-34C	F-Atlanta	18,456,000	30.00	50.00
F20-34C	G-Chicago	25,716,000	30.00	50.00
F20-34C	H-St. Louis	13,680,000	30.00	50.00
F20-34C	I-Minneapolis	3,282,000	35.00	60.00
F20-34C	J-Kansas City	8,880,000	30.00	55.00
F20-34C	K-Dallas	9,948,000	30.00	50.00
F20-34C	L-San Francisco	20,088,000	30.00	50.00

TWENTY DOLLAR FEDERAL RESERVE NOTES

$20 FEDERAL RESERVE NOTES—SERIES 1934C (12 Subject)
Secretary-Treasurer: Snyder-Julian

Federal Reserve District	First Serial Number Printed	Last Serial Number Printed	First Note Delivered	Last Note Delivered
Boston	A41 382 001A	A49 584 000A	3-12-47	3- 6-50
New York	B37 980 001B	B55 860 000B	2- 4-47	1-13-50
Philadelphia	C50 568 001A	C62 556 000A	1- 7-47	1-31-50
Cleveland	D71 124 001A	D88 380 000A	3-19-47	4- 3-50
Richmond	E81 030 001A	E04 668 000B	1-23-47	1-13-50
Atlanta	F53 628 001A	F72 084 000A	4-14-47	1-27-50
Chicago	G15 036 001B	G40 752 000B	1-10-47	2- 3-50
St. Louis	H35 184 001A	H48 864 000A	1-18-47	1-17-50
Minneapolis	I 19 332 001A	I 22 614 000A	11- 3-47	3- 8-50
Kansas City	J33 000 001A	J41 880 000A	9-26-47	3- 6-50
Dallas	K25 044 001A	K34 992 000A	3-20-47	7- 3-50
San Francisco	L21 672 001B	L41 760 000B	3-13-47	2-16-50

Series 1934D, Clark-Snyder

No.	District	Printed	Ex.Fine	Unc.
F20-34D	A-Boston	4,352,000	30.00	50.00
F20-34D	B-New York	15,460,000	30.00	50.00
F20-34D	C-Philadelphia	3,888,000	30.00	50.00
F20-34D	D-Cleveland	8,704,000	30.00	50.00
F20-34D	E-Richmond	13,812,000	30.00	50.00
F20-34D	F-Atlanta	7,492,000	30.00	50.00
F20-34D	G-Chicago	12,500,000	30.00	50.00
F20-34D	H-St. Louis	6,200,000	30.00	50.00
F20-34D	I-Minneapolis	2,358,000	32.00	55.00
F20-34D	J-Kansas City	4,108,000	30.00	50.00
F20-34D	K-Dallas	3,612,000	30.00	50.00
F20-34D	L-San Francisco	13,416,000	30.00	50.00

$20 FEDERAL RESERVE NOTES—SERIES 1934D (12 Subject)
Secretary-Treasurer: Snyder-Clark

Federal Reserve District	First Serial Number Printed	Last Serial Number Printed	First Note Delivered	Last Note Delivered
Boston	A49 584 001A	A53 936 000A	3-10-50	1-26-51
New York	B55 860 001B	B71 320 000B	1-13-50	1-31-51
Philadelphia	C62 556 001A	C66 444 000A	5- 2-50	1- 2-51
Cleveland	D88 380 001A	D97 084 000A	5- 1-50	1-25-51
Richmond	E04 668 001B	E18 480 000B	1-13-50	1-26-51
Atlanta	F72 084 001A	F79 576 000A	1-31-50	1-29-51
Chicago	G40 752 001B	G53 252 000B	2- 3-50	1-29-51
St. Louis	H48 864 001A	H55 064 000A	1-27-50	1-26-51
Minneapolis	I 22 614 001A	I 24 972 000A	3- 8-50	1-15-51
Kansas City	J41 880 001A	J45 988 000A	4- 4-50	1-25-51
Dallas	K34 992 001A	K38 604 000A	7-11-50	1-18-51
San Francisco	L41 760 001B	L55 176 000B	2-17-50	1-19-51

TWENTY DOLLAR FEDERAL RESERVE NOTES

Face Design $20.00 with Smaller Seal introduced on 1950 Series

Series 1950, Clark-Snyder. Smaller seal and letter indicating Bank of issue. Serial numbers for each District start with 00000001A with Bank letter as prefix and were consecutive through series 1950E.

No.	District	Printed	Ex.Fine	Unc.
F20-50	A-Boston	23,184,000	30.00	40.00
F20-50	B-New York	80,064,000	30.00	40.00
F20-50	C-Philadelphia	29,520,000	30.00	40.00
F20-50	D-Cleveland	51,120,000	30.00	40.00
F20-50	E-Richmond	67,536,000	30.00	40.00
F20-50	F-Atlanta	39,312,000	30.00	40.00
F20-50	G-Chicago	70,464,000	30.00	40.00
F20-50	H-St. Louis	27,352,000	30.00	40.00
F20-50	I-Minneapolis	9,216,000	32.00	45.00
F20-50	J-Kansas City	22,752,000	30.00	40.00
F20-50	K-Dallas	22,656,000	30.00	40.00
F20-50	L-San Francisco	70,272,000	30.00	40.00

$20 FEDERAL RESERVE NOTES—SERIES 1950 (12 Subject)
Secretary-Treasurer: Snyder-Clark

Federal Reserve District	First Serial Number Printed	Last Serial Number Printed	First Note Delivered	Last Note Delivered
Boston	A00 000 001A	A23 184 000A	2-16-51	8- 3-53
New York	D00 000 001A	B80 064 000A	2- 7-51	8- 7-53
Philadelphia	C00 000 001A	C29 520 000A	3- 5-51	7-23-53
Cleveland	D00 000 001A	D51 120 000A	2- 5-51	8- 3-53
Richmond	E00 000 001A	E67 536 000A	11- 7-50	8- 3-53
Atlanta	F00 000 001A	F39 312 000A	3-25-51	8-14-53
Chicago	G00 000 001A	G70 560 000A*	2- 1-51	8-31-53
St. Louis	H00 000 001A	H27 360 000A*	3-22-51	7- 7-53
Minneapolis	I 00 000 001A	I 09 216 000A	4-11-51	9- 1-53
Kansas City	J00 000 001A	J22 752 000A	3- 6-51	8- 7-53
Dallas	K00 000 001A	K22 752 000A*	4-24-51	7- 8-53
San Francisco	L00 000 001A	L70 272 000A	2- 6-51	8- 5-53

Remarks: *Serial Numbers G70 464 001A through G70 560 001A, H27 352 001A through H 27 360 000A and K 22 656 001A through K 22 752 000A were assigned for Chicago, St. Louis and Dallas notes, respectively, but were never used.

TWENTY DOLLAR FEDERAL RESERVE NOTES

Series 1950A, Priest-Humphrey

No.	District	Printed	Ex.Fine	Unc.
F20-50A	A-Boston	19,656,000	27.50	35.00
F20-50A	B-New York	*82,568,000	27.50	55.00
F20-50A	C-Philadelphia	16,560,000	27.50	35.00
F20-50A	D-Cleveland	50,320,000	27.50	35.00
F20-50A	E-Richmond	69,544,000	27.50	35.00
F20-50A	F-Atlanta	27,648,000	27.50	35.00
F20-50A	G-Chicago	73,720,000	27.50	35.00
F20-50A	H-St. Louis	22,680,000	27.50	35.00
F20-50A	I-Minneapolis	5,544,000	30.00	35.00
F20-50A	J-Kansas City	22,968,000	27.50	55.00
F20-50A	K-Dallas	10,728,000	27.50	35.00
F20-50A	L-San Francisco	85,528,000	27.50	35.00

*8000 additional notes were printed for New York and destroyed.

$20 FEDERAL RESERVE NOTES—SERIES 1950A (18 Subject)
Secretary-Treasurer: Humphrey-Priest

Federal Reserve District	First Serial Number Printed	Last Serial Number Printed	First Note Delivered	Last Note Delivered
Boston	A23 184 001A	A42 840 000A	8-26-53	8-27-57
New York	B80 064 001A*	B62 640 000A	8-25-53	8-30-57
Philadelphia	C29 520 001A	C46 080 000A	8-26-53	6- 6-55
Cleveland	D51 120 001A	D51 440 000B	8-13-53	5-31-57
Richmond	E67 536 001A	E37 080 000B	8-19-53	8-30-57
Atlanta	F39 312 001A	F66 960 000A	8-24-53	9-11-57
Chicago	G70 560 001A	G44 280 000B	8-31-53	9-18-57
St. Louis	H27 360 001A	H50 040 000A	8-28-53	9-17-57
Minneapolis	I 09 216 001A	I 14 760 000A	9-29-53	6-27-55
Kansas City	J22 752 001A	J45 720 000A	8-27-53	8- 6-56
Dallas	K22 752 001A	K33 480 000A	8-28-53	8- 1-57
San Francisco	L70 272 001A	L55 800 000B	8-24-53	6-21-57

Remarks: *New York—B90 236 001A to B90 240 000A and B90 252 001A to B90 256 000A were not delivered. They were reported missing because of theft. When recovered they were destroyed.
  $160,000.00—Total worth
  127,000.00—Recovered intact
   32,160.00—Still outstanding—was settled by check from Bureau to Treasurer
   17,000.00—Since recovered through banks as of 12-31-54

Series 1950B, Priest-Anderson

No.	District	Printed	Ex.Fine	Unc.
F20-50B	A-Boston	5,040,000	27.50	40.00
F20-50B	B-New York	49,960,000	27.50	35.00
F20-50B	C-Philadelphia	7,920,000	27.50	40.00
F20-50B	D-Cleveland	38,160,000	27.50	35.00
F20-50B	E-Richmond	42,120,000	27.50	35.00
F20-50B	F-Atlanta	40,240,000	27.50	35.00
F20-50B	G-Chicago	80,560,000	27.50	35.00
F20-50B	H-St. Louis	19,440,000	27.50	35.00
F20-50B	I-Minneapolis	12,240,000	27.50	40.00
F20-50B	J-Kansas City	28,440,000	27.50	35.00
F20-50B	K-Dallas	11,880,000	27.50	40.00
F20-50B	L-San Francisco	51,040,000	27.50	35.00

TWENTY DOLLARS FEDERAL RESERVE NOTES

$20 FEDERAL RESERVE NOTES—SERIES 1950B (18 Subject)
Secretary-Treasurer: Anderson-Priest

Federal Reserve District	First Serial Number Printed	Last Serial Number Printed	First Note Delivered	Last Note Delivered
Boston	A42 840 001A	A47 880 000A	7-10-58	10-24-60
New York	B62 640 001B	B12 600 000C	10-11-57	2-10-61
Philadelphia	C46 080 001A	C54 000 000A	11-24-58	3-31-61
Cleveland	D01 440 001B	D39 600 000B	9-25-57	2-17-61
Richmond	E37 080 001B	E79 200 000B	1-20-58	6-16-61
Atlanta	F66 960 001A	F07 200 000B	9- 2-58	4-28-61
Chicago	G44 280 001B	G24 840 000C	9-25-57	3- 7-61
St. Louis	H50 040 001A	H69 480 000A	9-25-57	4-21-61
Minneapolis	I 14 760 001A	I 27 000 000A	7-24-58	3-14-60
Kansas City	J45 720 001A	J74 160 000A	10-16-57	9-13-60
Dallas	K33 480 001A	K45 360 000A	8-18-58	1-24-61
San Francisco	L55 800 001B	L06 840 000C	7- 1-58	3-17-61

Series 1950C, Smith-Dillon

No.	District	Printed	Unc.
F20-50C	A-Boston	7,200,000	35.00
F20-50C	B-New York	43,200,000	32.50
F20-50C	C-Philadelphia	7,560,000	35.00
F20-50C	D-Cleveland	28,440,000	32.50
F20-50C	E-Richmond	37,000,000	32.50
F20-50C	F-Atlanta	19,080,000	32.50
F20-50C	G-Chicago	29,160,000	32.50
F20-50C	H-St. Louis	12,960,000	32.50
F20-50C	I-Minneapolis	6,480,000	40.00
F20-50C	J-Kansas City	18,360,000	35.00
F20-50C	K-Dallas	9,000,000	40.00
F20-50C	L-San Francisco	45,360,000	32.50

$20 FEDERAL RESERVE NOTES—SERIES 1950C (18 Subject)
Secretary-Treasurer: Dillon-Smith

Federal Reserve District	First Serial Number Printed	Last Serial Number Printed	First Note Delivered	Last Note Delivered
Boston	A47 880 001A	A55 080 000A	9-20-61	1-14-63
New York	B12 600 001C	B55 800 000C	2-28-61	1-11-63
Philadelphia	C54 000 001A	C61 560 000A	6-23-61	9-13-62
Cleveland	D39 600 001B	D68 040 000B	5-25-61	1- 2-63
Richmond	E79 200 001B	E16 200 000C	6-19-61	3-21-63
Atlanta	F07 200 001B	F26 280 000B	5- 1-61	3- 4-63
Chicago	G24 840 001C	G54 000 000C	4- 3-61	12- 5-62
St. Louis	H69 480 001A	H82 440 000A	7-17-61	3-19-63
Minneapolis	I 27 000 001A	I 33 480 000A	10-10-61	9- 7-62
Kansas City	J74 160 001A	J92 520 000A	9-22-61	3-19-63
Dallas	K45 360 001A	K54 360 000A	7-10-61	1- 2-63
San Francisco	L06 840 001C	L52 200 000C	9- 6-61	3-12-63

TWENTY DOLLAR FEDERAL RESERVE NOTES

Series 1950D, Granahan-Dillon

No.	District	Printed	Unc.
F20-50D	A-Boston	9,320,000	35.00
F20-50D	B-New York	64,280,000	35.00
F20-50D	C-Philadelphia	5,400,000	35.00
F20-50D	D-Cleveland	23,760,000	35.00
F20-50D	E-Richmond	30,240,000	35.00
F20-50D	F-Atlanta	22,680,000	35.00
F20-50D	G-Chicago	67,960,000	35.00
F20-50D	H-St. Louis	6,120,000	35.00
F20-50D	I-Minneapolis	3,240,000	45.00
F20-50D	J-Kansas City	8,200,000	35.00
F20-50D	K-Dallas	6,480,000	35.00
F20-50D	L-San Francisco	69,400,000	35.00

$20 FEDERAL RESERVE NOTES—SERIES 1950D (18 Subject)
Secretary-Treasurer: Dillon-Granahan

Federal Reserve District	First Serial Number Printed	Last Serial Number Printed	First Note Delivered	Last Note Delivered
Boston	A55 080 001A	A64 440 000A	5-28-63	1-25-65
New York	B55 800 001C	B10 080 000D	2-25-63	6-24-65
Philadelphia	C61 560 001A	C66 960 000A	4-26-63	7-21-65
Cleveland	D68 040 001B	D91 800 000B	2-12-63	4- 7-65
Richmond	E16 200 001B	E46 440 000C	3-21-63	6-29-65
Atlanta	F26 280 001B	F48 960 000B	4-19-63	4-30-65
Chicago	G54 000 001C	G21 960 000D	2-18-63	7- 2-65
St. Louis	H82 440 001A	H86 560 000A	8-30-63	11-30-65
Minneapolis	I 33 480 001A	I 36 720 000A	8- 9-63	8-25-65
Kansas City	J92 520 001A	J00 720 000B	10-21-63	7-26-65
Dallas	K54 360 001A	K60 840 000A	11-29-63	2-23-65
San Francisco	L52 200 001C	L21 680 000D	4-16-63	6-30-65

Series 1950E, Granahan-Fowler

This series printed for three Districts only; was released after 1963.

No.	District	Printed	Unc.
F20-50E	B-New York	8,640,000	35.00
F20-50E	G-Chicago	9,360,000	35.00
F20-50E	L-San Francisco	8,640,000	35.00

$20 FEDERAL RESERVE NOTES—SERIES 1950E (18 Subject)

Federal Reserve District	First Serial Number Printed	Last Serial Number Printed	First Note Delivered	Last Note Delivered
New York	B10 080 001D	B18 720 000D	11-22-65	7-15-66
Chicago	G21 960 001D	G31 320 000D	9- 1-65	4-20-66
San Francisco	L21 600 001D	L30 240 000D	9-23-65	6-22-66

TWENTY DOLLAR FEDERAL RESERVE NOTES

Face Design $20.00, Series 1950E and 1963

$20.00 Motto added. Back Design introduced on 1963 Series

Series 1963, Granahan-Dillon

Motto "In God We Trust" added to back design. Serial numbers for each District start with 00000001A with Bank letter as prefix. Numbering is consecutive through series 1963A.

No.	District	Printed	Unc.
F20-63	A-Boston	2,560,000	35.00
F20-63	B-New York	16,640,000	32.50
F20-63	C-Philadelphia	None	—
F20-63	D-Cleveland	7,680,000	32.50
F20-63	E-Richmond	4,480,000	35.00
F20-63	F-Atlanta	10,240,000	32.50
F20-63	G-Chicago	2,560,000	40.00
F20-63	H-St. Louis	3,200,000	35.00
F20-63	I-Minneapolis	None	—
F20-63	J-Kansas City	3,840,000	35.00
F20-63	K-Dallas	2,560,000	35.00
F20-63	L-San Francisco	7,040,000	32.50

TWENTY DOLLAR FEDERAL RESERVE NOTES

$20 FEDERAL RESERVE NOTES—SERIES 1963

Federal Reserve District	First Serial Number Printed	Last Serial Number Printed	First Note Delivered	Last Note Delivered
Boston	A00 000 001A	A02 560 000A	1-25-65	7- 2-65
New York	B00 000 001A	B16 640 000A	1-28-65	5-26-65
Philadelphia	None Printed			
Cleveland	D00 000 001A	D07 680 000A	10- 7-64	10-15-64
Richmond	E00 000 001A	E04 480 000A	1-18-65	1-25-65
Atlanta	F00 000 001A	F10 240 000A	4-19-65	7- 2-65
Chicago	G00 000 001A	G02 560 000A	4-30-65	5- 3-65
St. Louis	H00 000 001A	H03 200 000A	2-11-65	2-16-65
Minneapolis	None Printed			
Kansas City	J00 000 001A	J03 840 000A	5-26-65	5-28-65
Dallas	K00 000 001A	K02 560 000A	4-29-65	4-30-65
San Francisco	L00 000 001A	L07 040 000A	1-26-65	4-12-65

Series 1963A, Granahan-Fowler

No.	District	Printed	Unc.
F20-63A	A-Boston	23,680,000	32.50
F20-63A	B-New York	93,600,000	32.50
F20-63A	C-Philadelphia	17,920,000	32.50
F20-63A	D-Cleveland	68,480,000	32.50
F20-63A	E-Richmond	128,800,000	32.50
F20-63A	F-Atlanta	42,880,000	32.50
F20-63A	G-Chicago	156,320,000	32.50
F20-63A	H-St. Louis	34,560,000	32.50
F20-63A	I-Minneapolis	10,240,000	35.00
F20-63A	J-Kansas City	37,120,000	32.50
F20-63A	K-Dallas	38,400,000	32.50
F20-63A	L-San Francisco	169,120,000	32.50

$20 FEDERAL RESERVE NOTES—SERIES 1963A

Federal Reserve District	First Serial Number Printed	Last Serial Number Printed	First Note Delivered	Last Note Delivered
Boston	A02 560 001A	A26 240 000A	7-27-65	4-24-69
New York	B16 640 001A	B10 240 000B	6-25-65	7-30-69
Philadelphia	C00 000 001A	C17 920 000A	10-11-66	5-28-69
Cleveland	D07 680 001A	D76 160 000A	9-30-65	7-31-69
Richmond	E04 480 001A	E33 280 000B	6- 8-65	5-15-69
Atlanta	F10 240 001A	F53 120 000A	9-23-65	4-29-68
Chicago	G02 560 001A	G58 880 000B	6-30-65	5-26-69
St. Louis	H03 200 001A	H37 760 000A	8-31-65	8-21-69
Minneapolis	I 00 000 001A	I 10 240 000A	7-22-66	10-31-68
Kansas City	J03 840 001A	J40 960 000A	7-29-65	9-17-68
Dallas	K02 560 001A	K40 960 000A	8-17-65	8-29-69
San Francisco	L07 040 001A	L76 160 000B	5-20-65	7-24-69

TWENTY DOLLAR FEDERAL RESERVE NOTES

$20.00 Face Design, Series 1969 showing New Treasury Seal

Series 1969, Elston-Kennedy

No.	District	Printed	Unc.
F20-69	A-Boston	19,200,000	28.50
F20-69	B-New York	106,400,000	28.50
F20-69	C-Philadelphia	10,880,000	28.50
F20-69	D-Cleveland	60,160,000	28.50
F20-69	E-Richmond	66,560,000	28.50
F20-69	F-Atlanta	36,840,000	28.50
F20-69	G-Chicago	107,680,000	28.50
F20-69	H-St. Louis	19,200,000	28.50
F20-69	I-Minneapolis	12,160,000	28.50
F20-69	J-Kansas City	39,040,000	28.50
F20-69	K-Dallas	25,600,00	28.50
F20-69	L-San Francisco	103,840,000	28.50

$20 FEDERAL RESERVE NOTES—SERIES 1969

Federal Reserve District	First Serial Number Printed	Last Serial Number Printed	First Note Delivered	Last Note Delivered
Boston	A00 000 001A	A19 200 000A	8-27-69	7-19-71
New York	B00 000 001A	B06 400 000B	8- 6-69	6-16-71
Philadelphia	C00 000 001A	C10 880 000A	9-16-69	5-19-71
Cleveland	D00 000 001A	D60 160 000A	9- 2-69	8- 2-71
Richmond	E00 000 001A	E66 560 000A	10- 3-69	8- 6-71
Atlanta	F00 000 001A	F36 480 000A	8-19-69	9- 9-71
Chicago	G00 000 001A	G07 680 000B	7-30-69	5-27-71
St. Louis	H00 000 001A	H19 200 000A	9- 4-69	6-15-71
Minneapolis	I00 000 001A	I 12 160 000A	8-27-69	6- 7-71
Kansas City	J00 000 001A	J39 040 000A	8-19-69	7- 7-71
Dallas	K00 000 001A	K25 600 000A	9-30-69	6-29-71
San Francisco	L00 000 001A	L03 840 000B	9-22-69	9-15-71

TWENTY DOLLAR FEDERAL RESERVE NOTES

Series 1969A, Kabis-Connally

No.	District	No. Printed	Unc.	No.	District	No. Printed	Unc.
F20-69A	A-Boston	13,440,00	28.50	F20-69A	G-Chgo	81,640,000	28.50
F20-69A	B-N.Y.	69,760,000	28.50	F20-69A	H-St. L.	14,080,000	28.50
F20-69A	C-Phila.	13,440,000	28.50	F20-69A	I-Minn.	7,040,000	28.50
F20-69A	D-Clevel'd	29,440,000	28.50	F20-69A	J-K. C.	16,040,000	28.50
F20-69A	E-Rich.	42,400,000	28.50	F20-69A	K-Dallas	14,720,000	28.50
F20-69A	F-Atl'ta	13,440,000	28.50	F20-69A	L-San F.	50,560,000	28.50

$20 FEDERAL RESERVE NOTES—SERIES 1969A

Federal Reserve District	First Serial Number Printed	Last Serial Number Printed	First Note Delivered	Last Note Delivered
Boston	A19 200 001A	A32 640 000A	7-19-71	7-19-72
New York	B06 400 001B	B76 160 000B	6-16-71	8-14-72
Philadelphia	C10 880 001A	C24 320 000A	6-15-71	7-11-72
Cleveland	D60 160 001A	D89 600 000A	8- 2-71	10- 3-72
Richmond	E66 560 001A	E08 960 000A	8- 6-71	7-24-72
Atlanta	F36 480 001A	F49 920 000A	9- 9-71	7-18-72
Chicago	G07 680 001B	G88 320 000B	6-16-71	7-26-72
St. Louis	H19 200 001A	H33 280 000A	9-13-71	6-13-72
Minneapolis	I 12 160 001A	I 19 200 000A	6-27-71	3-21-73
Kansas City	J39 040 001A	J55 680 000A	7-28-71	10- 3-72
Dallas	K25 600 001A	K40 320 000A	7-13-71	4-27-72
San Francisco	L03 840 001B	L54 400 000B	9-15-71	5-31-72

Series 1969B, Banuelos-Connally

No.	District	No. Printed	Unc.	No.	District	No. Printed	Unc.
F20-69B	A-Boston	None	—	F20-69B	G-Chgo	14,240,000	28.50
F20-69B	B-N.Y.	39,200,000	28.50	F20-69B	H-St. L.	5,120,000	28.50
F20-69B	C-Phila.	None	—	F20-69B	I-Minn.	2,560,000	28.50
F20-69B	D-Clevel'd	6,400,000	28.50	F20-69B	J-K. C.	3,840,000	28.50
F20-69B	E-Rich.	27,520,000	28.50	F20-69B	K-Dallas	12,160,000	28.50
F20-69B	F-Atl'ta	14,080,000	28.50	F20-69B	L-San F.	26,000,000	28.50

$20 FEDERAL RESERVE NOTES—SERIES 1969B

Federal Reserve District	First Serial Number Printed	Last Serial Number Printed	First Note Delivered	Last Note Delivered
Boston	None Printed			
New York	B76 160 001B	B15 360 000C	8-14-72	1- 3-73
Philadelphia	None Printed			
Cleveland	D89 600 001A	D96 000 000A	10- 3-72	12-11-72
Richmond	E08 960 001B	E36 480 000B	7-24-72	1- 6-73
Atlanta	F49 920 001A	F64 000 000A	7-18-72	3-22-73
Chicago	G88 320 001B	G02 560 000C	7-26-72	10- 2-72
St. Louis	H33 280 001A	H38 400 000A	6-20-72	12- 7-72
Minneapolis	I 19 200 001A	I 21 760 000A	3-21-73	4-25-73
Kansas City	J55 680 001A	J59 520 000A	10- 3-72	11-15-72
Dallas	K40 320 001A	K52 480 000A	6- 6-72	2-20-73
San Francisco	L54 400 001B	L80 640 000B	5-31-72	11- 6-72

TWENTY DOLLAR FEDERAL RESERVE NOTES

Series 1969C, Banuelos-Shultz

No.	District	Unc.	No.	District	Unc.
F20-69C	A-Boston	27.50	F20-69C	G-Chgo	27.50
F20-69C	B-N.Y.	27.50	F20-69C	H-St. L.	27.50
F20-69C	C-Phila.	27.50	F20-69C	I-Minn.	27.50
F20-69C	D-Clevel'd	27.50	F20-69C	J-K. C.	27.50
F20-69C	E-Rich.	27.50	F20-69C	K-Dallas	27.50
F20-69C	F-Atl'ta	27.50	F20-69C	L-San F.	27.50

$20 FEDERAL RESERVE NOTES—SERIES 1969C (32 Subject)

Federal Reserve District	First Serial Number Printed	Last Serial Number Printed	First Note Delivered	Last Note Delivered
Boston	A32 640 001A	A49 920 000A	11- 7-72	8-21-74
New York	B15 360 001C	B50 560 000D	1- 3-72	9-11-74
Philadelphia	C24 320 001A	C65 280 000A	9-27-72	10-22-74
Cleveland	D96 000 001A	D53 760 000B	12-20-72	10- 1-74
Richmond	E36 480 001B	E16 640 000A	11- 2-72	11-26-74
Atlanta	F64 000 001A	F99 840 000C	3-22-73	11-14-74
Chicago	G02 560 001C	G81 280 000A	10- 2-72	12-13-74
St. Louis	H38 400 001A	H72 320 000A	12- 7-72	10- 1-74
Minneapolis	I 21 760 001A	I 35 840 000A	4-25-73	5- 2-74
Kansas City	J59 520 001A	J91 520 000A	11-15-72	
Dallas	K52 480 001A	K83 840 000A	2-20-73	
San Francisco	L80 640 001B	L62 720 000C	11- 6-72	

Series 1974, Neff-Simon

No.	District	Unc.	No.	District	Unc.
F20-74	A-Boston	25.00	F20-74	G-Chgo	25.00
F20-74	B-N.Y.	25.00	F20-74	H-St. L.	25.00
F20-74	C-Phila.	25.00	F20-74	I-Minn.	25.00
F20-74	D-Clevel'd	25.00	F20-74	J-K. C.	25.00
F20-74	E-Rich.	25.00	F20-74	K-Dallas	25.00
F20-74	F-Atl'ta	25.00	F20-74	L-San F.	25.00

$20 FEDERAL RESERVE NOTES—SERIES 1974 (32 Subject)

Federal Reserve District	First Serial Number Printed	Last Serial Number Printed	First Note Delivered
Boston	A49 920 001A	A07 040 000B	
New York	B50 560 001D	B47 360 000G	9-11-74
Philadelphia	C65 280 001A	C24 960 000B	10-22-74
Cleveland	D53 760 001B	D01 920 000D	10- 1-74
Richmond	E16 640 001C	E40 320 000D	9-11-74
Atlanta	F99 840 001A	F53 120 000B	12-12-74
Chicago	G81 280 001C	G31 360 000F	12-13-74
St. Louis	H72 320 001A	H45 440 000B	11-14-74
Minneapolis	I 35 840 001A	I 74 880 000A	12-16-74
Kansas City	J91 520 001A	J65 920 000A	10-24-74
Dallas	K83 840 001A	K52 480 000B	
San Francisco	L62 720 001A	L90 880 000D	

Series 1977 currently being printed all start with 00 000 001.

FIFTY DOLLAR FEDERAL RESERVE NOTES

Face Design $50.00, Series 1928

Series 1928, Woods-Mellon Large numeral in seal indicating issuing Bank.

No.	District	Ex.Fine	Unc.	No.	District	Ex.Fine	Unc.
F50-28	A-Boston	80.00	135.00	F50-28	G-Chicago	70.00	120.00
F50-28	B-New York	70.00	120.00	F50-28	H-St. Louis	80.00	140.00
F50-28	C-Phila.	70.00	120.00	F50-28	I-Minneapolis	95.00	175.00
F50-28	D-Cleveland	80.00	125.00	F50-28	J-Kansas City	80.00	130.00
F50-28	E-Richmond	80.00	125.00	F50-28	K-Dallas	95.00	175.00
F50-28	F-Atlanta	80.00	125.00	F50-28	L-San Fran.	70.00	125.00

Series 1928A, Woods-Mellon Large letter in seal replaces numeral.

No.	District	Ex.Fine	Unc.	No.	District	Ex.Fine	Unc.
F50-28A	A-Boston	75.00	100.00	F50-28A	G-Chicago	75.00	90.00
F50-28A	B-New York	75.00	100.00	F50-28A	H-St. Louis	85.00	120.00
F50-28A	C-Phila.	75.00	100.00	F50-28A	I-Minn.	100.00	135.00
F50-28A	D-Cleveland	75.00	100.00	F50-28A	J-K. C.	85.00	120.00
F50-28A	E-Richmond	75.00	100.00	F50-28A	K-Dallas	90.00	120.00
F50-28A	F-Atlanta	85.00	120.00	F50-28A	L-San Fran.	80.00	120.00

The Bureau of Engraving and Printing records do not separate the total number of notes in the series 1928 and 1928A. Experience has shown the 1928 to be the scarcer. The combined totals for the two series as given by the Bureau are as follows:

District	Quantity	District	Quantity
Boston	2,160,000	Chicago	6,360,000
New York	4,548,000	St. Louis	1,092,000
Philadelphia	3,372,000	Minneapolis	636,000
Cleveland	3,192,000	Kansas City	996,000
Richmond	1,800,000	Dallas	756,000
Atlanta	1,008,000	San Francisco	1,512,000

The starting number for each District in the 1928 series was 00000001A with prefix letter indicating Bank, and was consecutive through series 1928A.

FIFTY DOLLAR FEDERAL RESERVE NOTES

$50 FEDERAL RESERVE NOTES—SERIES 1928 and 1928A (12 Subject)
Secretary-Treasurer: Mellon-Woods

Federal Reserve District	First Serial Number Printed	Last Serial Number Printed	First Note Delivered	Last Note Delivered
Boston	A00 000 001A	A02 160 000A	6-13-29	3-28-33
New York	B00 000 001A	B04 548 000A	6-15-29	12-10-34
Philadelphia	C00 000 001A	C03 372 000A	6-14-29	3-13-33
Cleveland	D00 000 001A	D03 192 000A	6-14-29	7-21-33
Richmond	E00 000 001A	E01 800 000A	6-19-29	3-16-33
Atlanta	F00 000 001A	F01 008 000A	6-18-29	3-28-33
Chicago	G00 000 001A	G06 360 000A	6-13-29	3-11-33
St. Louis	H00 000 001A	H01 092 000A	6-19-29	3-18-33
Minneapolis	I 00 000 001A	I 00 636 000A	6-19-29	3-28-33
Kansas City	J00 000 001A	J00 996 000A	6-19-29	3-16-33
Dallas	K00 000 001A	K00 756 000A	6-20-29	3-28-33
San Francisco	L00 000 001A	L01 512 000A	6-14-29	3-12-33

Face Design $50.00, Series 1934 to 1934D

Series 1934, Julian-Morgenthau Light and dark green seals.

Research to date has not indicated the relative scarcity of LIGHT and DARK green seals in the 1934 series. Both are scarce and the light green seal is the scarcer of the two. Collectors are usually content to acquire either one.

No.	District	Ex.Fine	Unc.
F50-34	A-Boston	65.00	100.00
F50-34	B-New York	65.00	85.00
F50-34	C-Phila.	65.00	90.00
F50-34	D-Cleveland	65.00	90.00
F50-34	E-Richmond	65.00	90.00
F50-34	F-Atlanta	70.00	100.00
F50-34	G-Chicago	65.00	80.00
F50-34	H-St. Louis	70.00	100.00
F50-34	I-Minn.	75.00	100.00
F50-34	J-Kansas City	70.00	90.00
F50-34	K-Dallas	70.00	90.00
F50-34	L-San Fran.	65.00	85.00

Series 1934A, Julian-Morgenthau

No.	District	Ex.Fine	Unc.
F50-34A	A-Boston	67.50	90.00
F50-34A	B-New York	57.50	90.00
F50-34A	C-Phila.		None
F50-34A	D-Cleveland	60.00	90.00
F50-34A	E-Richmond	60.00	90.00
F50-34A	F-Atlanta	67.50	110.00
F50-34A	G-Chicago	60.00	95.00
F50-34A	H-St. Louis	70.00	115.00
F50-34A	I-Minn.	100.00	140.00
F50-34A	J-Kansas City	70.00	110.00
F50-34A	K-Dallas	70.00	100.00
F50-34A	L-San Fran.	70.00	110.00

FIFTY DOLLAR FEDERAL RESERVE NOTES

The Bureau of Engraving and Printing records do not separate the total number of notes in the 1934 and 1934A series. The combined totals for the two series as given by the Bureau are as follows:

District	Quantity	District	Quantity
Boston	2,940,000	Chicago	9,132,000
New York	16,404,000	St. Louis	1,740,000
Philadelphia	5,604,000	Minneapolis	576,000
Cleveland	9,420,000	Kansas City	1,224,000
Richmond	6,648,000	Dallas	1,392,000
Atlanta	3,276,000	San Francisco	7,824,000

$50 FEDERAL RESERVE NOTES—SERIES 1934 & 1934A (12 Subject)
Secretary-Treasurer: Morgenthau-Julian

Federal Reserve District	First Serial Number Printed	Last Serial Number Printed	First Note Delivered	Last Note Delivered
Boston	A00 000 001A	A02 940 000A	12-18-35	7-19-44
New York	B00 000 001A	B16 404 000A	3- 9-35	1- 2-49
Philadelphia	C00 000 001A	C05 604 000A	12-19-35	7-31-44
Cleveland	D00 000 001A	D09 420 000A	12-20-35	7-27-45
Richmond	E00 000 001A	E06 648 000A	12-19-35	7-31-45
Atlanta	E00 000 001A	F03 276 000A	12-18-35	7-13-46
Chicago	G00 000 001A	G09 132 000A	12-23-35	7-31-44
St. Louis	H00 000 001A	H01 740 000A	12-23-35	11-16-45
Minneapolis	I 00 000 001A	I 00 576 000A	12-24-35	7-11-44
Kansas City	J00 000 001A	J01 224 000A	12-27-35	7-13-45
Dallas	K00 000 001A	K01 392 000A	12-26-35	7-17-45
San Francisco	L00 000 001A	L07 824 000A	12-26-35	1-21-46

Series 1934B, Julian-Vinson

No.	District	Printed	Ex.Fine	Unc.
F50-34B	A-Boston	None	—	—
F50-34B	B-New York	None	—	—
F50-34B	C-Philadelphia	276,000	70.00	125.00
F50-34B	D-Cleveland	24,000	80.00	125.00
F50-34B	E-Richmond	120,000	70.00	120.00
F50-34B	F-Atlanta	96,000	70.00	120.00
F50-34B	G-Chicago	12,000	75.00	140.00
F50-34B	H-St. Louis	300,000	65.00	130.00
F50-34B	I-Minneapolis	120,000	70.00	140.00
F50-34B	J-Kansas City	180,000	70.00	130.00
F50-34B	K-Dallas	120,000	70.00	130.00
F50-34B	L-San Francisco	372,000	65.00	125.00

$50 FEDERAL RESERVE NOTES—SERIES 1934B (12 Subject)
Secretary-Treasurer: Vinson-Julian

Federal Reserve District	First Serial Number Printed	Last Serial Number Printed	First Note Delivered	Last Note Delivered
Boston	None Printed	None Printed	No Deliveries	
New York	None Printed	None Printed	No Deliveries	
Philadelphia	C05 604 001A	C05 880 000A	7-11-46	7- 3-47
Cleveland	D09 420 001A	D09 444 000A	8-19-47	8-19-47
Richmond	E06 648 001A	E06 768 000A	7-12-46	7-12-46
Atlanta	F03 276 001A	F03 372 000A	7-23-46	7-23-46
Chicago	G09 132 001A	G09 144 000A	7-11-49	7-11-49
St. Louis	H01 740 001A	H02 040 000A	1-17-47	1-20-47
Minneapolis	I 00 576 001A	I 00 696 000A	7-25-47	7-28-47
Kansas City	J01 224 001A	J01 404 000A	7-24-46	7-24-46
Dallas	K01 392 001A	K01 512 000A	7-29-47	7-29-47
San Francisco	L07 824 001A	L08 196 000A	7-25-46	1- 8-51

FIFTY DOLLAR FEDERAL RESERVE NOTES
Series 1934C, Julian-Snyder

No.	District	Printed	Ex.Fine	Unc.
F50-34C	A-Boston	180,000	75.00	115.00
F50-34C	B-New York	1,668,000	65.00	87.50
F50-34C	C-Philadelphia	1,380,000	65.00	115.00
F50-34C	D-Cleveland	2,740,000	65.00	90.00
F50-34C	E-Richmond	2,280,000	65.00	87.50
F50-34C	F-Atlanta	420,000	72.50	115.00
F50-34C	G-Chicago	408,000	72.50	100.00
F50-34C	H-St. Louis	548,000	67.50	90.00
F50-34C	I-Minneapolis	140,000	75.00	115.00
F50-34C	J-Kansas City	408,000	72.50	100.00
F50-34C	K-Dallas	324,000	72.50	100.00
F50-34C	L-San Francisco	None	—	—

$50 FEDERAL RESERVE NOTES—SERIES 1934C (12 Subject)
Secretary-Treasurer: Snyder-Julian

Federal Reserve District	First Serial Number Printed	Last Serial Number Printed	First Note Delivered	Last Note Delivered
Boston	A02 940 001A	A03 120 000A	8-11-48	7-19-49
New York	B16 404 001A	B18 072 000A	1- 2-49	7-20-50
Philadelphia	C05 880 001A	C07 260 000A	8-12-47	7-19-50
Cleveland	D09 444 001A	D12 184 000A	8-19-47	1-11-51
Richmond	E06 768 001A	E09 048 000A	8-19-47	7-19-50
Atlanta	F03 372 001A	F03 792 000A	10-27-47	10-28-47
Chicago	G09 144 001A	G09 552 000A	7-11-49	7-20-50
St. Louis	H02 040 001A	H02 588 000A	3-18-48	1- 9-51
Minneapolis	I00 696 001A	I00 836 000A	8-12-48	1- 8-51
Kansas City	J01 404 001A	J01 812 000A	8-22-47	7-21-50
Dallas	K01 512 001A	K01 836 000A	10-24-47	2- 1-50
San Francisco	None Printed	None Printed	No Deliveries	

Series 1934D, Clark-Snyder

No.	District	Printed	Ex.Fine	Unc.
F50-34D	A-Boston	348,000	75.00	115.00
F50-34D	B-New York	1,176,000	70.00	90.00
F50-34D	C-Philadelphia	744,000	70.00	90.00
F50-34D	D-Cleveland	None	—	—
F50-34D	E-Richmond	168,000	75.00	125.00
F50-34D	F-Atlanta	228,000	67.50	120.00
F50-34D	G-Chicago	636,000	65.00	110.00
F50-34D	H-St. Louis	None	—	—
F50-34D	I-Minneapolis	None	—	—
F50-34D	J-Kansas City	None	—	—
F50-34D	K-Dallas	148,000	75.00	130.00
F50-34D	L-San Francisco	None	—	—

$50 FEDERAL RESERVE NOTES—SERIES 1934D (12 Subject)
Secretary-Treasurer: Snyder-Clark

Federal Reserve District	First Serial Number Printed	Last Serial Number Printed	First Note Delivered	Last Note Delivered
Boston	A03 120 001A	A03 468 000A	8-18-50	1- 8-51
New York	B18 072 001A	B19 248 000A	9-28-50	1- 9-51
Philadelphia	C07 260 001A	C08 004 000A	12- 4-50	1-12-51
Cleveland	None Printed	None Printed	No Deliveries	
Richmond	E09 048 001A	E09 216 000A	1- 9-51	1-11-51
Atlanta	F03 792 001A	F04 020 000A	7-21-50	1-11-51
Chicago	G09 552 001A	G10 188 000A	12- 4-50	1-11-51
St. Louis	None Printed	None Printed	No Deliveries	
Minneapolis	None Printed	None Printed	No Deliveries	
Kansas City	None Printed	None Printed	No Deliveries	
Dallas	K01 836 001A	K01 934 000A	7-12-50	1- 9-51
San Francisco	None Printed	None Printed	No Deliveries	

FIFTY DOLLAR FEDERAL RESERVE NOTES

Face Design $50.00, Series 1950 to 1950E

Series 1950, Clark-Snyder. Seals and serial numbers smaller.

Starting serial number for each District in the 1950 series was 00000001A with prefix letter indicating issuing bank. Numbering was consecutive through series 1950E.

No.	District	Printed	Ex.Fine	Unc.
F50-50	A-Boston	1,248,000	60.00	85.00
F50-50	B-New York	10,236,000	60.00	80.00
F50-50	C-Philadelphia	2,352,000	60.00	80.00
F50-50	D-Cleveland	6,180,000	60.00	80.00
F50-50	E-Richmond	5,064,000	60.00	80.00
F50-50	F-Atlanta	1,812,000	60.00	85.00
F50-50	G-Chicago	4,212,000	60.00	80.00
F50-50	H-St. Louis	892,000	62.50	85.00
F50-50	I-Minneapolis	384,000	65.00	95.00
F50-50	J-Kansas City	696,000	62.50	85.00
F50-50	K-Dallas	1,100,000	60.00	85.00
F50-50	L-San Francisco	3,996,000	60.00	80.00

$50 FEDERAL RESERVE NOTES—SERIES 1950 (12 Subject)
Secretary-Treasurer: Snyder-Clark

Federal Reserve District	First Serial Number Printed	Last Serial Number Printed	First Note Delivered	Last Note Delivered
Boston	A00 000 001A	A01 296 000A*	10-26-51	7-28-53
New York	B00 000 001A	B10 368 000A*	5-28-51	8-28-53
Philadelphia	C00 000 001A	C02 448 000A*	5- 9-51	7-28-53
Cleveland	D00 000 001A	D06 192 000A*	7-13-51	7-23-53
Richmond	E00 000 001A	E05 184 000A*	4-23-51	7-14-53
Atlanta	F00 000 001A	F01 812 000A*	5-23-51	2- 6-53
Chicago	G00 000 001A	G04 320 000A*	11-26-51	7-17-53
St. Louis	H00 000 001A	H00 892 000A*	2-21-51	7- 9-53
Minneapolis	I 00 000 001A	I 00 384 000A*	11- 5-51	7-23-53
Kansas City	J00 000 001A	J00 720 000A*	5-21-51	7-21-53
Dallas	K00 000 001A	K01 152 000A*	2-27-51	7-10-53
San Francisco	L00 000 001A	L04 032 000A*	4-23-51	7-31-53

Remarks: *Serial Numbers—
A01 248 001A through A01 296 000A, B10 236 001A through B10 368 000A, C02 352 001A through C02 448 000A, D06 180 001A through D06 192 000A, E05 064 001A through E05 184 000A, F01 812 001A through F01 872 000A, G04 212 001A through G04 320 000A and H00 892 001A through H01 008 000A were not printed due to change from 12-subject to 18-subject sheets.
K01 104 001A through K01 152 000A and L03 996 001A through L04 032 000A were not printed.
H00 892 000A through H01 008 000A, H00 892 001A through H00 900 000A, I 00 384 001A through I 00 432 000A, J00 696 001A through J00 720 000A and K01 100 001A through K01 104 000A were transferred to stock cage and delivered as mutilated 10-30-53.

FIFTY DOLLAR FEDERAL RESERVE NOTES

Series 1950A, Priest-Humphrey

No.	District	Printed	Ex.Fine	Unc.
F50-50A	A-Boston	720,000	60.00	80.00
F50-50A	B-New York	6,480,000	60.00	80.00
F50-50A	C-Philadelphia	1,728,000	60.00	80.00
F50-50A	D-Cleveland	1,872,000	60.00	80.00
F50-50A	E-Richmond	2,016,000	60.00	80.00
F50-50A	F-Atlanta	288,000	60.00	90.00
F50-50A	G-Chicago	2,016,000	60.00	80.00
F50-50A	H-St. Louis	576,000	62.50	80.00
F50-50A	I-Minneapolis	None	—	—
F50-50A	J-Kansas City	144,000	62.50	95.00
F50-50A	K-Dallas	864,000	60.00	80.00
F50-50A	L-San Francisco	576,000	60.00	80.00

$50 FEDERAL RESERVE NOTES—SERIES 1950A (18 Subject)
Secretary-Treasurer: Humphrey-Priest

Federal Reserve District	First Serial Number Printed	Last Serial Number Printed	First Note Delivered	Last Note Delivered
Boston	A01 296 001A	A02 016 000A	12-28-54	8-12-57
New York	B10 368 001A	B16 848 000A	12-7-54	1-23-57
Philadelphia	C02 448 001A	C04 176 000A	12-27-54	8-20-57
Cleveland	D06 192 001A	D08 064 000A	12-21-54	1-16-57
Richmond	E05 184 001A	E07 200 000A	12-23-54	8-15-57
Atlanta	F01 872 001A	F02 160 000A	12-10-54	12-10-54
Chicago	G04 320 001A	G06 336 000A	12-20-54	1-23-57
St. Louis	H01 008 001A	H01 584 000A	12-13-54	1-11-57
Minneapolis	None Printed	None Printed	No Deliveries	
Kansas City	J00 720 001A	J00 864 000A	12-28-54	12-28-54
Dallas	K01 152 001A	K02 016 000A	12-16-54	10-14-55
San Francisco	L04 032 001A	L04 608 000A	12-23-54	12-23-54

Back Design $50.00, Series 1950 to 1950E

FIFTY DOLLAR FEDERAL RESERVE NOTES

Series 1950B, Priest-Anderson

No.	District	Printed	Unc.
F50-50B	A-Boston	864,000	85.00
F50-50B	B-New York	8,352,000	80.00
F50-50B	C-Philadelphia	2,592,000	80.00
F50-50B	D-Cleveland	1,728,000	80.00
F50-50B	E-Richmond	1,584,000	80.00
F50-50B	F-Atlanta	None	—
F50-50B	G-Chicago	4,320,000	80.00
F50-50B	H-St. Louis	576,000	85.00
F50-50B	I-Minneapolis	None	—
F50-50B	J-Kansas City	1,008,000	85.00
F50-50B	K-Dallas	1,008,000	85.00
F50-50B	L-San Francisco	1,872,000	80.00

$50 FEDERAL RESERVE NOTES—SERIES 1950B (18 Subject)
Secretary-Treasurer: Anderson-Priest

Federal Reserve District	First Serial Number Printed	Last Serial Number Printed	First Note Delivered	Last Note Delivered
Boston	A02 016 001A	A02 880 000A	11-21-58	9- 1-60
New York	B16 848 001A	B25 200 000A	11- 5-57	10-31-60
Philadelphia	C04 176 001A	C06 768 000A	11-28-58	11-29-60
Cleveland	D08 064 001A	D09 792 000A	10-13-58	12- 8-60
Richmond	E07 200 001A	E08 784 000A	7-28-58	8- 1-60
Atlanta	None Printed	None Printed	No Deliveries	
Chicago	G06 336 001A	G10 656 000A	9-30-57	9- 7-60
St. Louis	H01 584 001A	H02 160 000A	9-25-57	9-25-59
Minneapolis	None Printed	None Printed	No Deliveries	
Kansas City	J00 864 001A	J01 872 000A	10-28-57	8- 9-60
Dallas	K02 016 001A	K03 024 000A	11-21-58	9- 4-59
San Francisco	L04 608 001A	L06 480 000A	10-14-57	8- 8-60

Series 1950C, Smith-Dillon

No.	District	Printed	Unc.
F50-50C	A-Boston	720,000	80.00
F50-50C	B-New York	5,328,000	80.00
F50-50C	C-Philadelphia	1,296,000	80.00
F50-50C	D-Cleveland	1,296,000	80.00
F50-50C	E-Richmond	1,296,000	80.00
F50-50C	F-Atlanta	None	—
F50-50C	G-Chicago	1,728,000	80.00
F50-50C	H-St. Louis	576,000	85.00
F50-50C	I-Minneapolis	144,000	90.00
F50-50C	J-Kansas City	432,000	80.00
F50-50C	K-Dallas	720,000	80.00
F50-50C	L-San Francisco	1,152,000	80.00

$50 FEDERAL RESERVE NOTES—SERIES 1950C (18 Subject)
Secretary-Treasurer: Dillon-Smith

Federal Reserve District	First Serial Number Printed	Last Serial Number Printed	First Note Delivered	Last Note Delivered
Boston	A02 880 001A	A03 600 000A	9-20-61	9-11-62
New York	B25 200 001A	B30 528 000A	8- 2-61	12- 4-62
Philadelphia	C06 768 001A	C08 064 000A	7-31-61	10-17-62
Cleveland	D09 792 001A	D11 088 000A	10-18-61	8- 1-62
Richmond	E08 784 001A	E10 080 000A	7-26-61	11-14-62
Atlanta	None Printed	None Printed	No Deliveries	
Chicago	G10 656 001A	G12 384 000A	9-21-61	11- 1-62
St. Louis	H02 160 001A	H02 736 000A	7-12-61	7- 6-62
Minneapolis	I 00 432 001A	I 00 576 000A	10-23-61	10-23-61
Kansas City	J01 872 001A	J02 304 000A	10-26-61	9-13-62
Dallas	K03 024 001A	K03 744 000A	7-14-61	12- 3-62
San Francisco	L06 480 001A	L07 632 000A	10-11-61	10-31-62

FIFTY DOLLAR FEDERAL RESERVE NOTES

Series 1950D, Granahan-Dillon

No.	District	Printed	Unc.
F50-50D	A-Boston	1,728,000	80.00
F50-50D	B-New York	7,200,000	80.00
F50-50D	C-Philadelphia	2,736,000	80.00
F50-50D	D-Cleveland	2,880,000	80.00
F50-50D	E-Richmond	2,016,000	80.00
F50-50D	F-Atlanta	576,000	80.00
F50-50D	G-Chicago	4,176,000	80.00
F50-50D	H-St. Louis	1,440,000	80.00
F50-50D	I-Minneapolis	288,000	85.00
F50-50D	J-Kansas City	720,000	80.00
F50-50D	K-Dallas	1,296,000	80.00
F50-50D	L-San Francisco	2,150,000	80.00

$50 FEDERAL RESERVE NOTES—SERIES 1950D (18 Subject)
Secretary-Treasurer: Dillon-Granahan

Federal Reserve District	First Serial Number Printed	Last Serial Number Printed	First Note Delivered	Last Note Delivered
Boston	A03 600 001A	A05 328 000A	8-30-63	8-13-65
New York	B30 528 001A	B37 728 000A	9-20-63	7- 2-65
Philadelphia	C08 064 001A	C10 800 000A	10-29-63	7-30-65
Cleveland	D11 088 001A	D13 968 000A	9-16-63	8-27-65
Richmond	E10 080 001A	E12 096 000A	8-30-63	7-26-65
Atlanta	F02 160 001A	F02 736 000A	12-16-63	4-24-64
Chicago	G12 384 001A	G16 560 000A	7-31-63	8-26-65
St. Louis	H02 736 001A	H04 176 000A	9-24-63	7-30-65
Minneapolis	I 00 576 001A	I 00 864 000A	7-26-63	9-24-65
Kansas City	J02 304 001A	J03 024 000A	10-31-63	8-31-65
Dallas	K03 744 001A	K05 040 000A	11- 7-63	7-30-65
San Francisco	L07 632 001A	L09 782 000A	7-19-63	7-29-65

Series 1950E, Granahan-Fowler

Printed for three Districts only.

No.	District	Printed	Unc.
F50-50E	B-New York	3,024,000	90.00
F50-50E	G-Chicago	1,008,000	90.00
F50-50E	L-San Francisco	1,306,000	90.00

$50 FEDERAL RESERVE NOTES—SERIES 1950E

Federal Reserve District	First Serial Number Printed	Last Serial Number Printed	First Note Delivered	Last Note Delivered
New York	B37 728 001A	B40 752 000A	9-16-65	10-27-65
Chicago	G16 500 001A	G17 568 000A	11-24-65	11-30-65
San Francisco	L09 792 001A	L11 088 000A	9-10-65	11-30-65

FIFTY DOLLAR FEDERAL RESERVE NOTES

Face Design $50.00, Series 1963A and 1969

Inscription changed and obligation "will pay to Bearer on Demand" removed from lower border design.

Series 1963 $50. Federal Reserve notes were not printed. Numbering of 1963A series started with #1. Number printed indicates highest serial number. All have "A" suffix.

Back Design $50.00, with Motto added, introduced on Series 1963A

FIFTY DOLLAR FEDERAL RESERVE NOTES

Series 1963A, Granahan-Fowler

No.	District	Printed	Unc.
F50-63A	A-Boston	1,536,000	75.00
F50-63A	B-New York	11,008,000	75.00
F50-63A	C-Philadelphia	3,328,000	75.00
F50-63A	D-Cleveland	3,584,000	75.00
F50-63A	E-Richmond	3,072,000	75.00
F50-63A	F-Atlanta	768,000	80.00
F50-63A	G-Chicago	6,912,000	75.00
F50-63A	H-St. Louis	512,000	80.00
F50-63A	I-Minneapolis	512,000	80.00
F50-63A	J-Kansas City	512,000	80.00
F50-63A	K-Dallas	1,536,000	75.00
F50-63A	L-San Francisco	4,352,000	75.00

$50 FEDERAL RESERVE NOTES—SERIES 1963A

Federal Reserve District	First Serial Number Printed	Last Serial Number Printed	First Note Delivered	Last Note Delivered
Boston	A00 000 001A	A01 536 000A	11-22-66	7-29-68
New York	B00 000 001A	B12 288 000A	9-30-66	10- 7-68
Philadelphia	C00 000 001A	C03 328 000A	11- 8-66	9-16-68
Cleveland	D00 000 001A	D03 584 000A	9-28-66	7- 1-69
Richmond	E00 000 001A	E03 072 000A	11- 2-66	9-20-68
Atlanta	F00 000 001A	F00 768 000A	11- 8-66	11-15-68
Chicago	G00 000 001A	G06 912 000A	11-22-66	11-15-68
St. Louis	H00 000 001A	H00 512 000A	9-19-67	9-19-67
Minneapolis	I 00 000 001A	I 00 512 000A	12- 6-66	9- 8-67
Kansas City	J00 000 001A	J00 512 000A	11- 7-67	9- 3-68
Dallas	K00 000 001A	K01 536 000A	11-21-66	12-24-68
San Francisco	L00 000 001A	L04 352 000A	11- 8-66	7- 1-69

Series 1969, Elston-Kennedy, with new Treasury Seal.

No.	District	Printed	Unc.
F50-69	A-Boston	2,048,000	75.00
F50-69	B-New York	12,032,000	75.00
F50-69	C-Philadelphia	3,584,000	75.00
F50-69	D-Cleveland	3,584,000	75.00
F50-69	E-Richmond	2,560,000	75.00
F50-69	F-Atlanta	256,000	75.00
F50-69	G-Chicago	9,728,000	75.00
F50-69	H-St. Louis	256,000	85.00
F50-69	I-Minneapolis	512,000	80.00
F50-69	J-Kansas City	1,280,000	75.00
F50-69	K-Dallas	1,536,00	75.00
F50-69	L-San Francisco	6,912,000	75.00

FIFTY DOLLAR FEDERAL RESERVE NOTES

$50 FEDERAL RESERVE NOTES—SERIES 1969

Federal Reserve District	First Serial Number Printed	Last Serial Number Printed	First Note Delivered	Last Note Delivered
Boston	A00 000 001A	A02 048 000A	10-15-69	2-17-71
New York	B00 000 001A	B12 032 000A	10-22-69	4-12-72
Philadelphia	C00 000 001A	C02 584 000A	9-23-69	7-20-71
Cleveland	D00 000 001A	D03 584 000A	10-20-69	6-28-71
Richmond	E00 000 001A	E02 560 000A	11-21-69	9-17-71
Atlanta	F00 000 001A	F00 256 000A	6-24-71	4- 4-72
Chicago	G00 000 001A	G09 728 000A	10-30-69	9-13-71
St. Louis	H00 000 001A	H00 256 000A	12- 8-70	7-19-71
Minneapolis	I 00 000 001A	I 00 512 000A	10-15-69	9-20-72
Kansas City	J00 000 001A	J01 280 000A	7- 9-69	9- 9-71
Dallas	K00 000 001A	K01 536 000A	8-26-68	7-13-71
San Francisco	L00 000 001A	L06 912 000A	10- 6-69	7-28-71

Series 1969A, Kabis-Connally

No.	District	No. Printed	Unc.
F50-69A	A-Boston	1,536,00	70.00
F50-69A	B-New York	9,728,000	70.00
F50-69A	C-Phila.	2,560,000	70.00
F50-69A	D-Clevel'd	2,816,000	70.00
F50-69A	E-Rich.	2,304,000	70.00
F50-69A	F-Atlanta	256,000	75.00
F50-69A	G-Chgo	3,584,000	70.00
F50-69A	H-St. Louis	256,000	75.00
F50-69A	I-Minn.	512,000	70.00
F50-69A	J-Kan. City	256,000	75.00
F50-69A	K-Dallas	1,024,000	70.00
F50-69A	L-San F.	5,120,000	70.00

$50 FEDERAL RESERVE NOTES—SERIES 1969A

Federal Reserve District	First Serial Number Printed	Last Serial Number Printed	First Note Delivered	Last Note Delivered
Boston	A02 048 001A	A03 584 000A	10- 4-71	7-19-72
New York	B12 032 001A	B21 760 000A	4-12-72	8- 1-73
Philadelphia	C03 584 001A	C06 144 000A	10- 5-71	8- 1-72
Cleveland	D03 584 001A	D06 400 000A	10-18-71	9-21-72
Richmond	E02 560 001A	E04 864 000A	9-17-71	12- 6-72
Atlanta	F00 256 001A	F00 512 000A	4- 4-72	12-14-72
Chicago	G09 728 001A	G13 312 000A	10-19-71	7- 3-72
St. Louis	H00 256 001A	H00 512 000A	10- 5-71	7-27-72
Minneapolis	I 00 512 001A	I 01 024 000A	9-20-72	9-20-72
Kansas City	J01 280 001A	J01 536 000A	9- 9-71	5-17-72
Dallas	K01 536 001A	K02 560 000A	8-24-71	7-11-72
San Francisco	L06 912 001A	L12 032 000A	8-11-71	12-15-72

FIFTY DOLLAR FEDERAL RESERVE NOTES
Series 1969B, Banuelos-Connally

No.	District	No. Printed	Unc.	No.	District	No. Printed	Unc.
F50-69B	A-Boston	1,536,000	70.00	F50-69B	G-Chicago	1,124,000	70.00
F50-69B	B-New York	2,560,000	70.00	F50-69B	H-St. Louis	None	—
F50-69B	C-Philadelphia	None	—	F50-69B	I-Minneapolis	None	—
F50-69B	D-Cleveland	None	—	F50-69B	J-Kansas City	None	—
F50-69B	E-Rich.	1,536,000	70.00	F50-69B	K-Dallas	1,024,000	70.00
F50-69B	F-Atlanta	512,000	70.00	F50-69B	L-San Fran.	None	—

$50 FEDERAL RESERVE NOTES—SERIES 1969B (32 Subject)

Federal Reserve District	First Serial Number Printed	Last Serial Number Printed	First Note Delivered	Last Note Delivered
Boston	A03 584 001A	A04 608 000A	2-21-73	9-26-73
New York	B21 706 001B	B24 320 000C	8- 1-73	12- 5-73
Philadelphia	None Printed			
Cleveland	None Printed			
Richmond	E04 864 001A	E06 400 000A	12- 6-72	10-19-73
Atlanta	F00 512 001A	F01 024 000A	12-14-72	10-18-73
Chicago	G13 312 001A	G14 336 000A	9-27-72	12-11-72
St. Louis	None Printed			
Minneapolis	None Printed			
Kansas City	None Printed			
Dallas	K02 560 001A	K03 584 000A	9- 5-72	6-19-73
San Francisco	None Printed			

Series 1969C, Banuelos-Shultz

No.	District	Unc.	No.	District	Unc.
F50-69C	A-Boston	65.00	F50-69C	G-Chicago	65.00
F50-69C	B-New York	65.00	F50-69C	H-St. Louis	65.00
F50-69C	C-Philadelphia	65.00	F50-69C	I-Minneapolis	65.00
F50-69C	D-Cleveland	65.00	F50-69C	J-Kansas City	65.00
F50-69C	E-Richmond	65.00	F50-69C	K-Dallas	65.00
F50-69C	F-Atlanta	65.00	F50-69C	L-San Francisco	65.00

$50 FEDERAL RESERVE NOTES—SERIES 1969C (32 Subject)

Federal Reserve District	First Serial Number Printed	Last Serial Number Printed	First Note Delivered	Last Note Delivered
Boston	A04 608 001A	A06 400 000A	11-12-73	12-11-74
New York	B24 320 001A	B31 300 000A	8- 1-73	10-24-74
Philadelphia	C06 144 001A	C09 728 000A	10-17-72	7-10-74
Cleveland	D06 400 001A	D11 520 000A	10-26-72	6- 4-74
Richmond	E06 400 001A	E08 704 000A	10-19-73	9-20-74
Atlanta	F01 024 001A	F01 280 000A	10-18-73	9-30-74
Chicago	G14 336 001A	G21 120 000A	1-23-74	5- 6-74
St. Louis	H00 512 001A	H03 200 000A	11- 2-73	
Minneapolis	I01 024 001A	I01 280 000A	12- 6-73	7- 3-74
Kansas City	J01 536 001A	J02 816 000A	11-21-72	6-26-74
Dallas	K03 584 001A	K07 040 000A	11- 6-72	
San Francisco	L12 032 001A	L16 640 000A	12-15-72	7-24-74

FIFTY DOLLAR FEDERAL RESERVE NOTES

Series 1974, Neff-Simon

No.	District	Unc.	No.	District	Unc.
F50-74	A-Boston	55.00	F50-74	G-Chicago	55.00
F50-74	B-New York	55.00	F50-74	H-St. Louis	55.00
F50-74	C-Philadelphia	55.00	F50-74	I-Minneapolis	55.00
F50-74	D-Cleveland	55.00	F50-74	J-Kansas City	55.00
F50-74	E-Richmond	55.00	F50-74	K-Dallas	55.00
F50-74	F-Atlanta	55.00	F50-74	L-San Francisco	55.00

$50 FEDERAL RESERVE NOTES—SERIES 1974 (32 Subject)

Federal Reserve District	First Serial Number Printed	Last Serial Number Printed	First Note Delivered
Boston	A06 400 001A	A10 240 000A	
New York	B31 360 001A	B69 760 000A	10-24-74
Philadelphia	C09 728 001A	C17 280 000A	
Cleveland	D11 520 001A	D33 920 000A	8-29-74
Richmond	E08 704 001A	E23 040 000A	10-16-74
Atlanta	F01 280 001A	F02 560 000A	9-30-74
Chicago	G21 120 001A	G51 840 000A	10- 7-74
St. Louis	H03 200 001A	H05 120 000A	
Minneapolis	I 01 280 001A	I 04 480 000A	11-20-74
Kansas City	J02 816 001A	J07 680 000A	9-18-74
Dallas	K07 040 001A	K15 360 000A	
San Francisco	L16 640 001A	L24 320 000A	10-18-74

Series 1977 currently being printed all start with 00 000 001.

ONE HUNDRED DOLLAR FEDERAL RESERVE NOTES

Face Design $100.00, Series 1928

$100.00 Back Design, Series 1928 through 1950E

Series 1928, Woods-Mellon. Large numeral in seal indicating issuing Bank.

No.	District	Ex.Fine	Unc.
F100-28	A-Boston	135.00	235.00
F100-28	B-New York	135.00	235.00
F100-28	C-Phila.	135.00	235.00
F100-28	D-Cleveland	135.00	235.00
F100-28	E-Richmond	150.00	235.00
F100-28	F-Atlanta	150.00	235.00
F100-28	G-Chicago	135.00	235.00
F100-28	H-St. Louis	150.00	235.00
F100-28	I-Minneapolis	150.00	235.00
F100-28	J-Kansas City	135.00	235.00
F100-28	K-Dallas	150.00	235.00
F100-28	L-San Fran.	135.00	235.00

ONE HUNDRED DOLLAR FEDERAL RESERVE NOTES

Series 1928A, Woods-Mellon. Large letter replaces numeral in seal.

No.	District	Ex.Fine	Unc.	No.	District	Ex.Fine	Unc.
F100-28A	A-Boston	135.00	235.00	F100-28A	G-Chicago	135.00	235.00
F100-28A	B-New York	135.00	235.00	F100-28A	H-St. Louis	150.00	235.00
F100-28A	C-Phila.	135.00	235.00	F100-28A	I-Minn.	150.00	235.00
F100-28A	D-Clevel'd	135.00	235.00	F100-28A	J-Kans. City	150.00	235.00
F100-28A	E-Richm'd	135.00	235.00	F100-28A	K-Dallas	150.00	235.00
F100-28A	F-Atlanta	135.00	235.00	F100-28A	L-San Fran.	135.00	235.00

The Bureau of Engraving and Printing records do not give the separate totals for series 1928 and 1928A. The combined totals as given by the Bureau are as follows:

District	Quantity	District	Quantity
Boston	1,320,000	Chicago	4,140,000
New York	3,528,000	St. Louis	852,000
Philadelphia	1,704,000	Minneapolis	516,000
Cleveland	1,212,000	Kansas City	780,000
Richmond	828,000	Dallas	420,000
Atlanta	612,000	San Francisco	1,608,000

The starting number for each District in the 1928 series was 00000001A with prefix letter indicating bank of issue. The numbering was consecutive through the 1928A series.

$100 FEDERAL RESERVE NOTES—SERIES 1928 and 1928A (12 Subject)
Secretary-Treasurer—Mellon-Woods

Federal Reserve District	First Serial Number Printed	Last Serial Number Printed	First Note Delivered	Last Note Delivered
Boston	A00 000 001A	A01 320 000A	8-30-29	3-22-33
New York	B00 000 001A	B03 528 000A	9-21-29	12- 6-34
Philadelphia	C00 000 001A	C01 704 000A	8-30-29	3-21-33
Cleveland	D00 000 001A	D01 212 000A	8-30-29	3- 6-33
Richmond	E00 000 001A	E00 828 000A	9-23-29	3-23-33
Atlanta	F00 000 001A	F00 612 000A	9-23-29	3-28-33
Chicago	G00 000 001A	G04 140 000A	8-30-29	3- 7-33
St. Louis	H00 000 001A	H00 852 000A	9-23-29	3-28-33
Minneapolis	I 00 000 001A	I 00 516 000A	9-23-29	3-28-33
Kansas City	J00 000 001A	J00 780 000A	9-23-29	3-21-33
Dallas	K00 000 001A	K00 420 000A	11-25-29	3-24-33
San Francisco	L00 000 001A	L01 608 000A	11-25-29	7-24-33

No records available indicating Serial No. and delivery date of last note of 1928 Series or First Serial No. and delivery date of 1928A Series. The Serial Numbers and delivery dates listed hereon are the first of the 1928 Series and last of the 1928A Series.

Face Design $100.00, Series 1934 to 1934D

ONE HUNDRED DOLLAR FEDERAL RESERVE NOTES

Series 1934, Julian-Morgenthau. Light and dark green seals.

No.	District	Ex.Fine	Unc.	No.	District	Ex.Fine	Unc.
F100-34	A-Boston	135.00	200.00	F100-34	G-Chicago	135.00	200.00
F100-34	B-New York	135.00	200.00	F100-34	H-St. Louis	135.00	200.00
F100-34	C-Phila.	135.00	200.00	F100-34	I-Minn.	150.00	200.00
F100-34	D-Cleveland	135.00	200.00	F100-34	J-K. C.	135.00	200.00
F100-34	E-Richmond	135.00	200.00	F100-34	K-Dallas	135.00	200.00
F100-34	F-Atlanta	135.00	200.00	F100-34	L-San Fran.	135.00	200.00

Series 1934A, Julian-Morgenthau

No.	District	Ex.Fine	Unc.	No.	District	Ex.Fine	Unc.
F100-34A	A-Boston	150.00	190.00	F100-34A	G-Chicago	130.00	190.00
F100-34A	B-New York	130.00	190.00	F100-34A	H-St. Louis	130.00	190.00
F100-34A	C-Phila.	130.00	190.00	F100-34A	I-Minn.	150.00	190.00
F100-34A	D-Clevel'd	130.00	190.00	F100-34A	J-K. C.	130.00	190.00
F100-34A	E-Richm'd	130.00	190.00	F100-34A	K-Dallas	130.00	190.00
F100-34A	F-Atlanta	130.00	190.00	F100-34A	L-San Fran.	130.00	190.00

The Bureau of Engraving and Printing records do not give the separate totals of series 1934 and 1934A. The combined totals as given by the Bureau are as follows:

District	Quantity	District	Quantity
Boston	3,696,000	Chicago	10,188,000
New York	18,364,000	St. Louis	2,472,000
Philadelphia	3,420,000	Minneapolis	900,000
Cleveland	3,708,000	Kansas City	2,268,000
Richmond	4,332,000	Dallas	1,608,000
Atlanta	3,492,000	San Francisco	7,236,000

The starting number for each District in the 1934 series was 00000001A with prefix letter indicating issuing bank. Numbering was consecutive through series 1934D.

$100 FEDERAL RESERVE NOTES—SERIES 1934 & 1934A (12 Subject)
Secretary-Treasurer: Morgenthau-Julian

Federal Reserve District	First Serial Number Printed	Last Serial Number Printed	First Note Delivered	Last Note Delivered
Boston	A00 000 001A	No record	12-16-35	No record
New York	B00 000 001A	B18 364 000A	3- 9-35	1-19-51
Philadelphia	C00 000 001A	C03 420 000A	12-16-35	7-29-44
Cleveland	D00 000 001A	D03 708 000A	12-26-35	7-20-45
Richmond	E00 000 001A	E04 332 000A	12-30-35	8-25-45
Atlanta	E00 000 001A	F03 492 000A	12-31-35	8-25-45
Chicago	G00 000 001A	G10 188 000A	12-28-35	7-18-45
St. Louis	H00 000 001A	H02 472 000A	12-24-35	7-13-45
Minneapolis	I 00 000 001A	I 00 900 000A	12-26-35	7-24-45
Kansas City	J00 000 001A	J02 268 000A	12-28-35	7-16-45
Dallas	K00 000 001A	K01 608 000A	12-30-35	7-18-45
San Francisco	L00 000 001A	L07 236 000A	12-27-35	6- 1-49

The Serial Numbers and delivery dates listed hereon are the first of 1934 Series and last of 1934A. No records indicating further data were found.

Series 1934B, Julian-Vinson

No.	District	Printed	Ex.Fine	Unc.
F100-34B	A-Boston ....Printed	no record	—	Scarce*
F100-34B	B-New York	None	—	—
F100-34B	C-Philadelphia ......Printed	no record	—	Scarce*
F100-34B	D-Cleveland	12,000	185.00	250.00
F100-34B	E-Richmond	240,000	140.00	190.00
F100-34B	F-Atlanta...................	120,000	140.00	190.00
F100-34B	G-Chicago..................	12,000	155.00	190.00
F100-34B	H-St. Louis	132,000	140.00	190.00
F100-34B	I -Minneapolis.............	120,000	140.00	190.00
F100-34B	J-Kansas City	12,000	155.00	190.00
F100-34B	K-Dallas	40,000	150.00	190.00
F100-34B	L-San Francisco...........	None	—	—

*Standard Handbook reports 41,400 and 39,600 Philadelphia notes printed. A tentative value of $300.00 is placed on each of these.

$100 FEDERAL RESERVE NOTES—SERIES 1934B (12 Subject). Secretary-Treasurer: Vinson-Julian

Federal Reserve District	First Serial Number Printed	Last Serial Number Printed	First Note Delivered	Last Note Delivered
Boston	Printed, no record	No record	No Record	
New York	None Printed	None Printed	No Deliveries	
Philadelphia	Printed, no record	No record	No record	
Cleveland.................	D03 708 001A	D03 720 000A	7-13-49	7-13-49
Richmond	E04 332 001A	E04 572 000A	11-13-46	11-29-46
Atlanta...................	F03 492 001A	F03 612 000A	7-17-46	7-17-46
Chicago	G10 188 001A	G10 200 000A	8- 4-47	8- 4-47
St. Louis..................	H02 472 001A	H02 604 000A	7-17-46	12-17-46
Minneapolis...............	I 00 000 001A	I 01 020 000A	7-23-46	7-23-46
Kansas City	J02 268 001A	J02 280 000A	7-31-47	7-31-47
Dallas....................	K01 608 001A	K01 648 000A	7-23-46	7-23-46
San Francisco	None Printed	None Printed	No Deliveries	

Series 1934C, Julian-Snyder

No.	District	Printed	Ex.Fine	Unc.
F100-34C	A-Boston ....Printed	no record	—	Scarce*
F100-34C	B-New York ....Printed	no record	—	190.00
F100-34C	C-Philadelphia ......Printed	no record	—	Scarce*
F100-34C	D-Cleveland	240,000	145.00	190.00
F100-34C	E-Richmond ....See Note	—	—	—
F100-34C	F-Atlanta...................	960,000	145.00	190.00
F100-34C	G-Chicago..................	828,000	140.00	190.00
F100-34C	H-St. Louis	1,248,000	140.00	190.00
F100-34C	I -Minneapolis.............	632,000	145.00	190.00
F100-34C	J-Kansas City	728,000	145.00	190.00
F100-34C	K-Dallas	680,000	145.00	190.00
F100-34C	L-San Francisco...........	572,000	145.00	190.00

Note: Bureau records indicate no Series 1934C were printed for Richmond; a mule note for this series for Richmond has been reported. *Standard Handbook reports 13,800 Boston and 13,200 Philadelphia notes printed. A tentative value of $275.00 is placed on each of these.

$100 FEDERAL RESERVE NOTES—SERIES 1934C (12 Subject). Secretary-Treasurer: Snyder-Julian

Federal Reserve District	First Serial Number Printed	Last Serial Number Printed	First Note Delivered	Last Note Delivered
Boston	No record	No record	No record	
New York	No record	No record	No record	
Philadelphia	No record	No record	No record	
Cleveland.................	D03 720 001A	D03 960 000A	7-13-49	1-18-51
Richmond	E04 572 001A	E06 844 000A	8- 4-47	1-16-51
Atlanta...................	F03 612 001A	F04 572 000A	8- 6-47	7-15-49
Chicago	G10 200 001A	G11 028 000A	8- 4-47	7-25-50
St. Louis..................	H02 604 001A	H03 852 000A	12-31-46	3-14-50
Minneapolis...............	I 01 020 001A	I 01 652 000A	7-30-47	1-17-51
Kansas City	J02 280 001A	J03 008 000A	7-31-47	1-17-51
Dallas....................	K01 648 001A	K02 328 000A	7-23-46	7-14-49
San Francisco	L07 236 001A	L07 808 000A	7-13-49	1-15-51

The last delivery of notes for Boston District, Series 1934 through 1934C, was made on Jan. 12, 1951. This delivery included serial Nos. A03 600 001A to A03 696 000A, indicating a total of 3,696,000 notes for Boston through Series 1934, 1934A, 1934B and 1934C.

ONE HUNDRED DOLLAR FEDERAL RESERVE NOTES

Series 1934D, Clark-Snyder. Released through five banks only.

No.	District	Printed	Ex.Fine	Unc.
F100-34D	A-Boston	None	—	—
F100-34D	B-New York	No record of printing*		
F100-34D	C-Philadelphia	360,000	140.00	190.00
F100-34D	D-Cleveland	None	—	—
F100-34D	E-Richmond	None	—	—
F100-34D	F-Atlanta	320,000	140.00	190.00
F100-34D	G-Chicago	340,000	150.00	215.00
F100-34D	H-St. Louis	384,000	140.00	190.00
F100-34D	I-Minneapolis	None	—	—
F100-34D	J-Kansas City	None	—	—
F100-34D	K-Dallas	152,000	145.00	215.00
F100-34D	L-San Francisco	None	—	—

*Standard Handbook reports 156 notes printed. No reports of sales.

$100 FEDERAL RESERVE NOTES—SERIES 1934D (12 Subject)
Secretary-Treasurer: Snyder-Clark

Federal Reserve District	First Serial Number Printed	Last Serial Number Printed	First Note Delivered	Last Note Delivered
Boston	None Printed	None Printed	No Deliveries	
New York	No record	No record	No record	
Philadelphia	C03 420 001A	C03 780 000A	7-24-50	1-17-51
Cleveland	None Printed	None Printed	No Deliveries	
Richmond	None Printed	None Printed	No Deliveries	
Atlanta	F04 572 001A	F04 892 000A	7-25-50	1-16-51
Chicago	G11 028 001A	G11 368 000A	1-15-51	1-16-51
St. Louis	H03 852 001A	H04 236 000A	1-16-51	1-17-51
Minneapolis	None Printed	None Printed	No Deliveries	
Kansas City	None Printed	None Printed	No Deliveries	
Dallas	K02 328 001A	K02 480 000A	8-17-50	1-16-51
San Francisco	None Printed	None Printed	No Deliveries	

Face Design $100.00, Series 1950 to 1950E

ONE HUNDRED DOLLAR FEDERAL RESERVE NOTES

Note: This denomination is seldom collected in other than new condition.

Series 1950, Clark-Snyder. Seals and serial numbers smaller.

No.	District	Printed	Unc.
F100-50	A-Boston	768,000	155.00
F100-50	B-New York	3,908,000	155.00
F100-50	C-Philadelphia	1,332,000	155.00
F100-50	D-Cleveland	1,632,000	155.00
F100-50	E-Richmond	4,076,000	155.00
F100-50	F-Atlanta	1,824,000	155.00
F100-50	G-Chicago	4,428,000	155.00
F100-50	H-St. Louis	1,284,000	155.00
F100-50	I-Minneapolis	564,000	155.00
F100-50	J-Kansas City	864,000	155.00
F100-50	K-Dallas	1,216,000	155.00
F100-50	L-San Francisco	2,524,000	155.00

$100 FEDERAL RESERVE NOTES—SERIES 1950 (12 Subject)
Secretary-Treasurer: Snyder-Clark

Federal Reserve District	First Serial Number Printed	Last Serial Number Printed	First Note Delivered	Last Note Delivered
Boston	A00 000 001A	A00 768 000A	11- 7-52	7-27-53
New York	B00 000 001A	B03 908 000A	11-10-52	9- 9-53
Philadelphia	C00 000 001A	C01 332 000A	5- 9-51	7-31-53
Cleveland	D00 000 001A	D01 632 000A	9- 6-51	7-27-53
Richmond	E00 000 001A	E04 076 000A	5-21-51	7-27-53
Atlanta	F00 000 001A	F01 824 000A	9- 4-51	7-16-53
Chicago	G00 000 001A	G04 428 000A	11-28-51	7-31-53
St. Louis	H00 000 001A	H01 284 000A	5-21-51	7-13-53
Minneapolis	I 00 000 001A	I 00 564 000A	2- 8-52	7-23-53
Kansas City	J00 000 001A	J00 864 000A	11- 6-51	7-16-53
Dallas	K00 000 001A	K01 216 000A	5-23-51	7-13-53
San Francisco	L00 000 001A	L02 524 000A	5-29-51	7-23-53

Series 1950A, Priest-Humphrey

No.	District	Printed	Unc.
F100-50A	A-Boston	1,008,000	150.00
F100-50A	B-New York	2,880,000	150.00
F100-50A	C-Philadelphia	576,000	150.00
F100-50A	D-Cleveland	228,000	150.00
F100-50A	E-Richmond	2,160,000	150.00
F100-50A	F-Atlanta	288,000	150.00
F100-50A	G-Chicago	864,000	150.00
F100-50A	H-St. Louis	432,000	150.00
F100-50A	I-Minneapolis	144,000	150.00
F100-50A	J-Kansas City	288,000	150.00
F100-50A	K-Dallas	432,000	150.00
F100-50A	L-San Francisco	720,000	150.00

ONE HUNDRED DOLLAR FEDERAL RESERVE NOTES

$100 FEDERAL RESERVE NOTES—SERIES 1950A (18 Subject)
Secretary-Treasurer: Humphrey-Priest

Federal Reserve District	First Serial Number Printed	Last Serial Number Printed	First Note Delivered	Last Note Delivered
Boston	A00 864 001A*	A01 872 000A	12-28-54	6-13-57
New York	B04 032 001A*	B06 012 000A	12-13-54	1-28-57
Philadelphia	C01 440 001A*	C02 016 000A	12-10-54	8-20-57
Cleveland	D01 728 001A*	D02 016 000A	12-17-54	12-17-54
Richmond	E04 176 001A*	E06 336 000A	12-20-54	8-20-57
Atlanta	F01 872 001A*	F02 160 000A	12- 8-54	8-10-54
Chicago	G04 464 001A*	G05 328 000A	12-16-54	12-16-54
St. Louis	H01 296 001A*	H01 728 000A	12-13-54	1- 4-57
Minneapolis	I 00 576 000A*	I 00 720 000A	12-28-54	12-28-54
Kansas City	J00 864 001A	J01 152 000A	12-28-54	1-28-57
Dallas	K01 296 001A	K01 728 000A	12-15-54	10-17-55
San Francisco	L02 592 001A	L03 312 000A	12-14-54	9-13-56

Remarks: *The following numbers were not printed: *A00 768 001A through A00 864 000A, *B03 908 001A through B04 032 000A, *C01 332 001A through C01 440 000A, *D01 632 001A through D01 728 000A, *E04 076 001A through E04 176 000A, *F01 824 001A through F01 872 000A, *G04 428 001A through G04 464 000A, *H01 284 001A through H01 296 000A, *I 00 564 001A through I 00 576 000A, *K01 216 001A through K01 296 000A, *L02 524 001A through L02 592 000A.

Series 1950B, Priest-Anderson

No.	District	Printed	Unc.
F100-50B	A-Boston	720,000	150.00
F100-50B	B-New York	6,336,000	150.00
F100-50B	C-Philadelphia	720,000	150.00
F100-50B	D-Cleveland	432,000	150.00
F100-50B	E-Richmond	1,008,000	150.00
F100-50B	F-Atlanta	576,000	150.00
F100-50B	G-Chicago	2,592,000	150.00
F100-50B	H-St. Louis	1,152,000	150.00
F100-50B	I -Minneapolis	228,000	150.00
F100-50B	J-Kansas City	720,000	150.00
F100-50B	K-Dallas	1,728,000	150.00
F100-50B	L-San Francisco	2,880,000	150.00

$100 FEDERAL RESERVE NOTES—SERIES 1950B (18 Subject)
Secretary-Treasurer: Anderson-Priest

Federal Reserve District	First Serial Number Printed	Last Serial Number Printed	First Note Delivered	Last Note Delivered
Boston	A01 872 001A	A02 592 000A	11-18-58	9- 2-60
New York	B06 912 001A	B13 248 000A	12-18-57	10-21-60
Philadelphia	C02 816 001A	C02 730 000A	10- 6-59	11-22-60
Cleveland	D02 016 001A	D02 448 000A	9-25-57	12- 9-60
Richmond	E06 336 001A	E07 344 000A	9- 3-59	12- 6-60
Atlanta	F02 160 001A	F02 736 000A	8- 4-59	9- 9-60
Chicago	G05 328 001A	G07 920 000A	9-25-57	11-30-59
St. Louis	H01 728 001A	H02 880 000A	10- 1-59	9- 8-60
Minneapolis	I 00 720 001A	I 01 008 000A	11-17-59	11-17-59
Kansas City	J01 152 001A	J01 872 000A	10-29-57	8-10-60
Dallas	K01 728 001A	K03 456 000A	9- 4-57	10-28-59
San Francisco	L03 312 001A	L06 192 000A	10-15-57	8- 2-60

ONE HUNDRED DOLLAR FEDERAL RESERVE NOTES

Series 1950C, Smith-Dillon

No.	District	Printed	Unc.
F100-50C	A-Boston	864,000	150.00
F100-50C	B-New York	2,448,000	150.00
F100-50C	C-Philadelphia	576,000	150.00
F100-50C	D-Cleveland	576,000	150.00
F100-50C	E-Richmond	1,440,000	150.00
F100-50C	F-Atlanta	1,296,000	150.00
F100-50C	G-Chicago	1,584,000	150.00
F100-50C	H-St. Louis	720,000	150.00
F100-50C	I-Minneapolis	288,000	150.00
F100-50C	J-Kansas City	432,000	150.00
F100-50C	K-Dallas	720,000	150.00
F100-50C	L-San Francisco	2,160,000	150.00

$100 FEDERAL RESERVE NOTES—SERIES 1950C (18 Subject)
Secretary-Treasurer: Dillon-Smith

Federal Reserve District	First Serial Number Printed	Last Serial Number Printed	First Note Delivered	Last Note Delivered
Boston	A02 592 001A	A03 456 000A	9-12-61	9-13-62
New York	B13 248 001A	B15 696 000A	9-28-61	12-14-62
Philadelphia	C02 736 001A	C03 312 000A	8-28-61	10-17-62
Cleveland	D02 448 001A	D03 024 000A	7-31-61	7-16-62
Richmond	E07 334 001A	E08 784 000A	7-14-61	11- 1-62
Atlanta	F02 736 001A	F04 032 000A	10-25-61	10- 5-62
Chicago	G07 920 001A	G09 504 000A	8-25-61	11- 1-62
St. Louis	H02 880 001A	H03 600 000A	7-12-61	8-21-62
Minneapolis	I 01 008 001A	I 01 296 000A	10-20-61	9- 5-61
Kansas City	J01 872 001A	J02 304 000A	9-20-61	9-14-62
Dallas	K03 456 001A	K04 176 000A	1-10-62	12- 3-62
San Francisco	L06 192 001A	L08 332 000A	11-29-61	10-31-62

Series 1950D, Granahan-Dillon

No.	District	Printed	Unc.
F100-50D	A-Boston	1,872,000	150.00
F100-50D	B-New York	7,632,000	150.00
F100-50D	C-Philadelphia	1,872,000	150.00
F100-50D	D-Cleveland	1,584,000	150.00
F100-50D	E-Richmond	2,880,000	150.00
F100-50D	F-Atlanta	1,872,000	150.00
F100-50D	G-Chicago	4,608,000	150.00
F100-50D	H-St. Louis	1,440,000	150.00
F100-50D	I-Minneapolis	432,000	150.00
F100-50D	J-Kansas City	864,000	150.00
F100-50D	K-Dallas	1,728,000	150.00
F100-50D	L-San Francisco	3,312,000	150.00

ONE HUNDRED DOLLAR FEDERAL RESERVE NOTES

$100 FEDERAL RESERVE NOTES—SERIES 1950D (18 Subject)
Secretary-Treasurer: Dillon-Granahan

Federal Reserve District	First Serial Number Printed	Last Serial Number Printed	First Note Delivered	Last Note Delivered
Boston	A03 456 001A	A05 328 000A	8-29-63	8-26-65
New York	B15 696 001A	B23 328 000A	8-16-63	6-30-65
Philadelphia	C03 312 001A	C05 184 000A	10-25-63	7-28-65
Cleveland	D03 024 001A	D04 608 000A	9-13-63	8-30-65
Richmond	E08 784 001A	E11 664 000A	7-31-63	7-21-65
Atlanta	F04 032 001A	F05 904 000A	11-26-63	7-12-65
Chicago	G09 504 001A	G14 112 000A	9-26-63	8-12-65
St. Louis	H03 600 001A	H05 040 000A	9-10-63	7-28-65
Minneapolis	I01 296 001A	I01 728 000A		8-30-65
Kansas City	J02 304 001A	J03 168 000A	10-29-63	8-27-65
Dallas	K04 176 001A	K05 904 000A	11-29-63	7-27-65
San Francisco	L08 352 001A	L11 664 000A	7-23-63	7-30-65

Series 1950E, Granahan-Fowler
Printed for three Districts only.

No.	District	Printed	Unc.
F100-50E	B-New York	3,024,000	150.00
F100-50E	G-Chicago	576,000	160.00
F100-50E	L-San Francisco	2,736,000	150.00

$100 FEDERAL RESERVE NOTES—SERIES 1950E

Federal Reserve District	First Serial Number Printed	Last Serial Number Printed	First Note Delivered	Last Note Delivered
New York	B23 328 001A	B26 352 000A	10- 1-65	7-27-66
Chicago	G14 112 001A	G14 688 000A	10-26-65	10-29-65
San Francisco	L11 664 001A	L14 400 000A	9- 3-65	11-30-65

Series 1963A, Granahan-Fowler

Series 1963 $100 denomination was not printed. Numbering of 1963A series started with #1. Number printed indicates highest serial number. All "A" suffix.

No.	District	Printed	Unc.
F100-63A	A-Boston	1,536,000	135.00
F100-63A	B-New York	13,568,000	135.00
F100-63A	C-Philadelphia	1,792,000	135.00
F100-63A	D-Cleveland	2,304,000	135.00
F100-63A	E-Richmond	2,816,000	135.00
F100-63A	F-Atlanta	1,280,000	135.00
F100-63A	G-Chicago	4,352,000	135.00
F100-63A	H-St. Louis	1,536,000	135.00
F100-63A	I-Minneapolis	512,000	135.00
F100-63A	J-Kansas City	1,024,000	135.00
F100-63A	K-Dallas	1,536,000	135.00
F100-63A	L-San Francisco	6,400,000	135.00

ONE HUNDRED DOLLAR FEDERAL RESERVE NOTES

Face Design $100.00, Series 1963A

Inscription changed and obligation "will pay to the Bearer on Demand" removed from lower border design.

$100 FEDERAL RESERVE NOTES—SERIES 1963A

Federal Reserve District	First Serial Number Printed	Last Serial Number Printed	First Note Delivered	Last Note Delivered
Boston	A00 000 001A	A01 536 000A	11-21-66	7-26-68
New York	B00 000 001A	B13 568 000A	10- 6-66	12-24-68
Philadelphia	C00 000 001A	C01 792 000A	11-18-66	9-19-68
Cleveland	D00 000 001A	D02 304 000A	12-21-66	7- 1-69
Richmond	E00 000 001A	E02 816 000A	9-27-66	11-27-68
Atlanta	F00 000 001A	F01 280 000A	9-27-66	10- 1-68
Chicago	G00 000 001A	G04 352 000A	9-30-66	10-15-68
St. Louis	H00 000 001A	H01 536 000A	9-30-66	9- 6-68
Minneapolis	I 00 000 001A	I 00 512 000A	12-21-66	9-26-67
Kansas City	J00 000 001A	J01 024 000A	9-30-66	9- 3-68
Dallas	K00 000 001A	K01 536 000A	11-28-66	11- 6-68
San Francisco	L00 000 001A	L06 400 000A	11-15-66	8- 2-68

$100.00 Motto. Back Design, introduced on Series 1963A

ONE HUNDRED DOLLAR FEDERAL RESERVE NOTES

Series 1969, Elston-Kennedy, with new Treasury Seal.

No.	District	Printed	Unc.
F100-69	A-Boston	2,048,000	125.00
F100-69	B-New York	11,520,000	125.00
F100-69	C-Philadelphia	2,560,000	125.00
F100-69	D-Cleveland	768,000	125.00
F100-69	E-Richmond	2,560,000	125.00
F100-69	F-Atlanta	2,304,000	125.00
F100-69	G-Chicago	5,888,000	125.00
F100-69	H-St. Louis	1,280,000	125.00
F100-69	I-Minneapolis	512,000	125.00
F100-69	J-Kansas City	1,792,000	125.00
F100-69	K-Dallas	2,048,00	125.00
F100-69	L-San Francisco	7,168,000	125.00

$100 FEDERAL RESERVE NOTES—SERIES 1969

Federal Reserve District	First Serial Number Printed	Last Serial Number Printed	First Note Delivered	Last Note Delivered
Boston	A00 000 001A	A02 048 000A	10- 6-69	3-24-71
New York	B00 000 001A	B11 520 000A	11- 3-69	11- 9-71
Philadelphia	C00 000 001A	C02 560 000A	10-28-69	6- 8-71
Cleveland	D00 000 001A	D00 768 000A	11-20-69	7-12-71
Richmond	E00 000 001A	E02 560 000A	11-28-69	10-29-71
Atlanta	F00 000 001A	F02 304 000A	8-28-69	6-24-71
Chicago	G00 000 001A	G05 888 000A	9-10-69	5-10-71
St. Louis	H00 000 001A	H01 280 000A	8-28-69	6-29-71
Minneapolis	I 00 000 001A	I 00 512 000A	8-13-69	6- 7-71
Kansas City	J00 000 001A	J01 792 000A	7- 9-69	11- 3-71
Dallas	K00 000 001A	K02 048 000A	8-19-69	6-27-71
San Francisco	L00 000 001A	L07 168 000A	10- 6-69	8-18-71

Series 1969A, Kabis-Connally

No.	District	Printed	Unc.	No.	District	Printed	Unc.
F100-69A	A-Boston	1,280,00	125.00	F100-69A	G-Chgo	5,376,000	125.00
F100-69A	B-N. Y.	11,264,000	125.00	F100-69A	H-St. L.	1,024,000	125.00
F100-69A	C-Phila.	2,048,000	125.00	F100-69A	I-Minn.	1,024,000	125.00
F100-69A	D-Cleve.	1,280,000	125.00	F100-69A	J-K. C.	512,000	125.00
F100-69A	E-Rich.	2,304,000	125.00	F100-69A	K-Dallas	3,328,000	125.00
F100-69A	F-Atl'ta	2,304,000	125.00	F100-69A	L-San F.	4,352,000	125.00

$100 FEDERAL RESERVE NOTES—SERIES 1969A

Federal Reserve District	First Serial Number Printed	Last Serial Number Printed	First Note Delivered	Last Note Delivered
Boston	A02 048 001A	A03 328 000A	10-18-71	6-12-72
New York	B11 520 001A	B22 784 000A	11- 9-71	8-15-73
Philadelphia	C02 560 001A	C04 608 000A	10-12-71	11- 1-72
Cleveland	D00 768 001A	D02 048 000A	10-18-71	9-21-72
Richmond	E02 560 001A	E04 864 000A	10-29-71	12- 5-72
Atlanta	F02 304 001A	F04 608 000A	9-23-71	7-17-73
Chicago	G05 888 001A	G11 264 000A	8- 9-71	11- 1-72
St. Louis	H01 280 001A	H02 304 000A	9- 9-71	8-22-72
Minneapolis	I 00 512 001A	I 01 536 000A	10-17-71	10- 3-73
Kansas City	J01 792 001A	J02 304 000A	11-18-71	7-25-72
Dallas	K02 048 001A	K05 376 000A	9-14-71	12- 4-73
San Francisco	L07 168 001A	L11 520 000A	9-15-71	11-27-72

ONE HUNDRED DOLLAR FEDERAL RESERVE NOTES

Series 1969B, Banuelos-Connally

None printed in this series (Regular or Star).

Series 1969C, Banuelos-Shultz

No.	District	Unc.	No.	District	Unc.
F100-69C	A-Boston	120.00	F100-69C	G-Chicago	120.00
F100-69C	B-New York	120.00	F100-69C	H-St. Louis	120.00
F100-69C	C-Philadelphia	120.00	F100-69C	I-Minneapolis	120.00
F100-69C	D-Cleveland	120.00	F100-69C	J-Kansas City	120.00
F100-69C	E-Richmond	120.00	F100-69C	K-Dallas	120.00
F100-69C	F-Atlanta	120.00	F100-69C	L-San Francisco	120.00

$100 FEDERAL RESERVE NOTES—SERIES 1969C (32 Subject)

Federal Reserve District	First Serial Number Printed	Last Serial Number Printed	First Note Delivered	Last Note Delivered
Boston	A03 328 001A	A05 376 000A	10-16-72	5- 8-74
New York	B22 784 001A	B33 400 000A	8-15-73	
Philadelphia	C04 608 001A	C07 936 000A	11- 1-72	9-17-74
Cleveland	D02 048 001A	D07 040 000A	10- 3-72	
Richmond	E04 864 001A	E12 160 000A	12- 5-72	
Atlanta	F04 608 001A	F07 040 000A	7-31-73	10-15-74
Chicago	G11 264 001A	G17 920 000A	12- 5-72	11-14-74
St. Louis	H02 304 001A	H07 680 000A	10-26-72	
Minneapolis	I 01 536 001A	I 02 048 000A	10- 3-73	7- 3-74
Kansas City	J02 304 001A	J07 040 000A	10-24-72	
Dallas	K05 376 001A	K08 320 000A	12- 4-73	
San Francisco	L11 520 001A	L21 760 000A	12- 6-72	10-31-74

Series 1974, Neff-Simon

No.	District	Unc.	No.	District	Unc.
F100-74	A-Boston	110.00	F100-74	G-Chicago	110.00
F100-74	B-New York	110.00	F100-74	H-St. Louis	110.00
F100-74	C-Philadelphia	110.00	F100-74	I-Minneapolis	110.00
F100-74	D-Cleveland	110.00	F100-74	J-Kansas City	110.00
F100-74	E-Richmond	110.00	F100-74	K-Dallas	110.00
F100-74	F-Atlanta	110.00	F100-74C	L-San Francisco	110.00

$100 FEDERAL RESERVE NOTES—SERIES 1974 (32 Subject)

Federal Reserve District	First Serial Number Printed	Last Serial Number Printed	First Note Delivered
Boston	A05 376 001A	A17 280 000A	
New York	B38 400 001A	B01 280 000A	
Philadelphia	C07 936 001A	C16 000 000A	
Cleveland	D07 040 001A	D15 360 000A	
Richmond	E12 160 001A	E23 680 000A	
Atlanta	F07 040 001A	F11 520 000A	10-15-74
Chicago	G17 920 001A	G44 160 000A	11- 4-74
St. Louis	H07 680 001A	H13 440 000A	
Minneapolis	I 02 048 001A	I 07 040 000A	11- 6-74
Kansas City	J07 040 001A	J12 800 000A	
Dallas	K08 320 001A	K18 560 000A	
San Francisco	L21 760 001A	L51 200 000A	10-31-74

Series 1977 currently being printed, all start with 00 000 001.

FIVE HUNDRED DOLLAR FEDERAL RESERVE NOTES

Face Design $500.00, William McKinley

Back Design $500.00

F500-28 **Woods-Mellon.** Large letter in seal denoting bank of issue. Issued by all twelve Federal Reserve Banks.

$500 FEDERAL RESERVE NOTES—SERIES 1928 and 1928A (12 Subject)
Secretary-Treasurer—Mellon-Woods

Federal Reserve District	First Serial Number Printed	Last Serial Number Printed	First Note Delivered	Last Note Delivered
Boston	A00 000 001A	A00 084 000A	11-18-29	3-12-33
New York	B00 000 001A	B00 340 000A	11- 8-29	3-16-33
Philadelphia	C00 000 001A	C00 126 000A	11-12-29	3-16-33
Cleveland	D00 000 001A	D00 154 320A	11-12-29	3-16-33
Richmond	E00 000 001A	E00 093 600A	11-12-29	3-13-33
Atlanta	F00 000 001A	F00 064 200A	11-13-29	3-15-33
Chicago	G00 000 001A	G00 633 000A	11-13-29	3-15-33
St. Louis	H00 000 001A	H00 092 400A	11-13-29	3-16-33
Minneapolis	I00 000 001A	I00 044 400A	11-13-29	3-15-33
Kansas City	J00 000 001A	J00 091 800A	11-14-29	3-16-33
Dallas	K00 000 001A	K00 091 800A	11-13-29	3-18-33
San Francisco	L00 000 001A	L00 105 000A	11-14-29	3-16-33

F500-34 **Julian-Morgenthau.** Letter in seal. Issued by all Federal Reserve banks. No $500.00 notes released since July 1945.

F500-34A **Julian-Morgenthau.** Not shown on early Bureau records but now reported by collectors owning Boston, New York, Philadelphia, Cleveland, Richmond, Atlanta, Chicago, Kansas City, Minneapolis and San Francisco.

FIVE HUNDRED DOLLAR FEDERAL RESERVE NOTES

$500 FEDERAL RESERVE NOTES—SERIES 1934 (12 Subject)
Secretary-Treasurer: Morgenthau-Julian

Federal Reserve District	First Serial Number Printed	Last Serial Number Printed	First Note Delivered	Last Note Delivered
Boston	A00 000 001A	A00 058 200A	12-23-35	7-25-40
New York	B00 000 001A	B00 526 800A	12-26-35	7-31-44
Philadelphia	C00 000 001A	C00 072 000A	12-23-35	7-18-44
Cleveland	D00 000 001A	D00 154 320A	11-12-29	3-18-33
Richmond	E00 000 001A	E00 093 600A	11-12-29	3-18-33
Atlanta	E00 000 001A	F00 103 200A	2- 8-36	7-19-44
Chicago	G00 000 001A	G00 385 200A	2- 8-36	7-31-44
St. Louis	H00 000 001A	H00 070 800A	2-12-36	8- 1-44
Minneapolis	I 00 000 001A	I 00 025 200A	2-12-36	7-18-44
Kansas City	J00 000 001A	J00 079 200A	2-13-36	7-21-45
Dallas	K00 000 001A	K00 054 000A	2-13-36	7-21-45
San Francisco	L00 000 001A	L00 158 400A	2-13-36	7-21-45

Remarks: Plates were engraved for Series 1934-A-B&C, but no $500 Notes have been printed or delivered since 7-21-45 to date.

ONE THOUSAND DOLLAR FEDERAL RESERVE NOTES

Face Design $1000.00, Grover Cleveland

Back Design $1000.00

ONE THOUSAND DOLLAR FEDERAL RESERVE NOTES

F1000-28 **Woods-Mellon.** Large letter in seal denoting bank of issue. Issued by twelve Federal Reserve Banks.

$1000 FEDERAL RESERVE NOTES—SERIES 1928 (12 Subject)
Secretary-Treasurer: Mellon-Woods

Federal Reserve District	First Serial Number Printed	Last Serial Number Printed	First Note Delivered	Last Note Delivered
Boston	A00 000 001A	A00 052 800A	11-14-29	3-17-33
New York	B00 000 001A	B00 199 200A	11-15-29	3-17-33
Philadelphia	C00 000 001A	C00 091 200A	11-15-29	3-17-33
Cleveland	D00 000 001A	D00 076 200A	11-15-29	3-14-33
Richmond	E00 000 001A	E00 055 200A	11-16-29	3-14-33
Atlanta	E00 000 001A	F00 044 400A	11-16-29	7-26-33
Chicago	G00 000 001A	G00 403 596A	11-16-29	3-11-33
St. Louis	H00 000 001A	H00 055 200A	11-16-29	3-17-33
Minneapolis	I 00 000 001A	I 00 023 400A	11-16-29	3-13-33
Kansas City	J00 000 001A	J00 058 200A	11-18-29	3-17-33
Dallas	K00 000 001A	K00 036 600A	11-18-29	3-17-33
San Francisco	L00 000 001A	L00 062 400A	11-18-29	3-17-33

F1000-34 **Julian-Morgenthau.** Letter in seal. Issued by all twelve Federal Reserve Banks.

$1000 FEDERAL RESERVE NOTES—SERIES 1934 (12 Subject)
Secretary-Treasurer: Morgenthau-Julian

Federal Reserve District	First Serial Number Printed	Last Serial Number Printed	First Note Delivered	Last Note Delivered
Boston	A00 000 001A	A00 036 600A	12-18-35	7-24-40
New York	B00 000 001A	B00 352 800A	12-17-35	12-27-42
Philadelphia	C00 000 001A	C00 036 000A	12-20-35	7-27-42
Cleveland	D00 000 001A	D00 027 000A	12-21-35	1-16-41
Richmond	E00 000 001A	E00 019 800A	2-14-36	11-17-43
Atlanta	F00 000 001A	F00 044 400A	1-31-35	6-19-42
Chicago	G00 000 001A	G00 116 400A	2-15-36	6-14-40
St. Louis	H00 000 001A	H00 022 800A	2-14-36	7-29-43
Minneapolis	I 00 000 001A	I 00 007 200A	2-14-36	7-27-42
Kansas City	J00 000 001A	J00 027 600A	2-15-36	7-20-43
Dallas	K00 000 001A	K00 036 600A	2-14-36	10-16-43
San Francisco	L00 000 001A	L00 067 200A	2-15-36	7-27-42

F1000-34A **Julian-Morgenthau.** Issued by all Federal Reserve Banks except Dallas. No $1000.00 notes have been printed or released since July 21, 1945.

$1000 FEDERAL RESERVE NOTES—SERIES 1934A (12 Subject)
Secretary-Treasurer: Morgenthau-Julian

Federal Reserve District	First Serial Number Printed	Last Serial Number Printed	First Note Delivered	Last Note Delivered
Boston	A00 036 001A	A00 059 000A	7-27-42	7-17-44
New York	B00 352 801A	B00 496 800A	12-27-42	6-24-44
Philadelphia	C00 036 001A	C00 096 000A	7-20-43	7-17-44
Cleveland	D00 027 001A	D00 051 000A	7-21-43	7-17-44
Richmond	E00 019 801A	E00 028 800A	10-13-44	10-13-44
Atlanta	F00 044 401A	F00 126 600A	7-20-43	7-21-45
Chicago	G00 116 401A	G00 279 600A	3-30-42	7-18-44
St. Louis	H00 022 801A	H00 054 000A	2- 3-44	8- 1-44
Minneapolis	I 00 007 201A	I 00 019 200A	5- 1-44	5- 1-44
Kansas City	J00 027 601A	J00 057 600A	1- 5-44	7-21-45
Dallas	None Printed	None Printed	No Deliveries	
San Francisco	L00 067 201A	L00 099 600A	8- 2-43	7-17-44

Remarks: No $1,000.00 Notes or delivered since 7-21-45.

$500. · $1,000. · $5,000. · $10,000. DISCONTINUED

On July 14, 1969, the Treasury Department and the Federal Reserve System announced that the issuance of currency in denominations of $500, $1,000, $5,000, and $10,000 would be discontinued immediately, stating that the use of these large denominations had declined sharply and that demand for them by the Federal Reserve Banks appeared to be insufficient to warrant cost of production and custody of the new supply.

As a result of the above decision all existing supplies of large denomination notes at the Federal Reserve Banks will be turned over to the Treasury for destruction, and all circulating notes of high denomination which find their way back to the Federal Reserve Banks will be destroyed.

An amendment to the Federal Reserve Act in 1918, first authorized the higher denomination notes primarily for interbank transactions. As the demand lessened printings of these notes was discontinued in 1946 the supply on hand being ample to take care of the demand. The supply having diminished to such an extent that new printings would have to be made, the above decision to discontinue was made. Surveys indicate that transactions for which the higher denominations have been used, can now be handled by other means, such as checks or $100 notes.

The Treasury Department will continue to print and to issue to all twelve of the Federal Reserve Bank notes in denominations of $1 to $100 as formerly.

FIVE THOUSAND DOLLAR FEDERAL RESERVE NOTES

Face Design $5000.00, James Madison

FIVE THOUSAND DOLLAR FEDERAL RESERVE NOTES

Back Design $5000.00

F5000-28 **Woods-Mellon.** Large letter in seal denoting bank of issue. Not issued by Philadelphia, St. Louis or Minneapolis.

$5000 FEDERAL RESERVE NOTES—SERIES 1928 (12 Subject)
Secretary-Treasurer: Mellon-Woods

Federal Reserve District	First Serial Number Printed	Last Serial Number Printed	First Note Delivered	Last Note Delivered
Boston	A00 000 001A	A00 000 960A	11-19-29	7-26-33
New York	B00 000 001A	B00 002 400A	1-20-29	1-20-29
Philadelphia	None Printed	None Printed	No Deliveries	
Cleveland	D00 000 001A	D00 002 400A	11-19-29	8-25-31
Richmond	E00 000 001A	E00 003 192A	11-21-29	7-20-32
Atlanta	F00 000 001A	F00 001 032A	8- 5-30	7-29-31
Chicago	G00 000 001A	G00 004 440A	3- 4-30	3- 8-33
St. Louis	None Printed	None Printed	No Deliveries	
Minneapolis	None Printed	None Printed	No Deliveries	
Kansas City	J00 000 001A	J00 000 480A	11-21-29	11-21-29
Dallas	K00 000 001A	K00 000 240A	3- 4-30	3- 4-30
San Francisco	L00 000 001A	L00 001 224A	11-19-29	7-23-30

F5000-34 **Julian-Morgenthau.** Letter in seal. Not issued by Minneapolis. No $5000.00 notes have been printed or released since Oct. 18, 1943.

$5000 FEDERAL RESERVE NOTES—SERIES 1934 (12 Subject)
Secretary-Treasurer: Morgenthau-Julian

Federal Reserve District	First Serial Number Printed	Last Serial Number Printed	First Note Delivered	Last Note Delivered
Boston	A00 000 001A	A00 006 000A	12-19-35	7-26-40
New York	B00 000 001A	B00 007 800A	12-19-35	5- 7-40
Philadelphia	C00 000 001A	C00 000 600A	12-19-35	7-26-40
Cleveland	D00 000 001A	D00 001 200A	12-19-36	No record
Richmond	E00 000 001A	E00 001 200A	2-17-36	No record
Atlanta	E00 000 001A	F00 001 200A	2-17-36	No record
Chicago	G00 000 001A	G00 004 800A	2-17-36	3-15-43
St. Louis	H00 000 001A	H00 002 400A	2-17-36	10-18-43
Minneapolis	None Printed	None Printed	No Deliveries	
Kansas City	J00 000 001A	J00 001 200A	2-17-36	No record
Dallas	K00 000 001A	K00 001 200A	2-17-36	No record
San Francisco	L00 000 001A	L00 003 000A	2-17-36	1-16-41

Remarks: No $5,000 notes have been printed or delivered since 10-18-43.

TEN THOUSAND DOLLAR FEDERAL RESERVE NOTES

Face Design $10,000.00, Salmon P. Chase

Back Design $10,000.00

F10000-28 **Woods-Mellon.** Large letter in seal denoting bank of issue. Not issued by Philadelphia, St. Louis or Minneapolis.

$10000 FEDERAL RESERVE NOTES—SERIES 1928 (12 Subject)
Secretary-Treasurer: Mellon-Woods

Federal Reserve District	First Serial Number Printed	Last Serial Number Printed	First Note Delivered	Last Note Delivered
Boston	A00 000 001A	A00 000 960A	11-22-29	7-26-33
New York	B00 000 001A	B00 002 400A	1-18-30	12- 6-33
Philadelphia	None Printed	None Printed	No Deliveries	
Cleveland	D00 000 001A	D00 000 600A	4- 7-30	4- 7-30
Richmond	E00 000 001A	E00 001 992A	11-22-29	3- 8-33
Atlanta	F00 000 001A	F00 001 032A	8- 5-30	7-29-32
Chicago	G00 000 001A	G00 002 400A	3- 8-33	3- 8-33
St. Louis	None Printed	None Printed	No Deliveries	
Minneapolis	None Printed	None Printed	No Deliveries	
Kansas City	J00 000 001A	J00 000 240A	11-22-29	11-22-29
Dallas	K00 000 001A	K00 000 240A	3- 4-30	3- 4-30
San Francisco	L00 000 001A	L00 001 224A	11-22-29	7-23-30

TEN THOUSAND DOLLAR FEDERAL RESERVE NOTES

F10000-34 **Julian-Morgenthau.** Letter in seal. Not issued by Cleveland, Richmond, Atlanta, Minneapolis or Dallas. Records indicate last release July 8, 1944.

$10000 FEDERAL RESERVE NOTES—SERIES 1934 (12 Subject)
Secretary-Treasurer: Morgenthau-Julian

Federal Reserve District	First Serial Number Printed	Last Serial Number Printed	First Note Delivered	Last Note Delivered
Boston	A00 000 001A	A00 003 600A	12-18-35	7-25-40
New York	B00 000 001A	B00 007 800A	12-18-35	4-23-40
Philadelphia	C00 000 001A	C00 000 600A	7-26-40	7-26-40
Cleveland	None Printed	None Printed	No Deliveries	
Richmond	None Printed	None Printed	No Deliveries	
Atlanta	None Printed	None Printed	No Deliveries	
Chicago	G00 000 001A	G00 003 600A	2-18-36	7- 8-44
St. Louis	H00 000 001A	H00 001 200A	2-18-36	10-18-43
Minneapolis	None Printed	None Printed	No Deliveries	
Kansas City	None Printed	None Printed	No Deliveries	
Dallas	None Printed	None Printed	No Deliveries	
San Francisco	L00 000 001A	L00 001 800A	2-18-36	1-16-41

Remarks: No records found which would indicate the denomination and series were ever printed after the above dates.

GOLD CERTIFICATES

ALL HAVE GOLD SEALS AND SERIAL NUMBERS AND GREEN BACKS

Series 1928 Gold Certificates had a very short life, and very few were preserved. They were issued in denominations of $10.00 to $10,000.00. The $10.00 and $20.00 denominations were released May 29, 1929, just a few months before the country found itself in the midst of its worst economic depression, which permanently closed many banks and caused many collectors to sell or spend their currency.

On Dec. 28, 1933, only four years after the 1928 series was issued, Acting Secretary of the Treasury Henry C. Morgenthau, Jr., issued an order prohibiting the holding of any Gold Certificates, large or small size. Banks were ordered to return their stock of these notes. Provision was made for the holding of gold coins as part of a collection, but no special permission was given for holding Gold Certificates.

Restrictions against the holding of Gold Certificates which had been in force thirty years, were removed April 24, 1964, with the signing of an order by the Secretary of the Treasury, C. Douglas Dillon. This order applied only to issues previous to Jan. 30, 1934. Gold Certificates of series 1928A and 1934 were never released for circulation. The 1934 series which includes the $100,000.00 denomination with likeness of Woodrow Wilson, were issued for use within the Federal Reserve system only.

FACE AND BACK DESIGNS

The basic face and back designs on all denominations of 1928 Gold Certificates, are the same as those used on like denominations of other series. The backs are green, not gold as on the large size Gold Certificates.

OBLIGATION AND INSCRIPTION

The obligation reads: "This certifies that there have been deposited in the Treasury of the United States of America (amount in large letters) Dollars in Gold Coin, payable to the bearer on demand."

The inscription at left of note reads: "This certificate is a legal tender in the amount thereof in payment of all debts public and private."

All current size Gold Certificates were printed in sheets of twelve. No uncut sheets are known to exist.

TEN DOLLAR GOLD CERTIFICATES
Gold seals and serial numbers and green backs.

Face Design $10.00, Hamilton

No.	Series	Treasurer-Sec'y	Printed	VF	EF	Unc.
G10-28	1928	Woods-Mellon	130,812,000	35.00	60.00	90.00
G10-28A	1928A	Woods-Mills	2,544,000	Printed, not released		

$10 GOLD CERTIFICATE

Series	Sec'y. & Treas.	First Serial Number Printed	Last Serial Number Printed	Deliveries First Note	Last Note	Total Notes
1928	Mellon-Woods	A00 000 001A	B30 812 000A	5-29-29	2- 6-33	130,812,000
1928A	Mills-Woods	B30 812 001A	B33 356 000A	3-28-33	4-14-33	2,544,00

TWENTY DOLLAR GOLD CERTIFICATES

Face Design $20.00, Jackson

No.	Series	Treasurer-Sec'y	Printed	VF	EF	Unc.
G20-28	1928	Woods-Mellon	66,204,000	45.00	65.00	100.00
G20-28A	1928A	Woods-Mills	1,500,000	Printed, not released		

$20 GOLD CERTIFICATE

Series	Sec'y. & Treas.	First Serial Number Printed	Last Serial Number Printed	Deliveries First Note	Last Note	Total Notes
1928	Mellon-Woods	A00 000 001A	B66 204 000A	5-29-29	2- 8-33	66,204,000
1928A	Mills-Woods	B66 204 001A	A67 704 000A	4-18-33	4-28-33	1,500,000

FIFTY DOLLAR GOLD CERTIFICATES

Face Design $50.00, Grant

No.	Series	Treasurer-Sec'y	Printed	VF	EF	Unc.
G50-28	1928	Woods-Mellon	5,520,00	110.00	130.00	265.00

$50 GOLD CERTIFICATE

Series	Sec'y. & Treas.	First Serial Number Printed	Last Serial Number Printed	Deliveries First Note	Last Note	Total Notes
1928	Mellon-Woods	A00 000 001A	B05 520 000A	8-21-29	10-26-31	5,520,000

ONE HUNDRED DOLLAR GOLD CERTIFICATES

Face Design $100.00, Franklin

No.	Series	Treasurer-Sec'y	Printed	VF	EF	Unc.
G100-28	1928	Woods-Mellon	3,240,000	210.00	250.00	425.00
G100-34	1934	Julian-Morgenthau. Printed but not released for circulation.				

$100 GOLD CERTIFICATE

Series	Sec'y. & Treas.	First Serial Number Printed	Last Serial Number Printed	Deliveries First Note	Last Note	Total Notes
1928	Mellon-Woods	A00 000 001A	B03 240 000A	10- 1-29	10-24-31	3,240,000
1934	Morgenthau-Julian	A00 000 001A	A00 120 000A	6-25-34	6-25-34	120,000

The highest denomination of small size notes formerly printed by the Bureau of Engraving Department was $100,000. This note bears the portrait of Woodrow Wilson and was issued strictly for transactions between the Federal Reserve Banks.

FIVE HUNDRED DOLLARS, Head of Wm. McKinley

G500-28 1928 Woods-Mellon. 420,000 printed

$500 GOLD CERTIFICATE

Series	Sec'y. & Treas.	First Serial Number Printed	Last Serial Number Printed	Deliveries First Note	Last Note	Total Notes
1928	Mellon-Woods	A00 000 001A	A00 420 000A	12- 2-29	10-20-30	420,000

ONE THOUSAND DOLLARS, Head of Grover Cleveland

G1000-28 1928 Woods-Mellon. 288,000 printed.
G1000-34 1934 Julian-Morgenthau. Printed but not released

$1,000 GOLD CERTIFICATE

Series	Sec'y. & Treas.	First Serial Number Printed	Last Serial Number Printed	Deliveries First Note	Last Note	Total Notes
1928	Mellon-Woods	A00 000 001A	A00 288 000A	12- 2-29	10-20-30	288,000
1934	Morgenthau-Julian	A00 000 001A	A00 084 000A	6-25-34	6-25-34	84,000

FIVE THOUSAND DOLLARS, Head of James Madison

G5000-28 1928 Woods-Mellon. 24,000 printed.

$5000 GOLD CERTIFICATE

Series	Sec'y. & Treas.	First Serial Number Printed	Last Serial Number Printed	Deliveries First Note	Last Note	Total Notes
1928	Mellon-Woods	A00 000 001A	A00 024 000A	11-29-29	12-10-29	24,000

TEN THOUSAND DOLLARS, Head of Salmon P. Chase

G10000-28 1928 Woods-Mellon. 48,000 printed.
G10000-34 1934 Julian-Morgenthau. Printed but not released.

$10000 GOLD CERTIFICATE

Series	Sec'y. & Treas.	First Serial Number Printed	Last Serial Number Printed	Deliveries First Note	Last Note	Total Notes
1928	Mellon-Woods	A00 000 001A	A00 048 000A	11-23-29	11-23-29	48,000
1934	Morgenthau-Julian	A00 000 001A	A00 036 000A	6-25-34	6-25-34	36,000

ONE HUNDRED THOUSAND DOLLARS, Head of Woodrow Wilson

G10000-34 1934 Julian-Morgenthau. Printed but not released.

$100,000 GOLD CERTIFICATE

Series	Sec'y. & Treas.	First Serial Number Printed	Last Serial Number Printed	Deliveries First Note	Last Note	Total Notes
1934	Morgenthau-Julian	A00 000 001A	A00 042 000A	1- 9-35	1- 9-35	42,000

All denominations of Gold Certificates are 12-Subject sheet

WORLD WAR II
EMERGENCY SERIES

HAWAIIAN ISSUE, BROWN SEALS AND SERIAL NUMBERS

With Hawaii overprint, face and back.

The $1.00 note is a Silver Certificate, series 1935A. The $5.00, $10.00 and $20.00 denominations are Federal Reserve notes, San Francisco district.

First issued June 8, 1942 in the Territory of Hawaii, and also on Midway, Johnston and Palmyra Islands, as a precautionary measure against possible invasion of the Islands by the Japanese. After August 15, 1942, no other United States currency could be held or used in the Territory, without special license. Restriction removed October 21, 1944.

Face Design $1.00, Hawaii

Back Design $1.00, Hawaii

No.			Printed	VF	EF	Unc.
H1-35A	1.00	1935A	35,052,000	10.00	14.00	30.00

See pages 25, 26, 27 for star number evaluation of above and other issues.

$1 OVERPRINTED "HAWAII" FOR USE DURING WORLD WAR II
12-subject sheet

| 1935A | Morgenthay-Julian | Y68 628 001B
Z99 000 001B
A99 000 001C
C00 000 001C
F41 964 001C
(This lot was delivered to the Treasurer in uncut sheets)
F41 967 997C
L75 996 001C
P31 992 001C
S39 996 001C | Y71 628 000B
Z99 999 999B
A99 999 999C
C07 000 000C
F41 967 996C

F41 976 000C
L78 996 000C
P37 032 000C
S54 996 000C | First lot delivered on June 8, 1942. Last lot delivered on June 8, 1944. Total notes delivered 35,052,000. |

UNCUT SHEETS EMERGENCY ISSUES

ONE DOLLAR, 12 subjects

| H1-35A | 1934A | Hawaii. W. A. Julian-Henry Morgenthau, Jr. | 3,250.00 |
| A1-35A | 1935A | North Africa. W. A. Julian-H. Morgenthau, Jr. | 3,000.00 |

Face Design $5.00, Hawaii

Back Design $5.00, Hawaii

No.			Printed	VF	EF	Unc.
H5-34	5.00	1934	3,000,000	35.00	55.00	150.00
H5-34A	5.00	1934A	6,416,000	15.00	25.00	90.00

EMERGENCY SERIES — HAWAII

$5 SAN FRANCISCO FEDERAL RESERVE NOTES—SERIES 1934 and 1934A

1934	L12 396 001A thru L14 996 000A	First lot delivered on June 8, 1942.
1934	L19 776 001A thru L20 176 000A	Last lot delivered on May 30, 1944.
1934A	L46 404 001A thru L47 804 000A	Total notes delivered — 9,416,000
1934A	L54 072 001A thru L56 088 000A	
1934A	L66 132 001A thru L69 132 000A	

Face Design $10.00, Hawaii Overprint

Back Design $10.00, Hawaii Overprint

No.			Printed	VF	EF	Unc.
H10-34A	10.00	1934A	10,424,000	25.00	40.00	90.00

$10 SAN FRANCISCO FEDERAL RESERVE NOTE—SERIES 1934A (12 Subject)
Secretary and Treasurer: Morgenthau, Julian

Serial Numbers	Serial Numbers	When Delivered
L65 856 001A thru L66 456 000A	L11 160 001B thru L12 664 000B	First lot June 8, 1942. Last lot July 12, 1944. Total delivered—10,424,000
L67 476 001A thru L69 076 000A	L28 212 001B thru L29 712 000B	
L69 736 001A thru L71 336 000A	L43 032 001B thru L45 532 000B	
L77 052 001A thru L77 172 000A	L50 292 001B thru L51 292 000B	

EMERGENCY SERIES — HAWAII

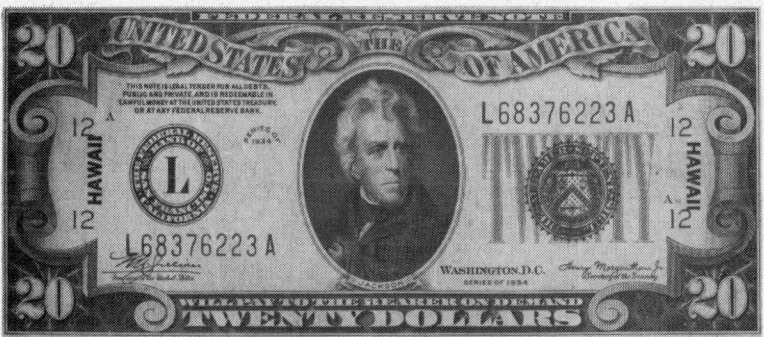

Face Design $20.00, Hawaii Overprint

Back Design $20.00, Hawaii Overprint

No.			Printed	VF	EF	Unc.
H20-34	20.00	1934	*	165.00	300.00	700.00
H20-34A	20.00	1934A	*	35.00	55.00	125.00

*Bureau record shows total of 11,246,000 for series 1934 and 1934A $20.00 notes. It is estimated that about 950,000 of this number were series 1934.

$20 FEDERAL RESERVE NOTES—SERIES 1934 and 1934A (12 Subject)
SAN FRANCISCO—$20.00
Secretary-Treasurer: Morgenthau-Julian

	Serial Numbers	When Delivered
1934 or 1934A	L30 540 001A thru L31 090 000A	
1934 or 1934A	L31 632 001A thru L32 032 000A	First lot delivered on June 8, 1942.
1934 or 1934A	L33 420 001A thru L34 220 000A	
1934A	L56 412 001A thru L56 912 000A	Last lot delivered on July 18, 1944.
1934A	L60 588 001A thru L61 592 000A	
1934A	L67 984 001A thru L69 976 000A	Total notes delivered — 11,246,000.
1934A	L76 980 001A thru L78 480 000A	
1934A	L85 536 001A thru L90 036 000A	

NORTH AFRICA and EUROPEAN INVASION SERIES

Yellow seals and blue serial numbers.

Issued in 1942 at the request of the War Department for use of armed forces in North Africa and later in the invasion of Sicily. Denominations $1.00, $5.00 and $10.00. After the end of WWII, troops leaving Europe for the Pacific Theater were paid in the yellow seals.

Unlike the Hawaii issue, only Silver Certificates were used for this special issue, and it was not countersigned in any way. The yellow seal which replaces the blue seal, is the only identifying marking.

Face Design as on other Silver Certificates, but with Yellow Seal

No.			Printed	VF	EF	Unc.
A1-35A	1.00	1935A	26,916,000	10.00	20.00	50.00

$1 OVERPRINTED WITH YELLOW SEALS (For North African Invasion in World War II)

Series	Sec'y & Treas.	First Serial Number Printed	Last Serial Number Printed	When Delivered
1935A	Morgenthau-Julian	B30 000 001C	B31 000 000C	First lot delivered on September 4, 1942. Last lot delivered on April 24, 1944. Total notes delivered 26,916,000.
		B51 624 001C	B52 624 000C	
		B99 000 001C	B99 999 999C	
		C60 000 001C	C62 000 000C	
		C78 000 001C	C79 904 000C	
		F41 952 001C	F41 955 996C	
		(This lot was delivered to the Treasurer in uncut sheets)		
		F41 955 997C	F41 964 000C	
		I 30 000 001C	I 40 000 000C	
		R90 000 001C	R99 999 999C	

A5-34	5.00	1934				None reported
A5-34A	5.00	1934A		15.00	20.00	45.00

A-34 is listed above, but none have been reported.

The Treasury Department records do not separate total for series 1934 and 1934A. The total of the $5. denomination for both series is given as 16,660,000.

NORTH AFRICA and EUROPEAN INVASION SERIES

Face Design $5.00. Yellow Seal does not show on black and white illustration

$5 OVERPRINTED WITH YELLOW SEALS (For North African Invastion in World War II)
12-subject Sheet

		Serial Numbers	When Delivered
1934 Morgenthau	K34 138 001A thru K34 508 000A		First lot delivered on September 4, 1942. Last lot delivered on May 8, 1944. Total notes printed — 16,600,000. Only 14,196,000 notes were released.
or 1934A Julian	K36 420 001A thru L36 740 000A		
	K37 464 001A thru K37 784 000A		
	K40 068 001A thru K42 068 000A		
	K43 152 001A thru K44 852 000A		
	K53 984 001A thru K65 984 000A		

Face Design $10.00 Silver Certificate with Yellow Seal

No.			Printed	VF	EF	Unc.
A10-34	10.00	1934	....	450.00	1000.00	3000.00
A10-34A	10.00	1934A	....	20.00	30.00	60.00

The Bureau records do not separate totals for series 1934 and 1934A. The total of the $10 denomination for both series is given at 21,860,000.

$10 OVERPRINTED WITH YELLOW SEALS (For North African Invasion in World War II)
12-subject Sheet

1934 Morgenthau	A91 044 001A	A92 764 000A	First lot delivered on September 4, 1942. Last lot delivered on May 8, 1944. Total notes delivered — 21,860,000.
or 1934A Julian			
1934A Morgenthau	A92 764 001A	A99 999 999A	
Julian	B00 000 001A	B00 904 000A	
	B01 564 001A	B13 564 000A	

SPECIAL PRINTING

EXPERIMENTAL ISSUE OF 1935A SILVER CERTIFICATES
Julian-Morgenthau, blue seals and serial numbers

These notes received this special overprint before delivery for the purpose of determining whether a special paper procured for use in currency printing had a longer life in circulation than the distinctive paper in regular use. The notes bearing the designation S were printed on the special paper, whereas those notes bearing the designation R were printed on regular distinctive paper and issued in the same manner in order to identify the notes when returned to the Treasury Department for redemption. Although some data was obtained as to the ratio of R to S notes returned as unfit, the Treasury Department and the Bureau of Engraving and Printing were unable to make a complete and accurate analysis of the results. Consequently, it was decided that the special paper furnished no material advantages over the regular stock. As a result, the Bureau continued the use of the regular paper for the printing of United States currency.

Face Design $1.00, "R" Experimental Series

Face Design $1.00, "S" Experimental Series

No.		Printed	VF	EF	Unc.
E1-35A	Red "R"	1,184,000	30.00	55.00	125.00
E1-35A	Red "S"	1,184,000	30.00	45.00	100.00

See pages 25-26-27 for star number evaluation of the above and other series.

Notes with red "R" are scarcer although an equal number were printed with "S". Beware of altered notes, with red "R" or "S" added to series 1935A.

EXPERIMENTAL ISSUES

| 1935A | Red "S" | S70 884 001C | S72 068 000C | 6-20-44 | 1,184,000 |
| 1935A | Red "S" | S73 884 001C | S75 068 000C | 6-20-44 | 1,184,000 |

ERRORS AND MISPRINTS
By JAMES GREBINGER

Largely due to careful methods and rigid inspections, relatively few specimens of misprinted currency leave the Bureau of Engraving and Printing. An opportunity to specialize and a desire to own unique items has helped to stimulate activity in error collecting, thereby creating a need for cataloging and pricing error notes.

All U.S. currency is printed by the intaglio (engraved plate) process. Backs are printed first and faces are printed a day or two later. The sheets are trimmed, overprinted with seals, signatures and serial numbers, then cut into individual notes. (1963 B and later series have signatures and series year engraved in the plates.) Considering the many separate phases involved, it is easily understood how a few pieces of currency can become spoiled.

One of the first to publish prices of error notes was James G. Johnson of Coin World. Any such pricing of these errors cannot, obviously, be as exact a matter as pricing regular notes. For one reason, there is no way to determine the number extant. Also, practically every misprinted note has individual features, there being no two exactly alike. Further, it is a relatively new field of collecting and is lacking precedence and experience. Therefore, generally speaking, the severity and singleness of the error will ultimately determine its curio value to the collector.

Prices shown in this book are based on the type of error only and have no reference to the denomination illustrated. In all cases the valuations represent the premium only, to be added to the face or normal value of the note.

(Contributors to this section are Aubrey E. Bebee, Harry M. Coleman, Wm. P. Donlon, William J. Doovas, Kurt E. Eckstein, Dennis Forgue, Nathan Goldstein II, Harry E. Jones, R. H. Rockholt, Bruno S. Rzepka, Glenn Smedley and Leonard Stark. Several photos furnished by Aubrey E. Bebee, Julian S. Marks, Tom McAfee and Grant H. Woldum.)

FIRST PRINT (BACK) ERRORS

No. 1-1—Crease on back, front and through the overprint is evidence that a small fold remained in the paper through all three printing procedures.
Fine-Very Fine .. 5.50   Extra Fine ..... 8.00   Uncirculated 17.00

No. 1-2—"Gutter" on back only creased during back printing, then became unfolded before the face impression, overprinting and cutting operations.

Fine-Very Fine ... 5.00   Extra Fine ...... 8.00   Uncirculated.... 15.00

No. 1-3—Blank area caused by a large fold in the moist paper during the back impression. Prior to cutting, the sheet became unfolded and the printed area was trimmed away.

Fine-Very Fine .. 20.00   Extra Fine ..... 30.00   Uncirculated.... 50.00

No. 1-4—This green smudge was caused by sheets rubbing during handling process while the ink was still wet.

Fine-Very Fine ... 8.00   Extra Fine ..... 10.00   Uncirculated.... 25.00

No. 1-5—Offset note, back printing on front. Caused by absence of sheet of paper on the impression roller when it made contact with plate. The plate transferring ink to impression roller, then when the next sheet of paper was fed, the ink made offset transfer from the impression roller. About a dozen impressions are required to completely eliminate the ink from the impression roller. Only on the first 3 or 4 sheets is the offset transfer sharp and complete; the image gradually fades away with each succeeding impression.

Fine-Very Fine .. 55.00   Extra Fine ..... 70.00   Uncirculated... 125.00
—Prices are for complete offsets. (100%).

1-5a—Offsets less than 50% coverage.
Fine-Very Fine .. 15.00   Extra Fine ..... 20.00   Uncirculated.... 30.00

No. 1-6—A two-part note in which a scrap of "Kraft counting strip" covered a portion of the note during printing. Extreme pressures associated with intaglio printing caused the scrap to adhere to the note while passing through inspections.

Fine-Very Fine . 220.00   Extra Fine .... 295.00   Uncirculated... 400.00

No. 1-7—Paired error notes. One has a large irregularly shaped hole, the result of defective paper delivered by the mill. The second note depicts the ink transfer, placed on the following sheet, after the roller had picked up the ink from the plate through the hole in the paper. For the defective note to be proven genuine, the companion note would have to be in evidence.

Fine-Very Fine .. 50.00   Extra Fine ..... 75.00   Uncirculated... 100.00

No. 1-8—Corner fold that remained intact through all printing, trimming and cutting operations.

Fine-Very Fine ... 9.00   Extra Fine ..... 12.00   Uncirculated.... 20.00

No. 1-9—Torn sheet error. The top note resulted from using defective paper delivered by the mill or otherwise torn. The other note depicts the ink transfers, offset on both sides of the succeeding sheet, by the roller after it had picked up an impression from the exposed plates. Several subsequent sheets would show the transfer, each successive one being fainter. For the defective note to be proven genuine, the comparison notes would have to be in evidence. The prices listed here are for a group of these notes.

Fine-Very Fine . 225.00   Extra Fine . . . . 395.00   Uncirculated . . . 500.00

No. 1-10—This defect in the printing was caused by a "broad break." The impression cylinders of the presses have what is referred to as a "rigging" consisting of sheets of strong heavy fiberboard with a rubber-covered textile "drawsheet." The board deteriorates under the extreme pressures of intaglio printing and sometimes break so that inadequate pressure is applied to certain areas.

Fine-Very Fine .. 25.00   Extra Fine ..... 50.00   Uncirculated.... 75.00

No. 1-11—Incomplete impression due to an insufficiently inked plate.
Fine-Very Fine .. 17.50   Extra Fine ..... 28.00   Uncirculated.... 45.00

SECOND PRINT (FACE) ERRORS

No. 2-1—Star note with small unprinted twin creases on the front only. It went through a normal back printing, became folded for face impression, overprinting and cutting operations.

Fine-Very Fine ... 9.00   Extra Fine ..... 12.00   Uncirculated.... 20.00

No. 2-2—This smeared note was the result of insufficient plate wiping prior to making the face impression.

Fine-Very Fine ... 7.00   Extra Fine ...... 9.00   Uncirculated.... 15.00

No. 2-3—$5.00 note, so-called "ghost of Lincoln over his tomb." Offset transfer of an obverse design over the reverse.
Fine-Very Fine .. 50.00   Extra Fine ..... 65.00   Uncirculated ... 100.00
—Prices are for complete offsets. (100%).

2-3a—Offsets less than 50% coverage.
Fine-Very Fine .. 10.00   Extra Fine ..... 15.00   Uncirculated 25.00

No. 2-4—Printed flag is the result of a fold that developed in the sheet prior to face printing, and remained through the cutting operation. There is a blank area on the face equal to the amount of printing shown on the tab.
Fine-Very Fine .. 17.00   Extra Fine ..... 22.00   Uncirculated 40.00

No. 2-5—Series of 1957 note with portion of face printing on back. The sheet was folded prior to face printing and unfold for cutting.
Fine-Very Fine .. 15.00   Extra Fine ..... 20.00   Uncirculated.... 30.00

No. 2-6—This misprint was caused by a large fold in the sheet prior to the face printing, the back being normal. The fold remained intact through the cutting operation.
Fine-Very Fine .. 15.00   Extra Fine ..... 25.00   Uncirculated.... 40.00

No. 2-7—Note with fold along the bottom. Pointed strip at the lower edge is from the face impression, thus an equal area of the face is blank.
Fine-Very Fine .. 20.00   Extra Fine ..... 30.00   Uncirculated.... 55.00

No. 2-7a—This misprint was caused by several large folds that gathered in the sheet, after the back was printed, and before the face impression was made. The folds remained intact through the overprinting, trimming and cutting operations.

Fine-Very Fine .. 45.00   Extra Fine ..... 55.00   Uncirculated.... 85.00

No.2-8—Misprint with portion of an adjacent note showing is caused by faulty alignment of the sheet for face printing.

Fine-Very Fine .. 12.00   Extra Fine ..... 15.00   Uncirculated.... 28.50

No. 2-9—This two-piece note resulted when part of a "tear-out" ticket became embedded in note paper at the paper mill. After passing into circulation, the strip became detached. While other notes may be spoiled in this manner, rarely do they reach circulation with the printed scrap attached.

Fine-Very Fine . 300.00   Extra Fine . . . . 400.00   Uncirculated . . . 600.00

No. 2-10—Incomplete impression due to an insufficiently inked plate.

Fine-Very Fine . . 12.00   Extra Fine . . . . . 17.00   Uncirculated 30.00

No. 2-11—The double denomination note is popularly thought of as the "king of errors." This highly unusual occurrence is the result of printing faces of one denomination on sheets with backs previously printed of a different denomination, such as $5 obverse with $10 reverse.

Fine-Very Fine .2000.00   Extra Fine . . . . 4000.00   Uncirculated . . . 5000.00

No. 2-12—So-called "inverted back." Actually the front is inverted since the backs are printed first. This error developed when the sheet was rotated 180 degrees prior to receiving the face printing.

Fine-Very Fine .. 60.00   Extra Fine . . . . . 85.00   Uncirculated . . . 130.00

No. 2-13—Partially double impression, the result of having gone through the face printing phase twice.
Fine-Very Fine . 145.00   Extra Fine .... 190.00   Uncirculated... 275.00

No. 2-13a—Complete double black face.—A Richmond $1.00 exists on which the black face plate has been printed twice. The first impression is with face plate #145 and overprint with face plate #126. Printing is slightly out-of-register giving a double effect to all the face black. The illustration shows a $1.00 1969D of St. Louis with plate 801 and 797.
Fine-Very Fine . 175.00   Extra Fine .... 225.00   Uncirculated... 475.00

THIRD PRINT (OVERPRINT) ERRORS

No. 3-1, 3-2, 3-3—These notes with seals, signatures and serial numbers misplaced are the result of faulty alignment of sheets for the overprinting operation. The dark square appearing in the lower right corner of the bottom note is an inspector's reject tag, inadvertently overlooked by the final inspector.

No. 3-1—
Fine-Very Fine ... 5.50   Extra Fine ...... 8.00   Uncirculated.... 15.00

No. 3-2—
Fine-Very Fine .. 27.50   Extra Fine ..... 45.00   Uncirculated.... 72.50

No. 3-3—More common than #3-2, except with an inspectors tab in corner.
Fine-Very Fine .. 27.50   Extra Fine ..... 45.00   Uncirculated.... 65.00

No. 3-4—This note with right hand signature, series designation, parts of seal and serial number missing was caused by an obstruction during overprinting.

Fine-Very Fine .. 22.00   Extra Fine ..... 35.00   Uncirculated.... 60.00

No. 3-5—On this note a very large portion of the sheet was covered during the overprinting, thus deleting most of the features of the overprint.

Fine-Very Fine .. 30.00   Extra Fine ..... 37.50   Uncirculated.... 70.00

No. 3-6—Mismatched prefix letters in the serial numbers. This was caused when the manual settings were improperly made.

Fine-Very Fine . 100.00   Extra Fine .... 120.00   Uncirculated ... 175.00

No. 3-7—Serial numbers mismatched in other than first two digits, caused by clogged numbering wheels, causing one or more wheels to stick or skip.

Fine-Very Fine . 100.00   Extra Fine .... 140.00   Uncirculated ... 200.00

No. 3-8—This series 1957 silver certificate has the second digits in the serial numbers mismatched. This is the result of incorrect manual setting of the numbering devices. This note is most common as 10,000 specimens were released. "U37" paired with "U47" is also common.

Fine-Very Fine .. 25.00   Extra Fine ..... 37.50   Uncirculated 55.00

No. 3-9—1928A note with overprint missing. Prior to 1950 all notes above $1 denomination had signatures and district signatures engraved in the plates.

Fine-Very Fine . 100.00   Extra Fine . . . . 130.00   Uncirculated . . . 240.00

No. 3-10—Note with overprint missing. Since 1938 all present overprinting features have been omitted from the engraved plates.

Fine-Very Fine . . 95.00   Extra Fine . . . . 120.00   Uncirculated . . . 225.00

No. 3-11—Inverted overprint, caused by a 180-degree rotation of the sheet before being fed into the overprinted press.

Fine-Very Fine . 120.00   Extra Fine . . . . 165.00   Uncirculated . . . 275.00

No. 3-11a. Inverted Cope Overprint. At press time of this edition the discovery of a considerable number of this type error on $1.00 note of Philadelphia, Kansas City, Atlanta and Dallas is being reported in the Numismatic press.

No. 3-12—This note with overprinting on the back is pictured with the fold as it occurred during printing. After the overprinting operation was completed the sheet became unfolded for cutting into individual notes. The back and face impressions are normal otherwise.

Fine-Very Fine . . 75.00   Extra Fine . . . . 100.00   Uncirculated . . . 185.00

No. 3-13—Partially turned digit in the serial number. One digit is replaced with parts of two separate numbers. This occurs when an impression was made while the machine lags in changing positions, usually due to foreign material in the number machine wheels.

Fine-Very Fine .. 25.00   Extra Fine ..... 35.00   Uncirculated ... 50.00

3-14—Note with double overprint.

Fine-Very Fine . 200.00   Extra Fine .... 275.00   Uncirculated ... 500.00

No. 3-15—Incorrect printing, such as, Federal Reserve note with silver certificate overprint.

Fine-Very Fine . 750.00   Extra Fine ....1000.00   Uncirculated ...1500.00

No. 3-16—Series 1935E note with signatures and series designation inverted. For many years the series number and signatures were engraved on the face plate, only the seals and serial numbers being added in the third printing process. During the conversion to adding the series number and signatures to the third printing, there was a period when these were printed in one press and the colored serial numbers and seals in another. This note resulted from a 180-degree rotation of the sheet between these two runs through overprinting presses.

Fine-Very Fine . 120.00   Extra Fine .... 190.00   Uncirculated... 345.00

No. 3-17—This series 1935E note went through the same printing sequences as note No. 3-16. However, the error resulted from a faulty alignment rather than a rotation of the sheet between printings.

Fine-Very Fine .. 22.50   Extra Fine ..... 38.50   Uncirculated.... 55.00

No. 3-18—Series of 1935E note with seal, signatures, serial numbers and series designation offset on back of the note. Back and face printings are normal otherwise.

Fine-Very Fine .. 70.00   Extra Fine ..... 90.00   Uncirculated... 145.00

No. 3-18a—$1.00 Federal Reserve Note with overprint on reverse (not an offset).
Fine-Very Fine .. 80.00   Extra Fine .... 100.00   Uncirculated... 145.00

No. 3-19—This note, one of the World War II emergency issues, has the HAWAII surcharge inverted on the reverse.
Fine-Very Fine . 360.00   Extra Fine .... 440.00   Uncirculated... 550.00

CUTTING ERRORS

No. C-1—This note with tab is the result of a large fold in the dampened paper. This type of tab is generally found on notes at the top or bottom of the sheet.

Fine-Very Fine .. 10.00   Extra Fine ..... 15.00   Uncirculated.... 25.00

(Note: Prices quoted are for the "error only" and represents premium to be added to denomination.)

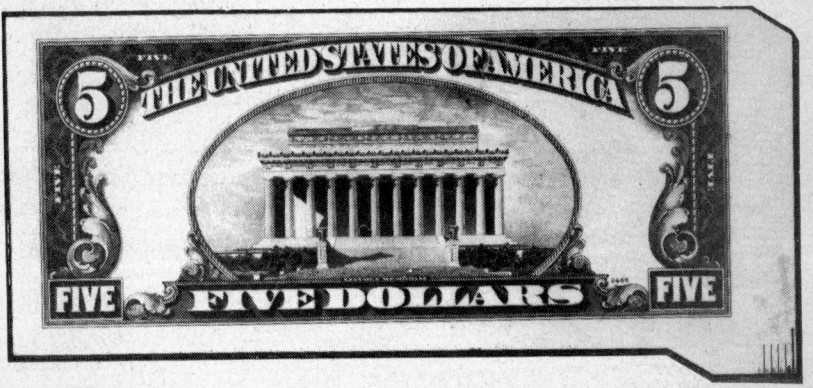

No. C-2—This cutting error was caused by a large fold that developed in the moist paper after back and face printing but prior to the cutting operation.

Fine-Very Fine .. 10.00   Extra Fine ..... 15.00   Uncirculated.... 25.00

No. C-3—Cutting error with portion of an adjacent note showing at the top edge. Due to one sheet in the stack being improperly jogged or printed off register. If the latter, an unusual occurrence as face side is inspected in full sheets.

Fine-Very Fine .. 15.00   Extra Fine ..... 20.00   Uncirculated.... 30.00

No. C-4—This error was caused by a large fold that developed in the moist paper prior to the cutting operation.

Fine-Very Fine .. 12.00   Extra Fine ..... 16.50   Uncirculated.... 30.00

OTHER IRREGULARITIES

No. O-1—Double error note, streak and portion of an adjacent note showing along right edge. The sheet became creased for back printing, unfolded for face impression and misaligned for cutting.

Fine-Very Fine .. 60.00   Extra Fine ..... 75.00   Uncirculated... 100.00

No. O-2—One of the true rarities in misprinted currency. This note went through its three normal printings and a fourth one as well, when the back received an inverted face design. This is a plate impression, not a wet ink transfer in offset.

Fine-Very Fine . 650.00   Extra Fine .... 800.00   Uncirculated...1000.00

No. O-4—Entire back impression missing. (Not a split note.)
Fine-Very Fine . 110.00   Extra Fine .... 140.00   Uncirculated... 225.00

No. O-5—Entire obverse impression missing, overprint normal.
Fine-Very Fine . 100.00   Extra Fine .... 140.00   Uncirculated... 250.00

anco COIN & STAMP SUPPLIES

No. 1850-CURRENCY ALBUM, 32 vinyl pages (9"x12") containing 96 pockets. Each pocket measures (9"x3¼") and will hold all small, large or fractional size currency. Durable, gold-stamped, padded hardcover $24.95

No. 1850A-CURRENCY ALBUM, 12 vinyl pages (9"x7") containing 36 pockets. Each pocket measures (2¾"x6¼") and will hold all small and fractional size currency. Durable gold-stamped vinyl cover .... $ 5.95

No. 1915-FRACTIONAL SIZE CURRENCY HOLDER, clear mylar, (5"x3") ..... $ .19

No. 1916-SMALL SIZE CURRENCY HOLDER, clear mylar, (6"½x3") .... $ .20

No. 1917-LARGE SIZE CURRENCY HOLDER, clear mylar, (8"x3½") .... $ .25

No. 1928-VINYL CURRENCY PAGE, (8½"x11½") with 3 pockets. Fits all small and fractional size currency .... $ .40

No. 1929-VINYL CURRENCY PAGE, (8½"x11½") with 3 pockets. Fits all large size currency .... $ .40

No. 1944-VINYL CURRENCY WALLET, 12 pockets (3¼"x6¾") with a flexible vinyl gold-stamped cover .... $ 2.25

No. 4206-3 RING BINDER with a durable metal edge and specially engineered piano type hinges for long lasting use. Will hold either the No. 1928 or No. 1929 vinyl currency pages .... $ 6.50

No. 17755-UNITED STATES DOLLAR STORY, framed coin card (8"x10"). This set provides mountings for every U.S. dollar issued (Morgan, Peace, Eisenhower, Anthony and Silver Certificate). The metal frame, w/glass, is available in either black or walnut color w/gold trim. The cards are available in white w/full color eagle, black or walnut w/gold stamped letters. Each frame comes fully assembled and packaged in a richly grained giftbox. Please state frame and card color. .... $ 3.95

These items may be purchased at your local numismatic dealer or order directly from:
ANCO COIN & STAMP SUPPLY, P. O. Box 782, Florence, Alabama, 35630.

The largest selling, most comprehensive, up-to-date OFFICIAL PRICE GUIDES...

THE OFFICIAL
1980 BLACKBOOK
PRICE GUIDE OF UNITED STATES
COINS
SEVENTEENTH EDITION

NEW • EXPANDED OFFICIAL A.N.A. GRADING SYSTEM

- over 16,000 *current* buying & selling prices
- covers ALL U.S. COINAGE -1616 TO DATE - COLONIAL -COMMEMORATIVE-CONFEDERATE- GOLD—U.S. PROOF SETS
- the history of THE AMERICAN NUMISMATIC ASSOCIATION
- fully illustrated for *easy* identification
- **NEW GOLD & SILVER COIN VALUE CHART** - tells what coins are worth based on *current* spot prices
- detecting altered coins section - makes identifying counterfeit coins easy
- inventory checklist system

BUY IT — USE IT — BECOME AN EXPERT

$1.95

4-1/8" × 5-1/2" 224 pages (paperback)

THE OFFICIAL
1980 BLACKBOOK
PRICE GUIDE OF UNITED STATES
PAPER MONEY
TWELFTH EDITION

NEW • COMPLETE CONFEDERATE CURRENCY SECTION

- over 6,200 buying & selling prices
- covers *U.S. CURRENCY - 1861 TO DATE* - DEMAND- NATIONAL BANK-GOLD & SILVER CERTIFICATES- TREASURY-FEDERAL RESERVE-FRACTIONAL- MULES-FREAKS & ERRORS
- comprehensive grading system
- fully illustrated for *easy* identification
- **FEDERAL RESERVE** district information
- inventory checklist system

BUY IT — USE IT — BECOME AN EXPERT

4-1/8" × 5-1/2" 224 pages (paperback) $1.95

THE OFFICIAL
1980 BLACKBOOK
PRICE GUIDE OF UNITED STATES
POSTAGE STAMPS
SECOND EDITION

NEW • ALL STAMPS ARE PICTURED IN A FULL COLOR, FAST-FIND-PHOTO INDEX

- over 15,000 current selling prices
- covers ALL U.S. STAMPS · 1861 TO DATE · GENERAL ISSUES-AIRMAILS-UNITED NATIONS-FIRST DAY COVERS-HAWAIIAN ISSUES
- **EXCLUSIVE DETAILED GRADING SECTION**
- stamps are listed using THE SCOTT NUMBERING SYSTEM
- information on investments/rarities/trends
- glossary of terminology
- inventory checklist system

BUY IT – USE IT – BECOME AN EXPERT

4-1/8" × 5-1/2" 208 pages (paperback)   **$1.95**

SIXTH EDITION

HOW TO DETECT ALTERED & COUNTERFEIT COINS AND PAPER MONEY

CAN YOU TELL THE DIFFERENCE BETWEEN AUTHENTIC AND FAKE??? HERE'S HOW IT'S DONE...

Authored by Bert Harshe, this book is designed so beginner and professional can ascertain counterfeit from genuine, fully illustrated and easy to understand.

- Featuring the most popular **altered coins from U.S. Cents thru Paper Money**
- Complete new section on counterfeit gold coins, detailed facts and techniques used in distinguishing authentic gold from "fakes"
- Every day the American public is victimized by counterfeit bills, learn how you can **protect yourself from accepting fraudulent paper money**
- With the high prices commanded by misstruck coins, counterfeits have become increasingly more common, learn to quickly identify imitations

BUY IT – USE IT – BECOME AN EXPERT

$2.95   5-3/8" × 8" 60 pages (paperback)

Send for our latest catalog or contact your local bookseller.

773 Kirkman Road, No. 120, Orlando, Florida 32811
Phone (305) 299-9343

BECOME AN EXPERT

The **HOUSE OF COLLECTIBLES** publishes the largest selling, most comprehensive, up-to-date **OFFICIAL PRICE GUIDES** on collectibles.

KEEPING UP WITH THE EXPANDING MARKET IN COLLECTIBLE IS OUR BUSINESS. Our series of OFFICIAL PRICE GUIDES covers virtually every facet of collecting with subjects that range from ANTIQUES to ZEPPELIN STAMPS. Each volume is devoted to a particular subject and is written by an expert in that field. The information is presented in an organized, easily understood format with the utmost care given to accuracy. This comprehensive approach offers valuable information to both the novice and the seasoned collector.
Send for our latest catalog or contact your local bookseller.

BUY IT • USE IT • BECOME AN EXPERT

773 Kirkman Road, No. 120, Orlando, Florida 32811
Phone (305) 299-9343